The Essential Evidence

Avery Love

The Essential Evidence

The 100 Landmark Trials in Medicine Every Clinician Should Know

Dr. Avery Love, DO
Department of Internal Medicine
The University of Texas Medical Branch
Galveston, TX, USA

ISBN 978-3-032-12398-5 ISBN 978-3-032-12399-2 (eBook)
https://doi.org/10.1007/978-3-032-12399-2

This Springer imprint is published by the registered company Springer Nature Switzerland AG
The registered company address is: Gewerbestrasse 11, 6330 Cham, Switzerland

Dedicated to my loving wife Ari, whose tremendous love and support allows me to flourish and pursue my dreams.

In memory of my role model, inspiration, and dear father,

Dr. Ralph W Love, DO

Foreword

In medicine, our ability to care for patients relies on far more than intuition or experience—it is anchored in the collective evidence painstakingly built through decades of clinical research. Landmark trials form the bedrock of this evidence. They shape our understanding of disease, inform the guidelines we follow, and ultimately guide the therapies we choose at the bedside. Yet in an era of information overload, the sheer volume and fragmentation of data can feel daunting, particularly to trainees and even to busy clinicians seeking clarity in daily practice.

The Essential Evidence: The 100 Landmark Trials in Medicine Every Clinician Should Know meets that challenge with precision and purpose. It distills the most influential clinical studies across disciplines into concise, clinically relevant summaries, transforming complex data into practical insights. The book is written with the modern clinician in mind—accessible enough for students and trainees, yet rigorous enough for educators and seasoned practitioners. Each trial is presented not just for its results, but for its impact—how it has shaped practice and continues to influence patient care today.

What I find most compelling about this work is its spirit of integration. Internal medicine—and indeed the art of medicine itself—requires drawing upon knowledge from cardiology, rheumatology, nephrology, infectious diseases, oncology, and beyond. This book embraces that interdisciplinary reality, helping readers connect pivotal evidence to the clinical scenarios they encounter every day. It is more than a compendium of research—it is a roadmap for applying evidence to patient-centered care, fostering deeper understanding and more meaningful dialogue on teaching rounds and in clinical discussions.

The clarity, focus, and scholarly integrity reflected in these pages are commendable. This book exemplifies the very essence of evidence-based medicine—bridging scientific discovery with the humanistic art of healing. I am confident that *The*

Essential Evidence will become a trusted companion for those striving to make informed, compassionate, and data-driven decisions. It reminds us that behind every landmark trial lies not just data but decades of progress—and, most importantly, the lives of patients whose care continues to benefit from this enduring pursuit of knowledge.

Hani Jneid

Professor & Chair, Department
of Cardiovascular Medicine
Director, Sealy Heart & Vascular Institute (SHVI),
Vice President, Cardiovascular Operations,
The University of Texas Medical Branch,
Galveston, TX, USA

Introduction

Purpose of This Book

During my clinical years in medical school and on into residency, I was always fascinated and inspired by some of my attendings amazing ability to recall any bit of research pertaining to any clinical scenario. We have all encountered many like this throughout our training.

The practice of medicine today is guided by expert opinions in societal guidelines, backed by numerous groundbreaking studies and years of research. It is these guidelines that allow us to provide care, ensuring the greatest likelihood of success in treating patient's ailments. However, in practice clinical scenarios are almost never by the book. This is when experience and further understanding behind the research that formed these guidelines guides our decisions. Thus, a solid understanding of these studies is not only important academically to understand what has guided the way we practice throughout the years but to also lead us when we may not know the exact answer in a challenging case.

The word "doctor," comes from the Latin word "docere," meaning scholar, or to teach. Physicians began being called doctors in the thirteenth to fifteenth centuries when medical education shifted to a university setting. Physicians were then referred to as a doctor, emphasizing that they had received a formal university education in medicine.

But the word "doctor" also highlights a physician is also a teacher. Every day we teach our patients the way their body works and the ways their illnesses affect their physiological homeostasis. We teach our patients correct lifestyle changes to attain their highest state of health. We teach our patients about medications, the way they work, why they should take them, and how to take them.

Aside from our patients we are also teachers to each other. Whether you work in academics, community, or private practice, we continuously pass on our knowledge to others in all healthcare professions and continuously learn from others as well. But to effectively teach others you must fully grasp the rationale and background to your methods, otherwise learning becomes superficial, and easily forgotten. Thus, stressing the importance of understanding the research behind current medical guidelines to not be of disservice to your learners.

The art of medicine can never truly be mastered. It requires constant studying and the ability to adapt to new technologies, changing world events, and the constant flow of practice changing research. Therefore, to strive to be the best physician you can be is to understand the studies behind the guidelines we follow and to be able to successfully teach it to others.

In conclusion, I was inspired to write this book due to my fascination with my attendings proficiency in teaching core concepts and successfully backing them by citing research. I wanted to create and share a resource where those of us, at any level of training, can have these most important studies in one place. Therefore, promoting the building of a strong foundational knowledge of the research that guides our practice and in return be able to teach others and stay up to date with the vast amount of novel research that comes out each year.

How to Use This Book

This book is written for those in any stage of their training who are interested in primary care. Though, this book is still beneficial for even the most experienced physicians, and to those in any healthcare profession who are just interested in evidence-based medicine.

The trials I have listed in this book are by no means a comprehensive list, and some might argue that there are some better landmark trials. The trials in this book are ones that I have personally encountered in my training so far and have learned about in my studies. I believe I offer a valuable perspective as a physician currently in residency. The patient cases I see day to day heavily rely on these trials for optimal management. By providing the trials that are most pertinent to my daily encounters, I can successfully prepare you, the reader, for what you too will see most in your practice.

For each trial listed in this book I provide a summary and background, as well as takeaway messages, clinical application pearls, and even a section on when you can discuss each trial on rounds. The discussion section is especially important for those in medical school and entering intern year, as it serves as a tool to create an educational discussion during rounds and to impress your attending.

During clinical years of training this book would be important to read prior to and during rotations of the specialties listed in this book. Doing so will allow you to further solidify the knowledge you gain on your rotation and help guide your decision making. Lastly, this book is valuable to those looking to be active in their journal club by providing landmark research to discuss and teach.

Contents

About the Author

Dr. Avery Love, DO The author of *100 Trials You Should Know in Medicine* is a dedicated physician with roots in Houston, Texas. He earned his undergraduate degree in Exercise Science from the University of Houston, where his passion for physiology and clinical care first took shape. He went on to work as an EMT in the Houston area for two years, gaining hands-on experience in acute care and patient triage that would later shape his approach to medicine.He attended A.T. Still University School of Osteopathic Medicine, where he graduated in the top three of his class, and is currently completing his internal medicine residency at the University of Texas Medical Branch in Galveston, Texas. He plans to pursue a fellowship in cardiology with the goal of becoming an interventional cardiologist.A strong advocate for evidence-based practice and academic teaching, he wrote this book to serve as a foundational resource for trainees seeking to bridge clinical knowledge with landmark trials. Outside the hospital, he enjoys spending time with his wife and pets, working out at the gym, golfing, and kayak fishing.

Abbreviations

ACS	Acute Coronary Syndrome
ADPKD	Autosomal Dominant Polycystic Kidney Disease
AE	Adverse Event
AF	Atrial Fibrillation
AIDS	Acquired Immunodeficiency Syndrome
AKI	Acute Kidney Injury
ALP	Alkaline Phosphatase
ALT	Alanine Transaminase
ANCA	Anti-Neutrophil Cytoplasmic Antibody
ARDS	Acute Respiratory Distress Syndrome
ARNI	Angiotensin Receptor Neprilysin Inhibitor
ART	Antiretroviral Therapy
AS	Aortic Stenosis
ASCVD	Atherosclerotic Cardiovascular Disease
AST	Aspartate Aminotransferase
BMI	Body Mass Index
BP	Blood Pressure
CA	Coronary Artery
CAD	Coronary Artery Disease
CAP	Community-Acquired Pneumonia
CHD	Coronary Heart Disease
CHOP	Cyclophosphamide, Hydroxydaunorubicin, Oncovin, Prednisone
CI	Confidence Interval
CKD	Chronic Kidney Disease
CM	Cardiomyopathy
CNS	Central Nervous System
COPD	Chronic Obstructive Pulmonary Disease
CPAP	Continuous Positive Airway Pressure
CPR	Cardiopulmonary Resuscitation
CRP	C-Reactive Protein
CT	Computed Tomography

CTPA	CT Pulmonary Angiography
CV	Cardiovascular
CVD	Cardiovascular Disease
DAPT	Dual Antiplatelet Therapy
DI	Diabetes Insipidus
DKD	Diabetic Kidney Disease
DLBCL	Diffuse Large B-Cell Lymphoma
DLCO	Diffusion Capacity for Carbon Monoxide
DM	Diabetes Mellitus
DMARD	Disease-Modifying AntiRheumatic Drugs
DOAC	Direct Oral Anticoagulant
DVT	Deep Vein Thrombosis
ED	Emergency Department
ER	Emergency Room
ESBL	Extended Spectrum Beta Lactamase
ESRD	End-Stage Renal Disease
FEV	Forced Expiratory Volume
FVC	Functional Vital Capacity
GDMT	Goal Directed Medical Therapy
GERD	Gastroesophageal Reflux Disease
GFR	Glomerular Filtration Rate
GI	Gastrointestinal
GLP	Glucagon-Like Peptide
HIT	Heparin-Induced Thrombocytopenia
HIV	Human Immunodeficiency Virus
HR	Heart Rate
HRT	Hormone Replacement Therapy
ICS	Inhaled Corticosteroids
ICU	Intensive Care Unit
IE	Infective Endocarditis
INR	International Normalized Ratio
IV	Intravenous
LABA	Long-Acting Beta Agonist
LAMA	Long-Acting Muscarinic Antagonist
LDL	Low-Density Lipoprotein
LMWH	Low Molecular Weight Heparin
LTBI	Latent Tuberculosis Infection
LV	Left Ventricle
LVEF	Left Ventricular Ejection Fraction
LVH	Left Ventricular Hypertrophy
MAP	Mean Arterial Pressure
MDD	Major Depressive Disorder
MDI	Meter Dose Inhaler
MDR	Multidrug Resistance
MI	Myocardial Infarction

MPA	Microscopic Polyangiitis
MR	Mitral Regurgitation
MTX	Methotrexate
NAFLD	Non-Alcoholic Fatty Liver Disease
NASH	Non-Alcoholic Steatohepatitis
NIDDM	Non-Insulin Dependent Diabetes Mellitus
NPV	Negative Predictive Value
NSTEMI	Non-ST Elevation Myocardial Infarction
OR	Odds Ratio
ORR	Objective Response Rate
OSA	Obstructive Sleep Apnea
PA	Pulmonary Artery
PAH	Pulmonary Arterial Hypertension
PBC	Primary Biliary Cholangitis
PCI	Percutaneous Coronary Intervention
PDE	Phosphodiesterase
PE	Pulmonary Embolism
PNA	Pneumonia
PPI	Proton Pump Inhibitor
PPV	Positive Predictive Value
PSA	Prostate-Specific Antigen
PT	Prothrombin Time
RA	Rheumatoid Arthritis
RAAS	Renin-Angiotensin-Aldosterone System
RR	Relative Risk
RRR	Relative Risk Reduction
RRT	Renal Replacement Therapy
SABA	Short-Acting Beta Agonist
SARS	Severe Acute Respiratory Syndrome
SBP	Spontaneous Bacterial Peritonitis
SLE	Systemic Lupus Erythematous
SSRI	Selective Serotonin Reuptake Inhibitor
STEMI	ST-Elevation Myocardial Infarction
TB	Tuberculosis
TIA	Transient Ischemic Attack
TIPS	Transjugular Intrahepatic Portosystemic Shunt
TNF	Tumor Necrosis Factor
TXA	Tranexamic Acid
UC	Ulcerative Colitis
VTE	Venous Thromboembolism
XDR	Extensively Drug Resistant

Chapter 1
General Internal Medicine

1 ALLHAT Trial Summary [1]

Full Title: Major Outcomes in High-Risk Hypertensive Patients Randomized to Angiotensin-Converting Enzyme Inhibitor or Calcium Channel Blocker vs Diuretic: The Antihypertensive and Lipid-Lowering Treatment to Prevent Heart Attack Trial
Publication Year: 2002
Journal: Journal of the American Medical Association

1.1 Background

Hypertension is a leading risk factor for cardiovascular disease. Multiple antihypertensive medications exist, and before this trial it was unclear as to which class of drugs should be the first line therapy to reduce cardiovascular events in high-risk patients.

1.2 Study Design

Type: Randomized, double-blind, multi-center trial.
Population: 42,418 adults aged ≥55 years with hypertension and at least one additional cardiovascular risk factor (e.g., diabetes, prior cardiovascular event).
Intervention: Chlorthalidone (thiazide diuretic) vs. amlodipine (calcium channel blocker) vs. lisinopril (ACE inhibitor) vs. doxazosin (alpha-adrenergic blocker)

- Doxazosin was stopped early in this study due to adverse outcomes.

A. Love, *The Essential Evidence*, https://doi.org/10.1007/978-3-032-12399-2_1

Primary Outcome: Fatal coronary heart disease or nonfatal myocardial infarction.
Secondary Outcomes:

- All-cause mortality
- stroke and nonfatal stroke
- Combined coronary heart disease (CHD) (Primary outcome + revascularization + angina with hospitalization)
- Combined cardiovascular disease (CVD) (Combined CHD + stroke + treated angina without hospitalization + HF + PAD)

1.3 Results

Primary Outcome: No significant difference in rate of fatal coronary heart disease or nonfatal myocardial infarction compared to the other medications.
Secondary Outcomes:

- All-Cause Mortality: No significant difference between treatment groups
- Fatal and Nonfatal Stroke: Higher rates with lisinopril compared to chlorthalidone (RR 1.15; [95% CI: 1.02–1.30; $p = 0.02$])
- Combined CHD: No significant difference observed with amlodipine or lisinopril vs. chlorthalidone
- Combined CVD: Lisinopril had higher rates of combined CVD vs. chlorthalidone (RR 1.10; [95% CI: 1.05-1.16; $p < 0.001$]). No significant difference with amlodipine vs. chlorthalidone.
  - Higher rates of HF with lisinopril (RR 1.19; [95% CI: 1.07-1.31; $p < 0.001$])

1.4 Key Takeaways

- Chlorthalidone was as effective as amlodipine and lisinopril in preventing major coronary events and all-cause mortality.
- Chlorthalidone was superior to amlodipine in reducing heart failure by about 25%.
- Chlorthalidone was superior to lisinopril in lowering blood pressure and reducing combined cardiovascular outcomes (notably stroke, heart failure, angina, and revascularization).
- Lisinopril was less effective in Black patients, with higher rates of stroke and heart failure compared to chlorthalidone.
- Diuretics outperformed ACE inhibitors and calcium channel blockers in reducing hypertension-related complications across diverse subgroups.
- Thiazide-type diuretics are well tolerated, cost-effective, and should be first-line therapy for most patients with hypertension.

- No increase in non-cardiovascular mortality with amlodipine, refuting older concerns about cancer or bleeding risk with CCBs.
- ALLHAT reinforced the need to include a diuretic in multi-drug regimens for optimal blood pressure control.

1.5 Clinical Application

- ALLHAT supports the use of thiazide diuretics as a first line antihypertensive for most patients, especially those with hypertension and additional cardiovascular risk factors.
- In multi-drug regimens, include a diuretic when possible to improve BP control and reduce cardiovascular outcomes.
- Avoid CCB monotherapy in patients at risk for heart failure, given the higher incidence compared to diuretics.
- Consider cost-effectiveness. Thiazides are less expensive and offer comparable or superior efficacy to newer agents.
- Monitor for metabolic effects (e.g., hypokalemia, increased glucose/cholesterol) with thiazides, but note these did not lead to worse cardiovascular outcomes.

1.6 When to Discuss on Rounds

Discuss this trial on rounds with the following scenarios:

- When choosing an initial antihypertensive for a new diagnosis of hypertension.
- When discussing blood pressure management in older patients with multiple comorbidities.
- When reviewing a patient with heart failure during rounds, recall that ALLHAT found amlodipine was associated with a higher risk of developing heart failure compared to chlorthalidone.
- When polypharmacy is being discussed on rounds, highlight that ALLHAT supports starting with a thiazide since it lowers cardiovascular risk and is cost-effective, limiting the need for multiple agents early on.

1.7 Relevant Guidelines

The ALLHAT trial heavily influenced the **American College of Cardiology/ American Heart Association (ACC/AHA)** hypertension guidelines, which recommends thiazide diuretics, ACE inhibitors, ARBs, and calcium channel blockers as first line agents, with thiazide diuretics often highlighted for broader use.

2 SPRINT Trial Summary [2]

Full Title: A Randomized Trial of Intensive versus Standard Blood-Pressure Control
Publication Year: 2015
Journal: New England Journal of Medicine

2.1 *Background*

Before the SPRINT trial, the optimal blood pressure target for reducing cardiovascular events and mortality was unclear. This trial aimed to determine if more intensive blood pressure control provided additional benefit compared to standard blood pressure control in those at high cardiovascular risk.

2.2 *Study Design*

Type: Randomized, open label, multicenter trial with blind endpoint adjudication
Population: 9361 adults aged ≥50 years with a systolic blood pressure ≥ 130 mmHg and at least one additional cardiovascular risk factor (e.g., CKD, prior cardiovascular event, high Framingham risk score). Patients with diabetes, previous stroke, severe orthostatic hypotension, or advanced CKD (eGFR <20) were excluded.
Interventions: Target SBP <120 mmHg (intensive treatment) vs. target SBP <140 mmHg (standard treatment)
Primary Outcome: Composite of myocardial infarction, acute coronary syndrome, stroke, heart failure, or cardiovascular death.
Secondary Outcomes:

- All-cause mortality
- Individual components of the primary outcome
- Adverse events

2.3 *Results*

Primary Outcome: Intensive treatment significantly reduced the composite primary outcome by 25% compared to standard treatment (1.65% vs. 2.19% per year; HR 0.75; [95% CI: 0.64–0.89; $p < 0.001$]).
Secondary Outcome:

- All-cause Mortality: Reduced by 27% in the intensive group (HR 0.73; [95% CI: 0.60–0.90; $p = 0.003$]).

- Individual Components: No significant differences except for a significant reduction in heart failure in the intensive group (HR 0.62; [95% CI: 0.45–0.84; p = 0.002]).
- Adverse Events: Higher rates of hypotension, syncope, electrolyte abnormalities, and acute kidney injury in the intensive group.

2.4 Key Takeaways

- Targeting SBP <120 mmHg significantly reduces cardiovascular events and all-cause mortality in high-risk patients with hypertension without diabetes.
- Intensive treatment was associated with more adverse events such as higher rates of hypotension, syncope, electrolyte abnormalities, and acute kidney injury.
- There was no difference in stroke or end-stage renal disease (ESRD) rates between groups; renal harm mostly reversible and not clearly permanent.
- SPRINT established <120 mmHg as a valid target for high-risk hypertensive patients without diabetes, although more medications and monitoring are needed to achieve it.
- SPRINT did not include patients with diabetes, stroke, or the institutionalized elderly, so findings may not apply to these populations.

2.5 Clinical Application

- Aim for a systolic BP target <120 mmHg in high-risk hypertensive patients without diabetes or prior stroke, especially older adults.
- Use SPRINT to justify more aggressive treatment when appropriate, recognizing that benefits extend to mortality reduction.
- Monitor closely for hypotension, syncope, and acute kidney injury, particularly in frail or elderly patients.
- Consider medication burden and patient tolerance when intensifying therapy; achieving <120 mmHg often requires multiple agents.

2.6 When to Discuss on Rounds

Discuss this trial on rounds with the following scenarios:

- When discussing BP goals for a patient with hypertension and additional risk factors (e.g., CKD< CAD, high Framingham risk score).
- When managing hypertension in geriatric patients, especially when balancing benefits vs risks of hypotension

- When discussing risks vs benefits of aggressive BP lowering, especially in patients with fall risk or CKD.
- When considering BP goals for patients with diabetes or prior stroke as the SPRINT trial excluded these populations.

2.7 Relevant Guidelines

The SPRINT Trial significantly influenced the **ACC/AHA** hypertension guidelines, which redefined hypertension and adopted a more aggressive blood pressure target of <130/80 mmHg for most adults, replacing the previous 140/90 threshold. It also shaped the **Kidney Disease Improving Global Outcomes (KDIGO)** guidelines, which recommended a systolic BP target of <120 mmHg in patients with CKD, while emphasizing individualized treatment and close monitoring when applying intensive BP control in CKD populations.

3 JUPITER Trial Summary [3]

Full Title: Rosuvastatin to Prevent Vascular Events in Men and Women with Elevated C-Reactive Protein
Publication Year: 2008
Journal: New England Journal of Medicine

3.1 Background

Prior to the JUPITER trial, statins were primarily recommended for the treatment of elevated LDL cholesterol or established cardiovascular disease. However, observational studies suggested a link between inflammation measured by high-sensitivity C-reactive protein (hs-CRP) and cardiovascular risk, despite having normal LDL levels. JUPITER sought to determine whether rosuvastatin (20 mg daily) could reduce cardiovascular events in apparently healthy individuals with normal LDL but elevated hs-CRP (>2.0 mg/L).

3.2 Study Design

Type: Multicenter, randomized, double-blind, placebo-controlled trial.
Population: 17,802 men (≥50 years) and women (≥60 years) with:

- LDL <130 mg/dl
- hs-CRP ≥2.0 mg/L
- No prior history of cardiovascular disease or diabetes

Intervention: Rosuvastatin 20 mg daily vs. Placebo.

Primary Outcome: Composite of nonfatal myocardial infarction, nonfatal stroke, hospitalization for unstable angina, an arterial revascularization procedure, or confirmed death from cardiovascular causes.

Secondary Outcomes:

- Individual components of the primary outcome
- All-cause mortality
- Adverse effects

3.3 *Results*

Primary Outcome: Rosuvastatin reduced the risk of cardiovascular events by 44% compared to placebo (HR 0.56; [95% CI 0.46–0.69; $p < 0.00001$]).

Secondary Outcomes:

- Stroke Reduction: There was a 48% reduction in stroke risk (HR 0.52; [95% CI 0.34–0.79; $p = 0.002$]).
- MI Reduction: Myocardial infarction risk was cut by 54% (HR 0.46; [95% CI 0.30–0.70; $p = 0.0002$]).
- All-Cause Mortality: Rosuvastatin was associated with a 20% reduction in all-cause mortality (HR 0.80; [95% CI 0.67–0.97; $p = 0.02$]).
- LDL and hs-CRP Reduction: Rosuvastatin lowered LDL by 50% and hs-CRP by 37% reinforcing the role of inflammation in atherosclerosis.
- Adverse Effects: Slightly increased incidence of new-onset diabetes in the statin group (HR 1.25; $p = 0.01$), raising concerns about statin-induced diabetes risk.

3.4 *Key Takeaways*

- Rosuvastatin significantly reduced the risk of first major cardiovascular events and all-cause mortality in individuals without hyperlipidemia but with elevated high-sensitivity CRP.
- Benefits were observed across all subgroups, including those with LDL ≤100 mg/dL, women, and Black and Hispanic participants.
- The magnitude of benefit exceeded what would be expected based on LDL reduction alone, supporting a role for inflammation (via hs-CRP) in cardiovascular risk.

- Rosuvastatin was well tolerated, though there was a small but statistically significant increase in physician-reported diabetes.
- The trial was stopped early after a median follow-up of 1.9 years due to clear benefit.

3.5 Clinical Application

- Consider statins in patients with normal LDL but elevated hs-CRP.
- Consider using hs-CRP as a risk-enhancing factor for borderline statin decisions as it can help identify patients who may benefit from statins despite normal cholesterol levels.
- Discuss the small increased risk of new-onset diabetes with statins.
- Recognize that statins reduce cardiovascular risk beyond just lowering LDL. This trial supports the idea that inflammation plays a key role in atherosclerosis.
- JUPITER justified statin use in patients without traditional LDL-based indications but with other risk factors.

3.6 When to Discuss on Rounds

Discuss this trial on rounds with the following scenarios:

- When discussing statin use in patients without traditional indications but with inflammatory risk markers.
- When considering hs-CRP testing in patients with borderline indications for statins.
- When discussing the ethics and interpretation of stopping trials early due to efficacy.
- When addressing patient concerns about diabetes risk with statins.
- When discussing non-LDL risk factors in cardiovascular prevention.

3.7 Relevant Guidelines

The JUPITER trial heavily influenced the **ACC/AHA** cholesterol guidelines, shifting the focus from LDL-based thresholds to overall cardiovascular risk assessment. The **United States Preventive Service Task Force (USPSTF)** guidelines on statin use for primary prevention also incorporated JUPITER's findings, recommending low-to-moderate intensity statins for adults aged 40–75 with at least one cardiovascular risk factor and a 10-year ASCVD risk ≥10%, even in the absence of elevated LDL.

4 DCCT/EDIC Trial Summary [4, 5]

Full Title: Diabetes Control and Complications Trial (DCCT) & Epidemiology of Diabetes Interventions and Complications (EDIC)
Publication Year: DCCT (1993), EDIC (2005, ongoing)
Journal: New England Journal of Medicine

4.1 Background

Before DCCT, the benefits of intensive glucose control in type 1 diabetes were uncertain. Many providers used conventional therapy (one or two insulin injections per day) because the risk of hypoglycemia was a concern. DCCT aimed to determine whether intensive glucose control could prevent microvascular and macrovascular complications in type 1 diabetes.

EDIC is the long-term follow-up study of DCCT participants to assess whether the benefits of early intensive therapy persisted over time (the concept of metabolic memory)

4.2 Study Design

DCCT (1983–1993)
Type: Multicenter, randomized controlled trial
Population: 1441 patients with type 1 diabetes aged 13–39 years
Intervention: Multiple daily insulin injections (MDI) or continuous subcutaneous insulin infusion (CSII) with a target HbA1c <6.05% (intensive group) vs. one or two daily insulin injections with no strict glucose targets (conventional group)
Primary Outcome: Development of progression of diabetic microvascular complications (retinopathy, nephropathy, neuropathy).

EDIC (1994–Present)
Type: Long-term observational study of DCCT participants.

- To assess whether the benefits of intensive therapy persist even after transitioning to standard care.

4.3 Results

DCCT Findings

- Retinopathy: Intensive therapy reduced the risk of retinopathy progression by 76%.
- Nephropathy: Intensive therapy lowered the risk of microalbuminuria by 39%.
- Neuropathy: Intensive therapy reduced the incidence of neuropathy by 60%.
- HbA1c Levels: Intensive therapy achieved an average HbA1c of ~7.2% vs. 9.1% in conventional therapy.
- Hypoglycemia Risk: Higher in the intensive group but the benefits outweighed risks.

EDIC Findings

- Cardiovascular Benefits: Patients originally in the intensive group had a 57% lower risk of cardiovascular events (MI, stroke, CV death), despite similar HbA1c levels after DCCT ended. This supports the concept of "metabolic memory"—early glucose control provides long-term cardiovascular benefits.
- Mortality Reduction: Intensive therapy was associated with lower overall mortality over time.
- Persistent Microvascular Benefits: Patients in the intensive group continued to have lower rates of retinopathy, nephropathy, and neuropathy.

4.4 Key Takeaways

- Intensive glycemic control significantly reduced the risk of microvascular complications (retinopathy, nephropathy, neuropathy) in patients with type 1 diabetes.
- Long-term follow-up (EDIC) showed that early intensive control also leads to sustained reductions in macrovascular complications, including myocardial infarction and stroke—an effect known as "metabolic memory."
- Even after HbA1c differences between groups diminished over time, patients originally assigned to intensive therapy continued to show lower rates of complications.
- The benefits of early, aggressive glucose control persist over decades, reinforcing the importance of tight glycemic control from the onset of type 1 diabetes.

4.5 Clinical Application

- Encourage early intensive glucose control in type 1 diabetes as it prevents retinopathy, nephropathy, and neuropathy.
- Reinforce that early good glucose control has lifelong benefits. The "metabolic memory" effect leads to lower cardiovascular risk later in life.

- Use multiple daily insulin injections (MDI) or insulin pumps—DCCT proved that strict control with these methods is superior to conventional therapy.
- Monitor for and manage potential adverse effects of intensive control, such as hypoglycemia and weight gain.

4.6 *When to Discuss on Rounds*

Discuss this trial on rounds with the following scenarios:

- When discussing insulin regimens in type 1 diabetes.
- When explaining why glucose control matters beyond just preventing microvascular complications, as EDIC later proved it also reduces cardiovascular events by 57%.
- When counseling newly diagnosed diabetics on the long-term importance of early glycemic control (metabolic memory).
- When balancing tight glucose control vs. hypoglycemia risk in patients.
- When discussing whether these findings apply to type 2 diabetes (UKPDS trial—discussed in endocrine chapter).

4.7 *Relevant Guidelines*

The **American Diabetes Association (ADA)** guidelines incorporated findings from the DCCT, as well as the **ADA/European Association for the Study of Diabetes (EASD) Consensus Statement** later including long-term follow-up data from the EDIC study, emphasizing that early glycemic control provides lasting cardiovascular protection—even after glycemic control worsens—introducing the concept of "metabolic memory."

5 SMART Trial Summary (Asthma) [6]

Full Title: The Salmeterol Multicenter Asthma Research Trial: a Comparison of Usual Pharmacotherapy for Asthma or Usual Pharmacotherapy Plus Salmeterol
Publication Year: 2006
Journal: Chest

5.1 Background

Before the SMART trial, long-acting beta-agonists (LABAs) like salmeterol were widely used for asthma control, often in combination with inhaled corticosteroids (ICS), However, concerns existed about the safety of LABAs, particularly regarding an increased risk of asthma-related death. The SMART trial aimed to evaluate whether salmeterol use increased the risk of serious asthma-related events, including death.

5.2 Study Design

Type: Multicenter, randomized, placebo-controlled trial.
Population: 26,355 patients with moderate to severe asthma ≥12 years old.
Intervention: 42 mcg of salmeterol twice daily in addition to their usual asthma therapy vs. placebo instead of salmeterol.
Primary Outcome: Combined respiratory-related deaths or life-threatening experiences (defined as intubation and mechanical ventilation due to asthma).
Secondary Outcomes:

- Combined asthma-related death or life-threatening experiences
- All-cause death
- All-cause hospitalization
- Respiratory-related death
- Asthma-related death
- Combined all-cause death or life-threatening experience.

5.3 Results

Primary Outcome: Occurrence of the primary outcome was low and there was no significant difference for salmeterol vs. placebo (50 vs 36; RR 1.40; [95% CI: 0.91–2.14])
Secondary Outcomes:

- Mortality: In patients receiving salmeterol vs. placebo there was a small but significant increase in respiratory-related deaths (24 vs 11; RR 2.16; [95% CI 1.06–4.41]), asthma-related deaths (13 vs 3; RR 4.37; [95% CI 1.25–15.34]), and in asthma-related deaths or life-threatening experiences (37 vs 22; RR 1.71; [95% CI 1.01–2.89]).

5.4 Key Takeaways

- The SMART trial found no significant difference in the primary outcome (respiratory-related death or life-threatening experiences) between salmeterol and placebo in the overall population.
- Salmeterol was associated with small but statistically significant increases in asthma-related deaths and life-threatening events.
- The increased risk was predominantly observed in African-American patients, a subgroup with worse baseline asthma control and less inhaled corticosteroid (ICS) use.
- The study was terminated early due to these safety concerns and enrollment challenges.
- Post hoc analyses suggested that salmeterol may be safer when used in combination with ICS, consistent with findings from prior observational studies.
- The results led to increased scrutiny over LABA monotherapy in asthma and shaped regulatory warnings and guideline updates.

5.5 Clinical Application

- Avoid LABA monotherapy in asthma. Long-acting beta-agonists like salmeterol should *always* be used in combination with inhaled corticosteroids (ICS) to reduce the risk of severe asthma events.
- Educate patients about adherence to controller medications, especially ICS, and reinforce that LABAs are not substitutes for anti-inflammatory therapy.
- Monitor high-risk populations closely, including African Americans and those with poor baseline asthma control or limited ICS use.
- Use SMART findings to justify stepping up to ICS/LABA combination therapy rather than LABA monotherapy in moderate to severe asthma.

5.6 When to Discuss on Rounds

Discuss this trial on rounds with the following scenarios:

- When discussing asthma treatment, particularly why LABAs must be combined with ICS.
- When explaining why LABAs are not first-line therapy for asthma.
- When discussing disparities or tailoring asthma treatment in minority populations.
- When explaining the rationale behind asthma prescribing guidelines.

5.7 *Relevant Guidelines*

The **National Institute of Health (NIH)/National Heart Lung and Blood Institute (NHLBI)** asthma guidelines incorporated findings from the SMART trial. This guidance was further reinforced by the **FDA Black Box Warning**, which mandated that LABA-containing inhalers must always be prescribed with ICS. The **Global Initiative for Asthma (GINA)** Guidelines echoed these recommendations, firmly discouraging LABA monotherapy in all asthma patients and emphasizing combination therapy to improve safety.

6 SMART Trial Summary (HIV) [7]

Full Title: CD4+ Count–Guided Interruption of Antiretroviral Treatment
Publication Year: 2006
Journal: New England Journal of Medicine

6.1 *Background*

Prior to the SMART trial, some clinicians used CD4-guided antiretroviral therapy (ART) interruptions to minimize drug toxicity, cost, and resistance. The trial aimed to determine whether intermittent ART (stopping and restarting based on CD4 count) was as effective and safe as continuous ART in HIV patients.

6.2 *Study Design*

Type: Multicenter, randomized controlled trial.
Population: 5472 adults with HIV and CD4 $\geq$ 350 cells/mm^3.
Intervention: Patients remained on ART regardless of CD4 count (viral suppression group, continuous ART) vs. ART was stopped when CD4 > 350 and restarted when CD4 dropped below 250 (drug conservation group, intermittent ART)
Primary Outcome: Opportunistic disease or death from any cause.
Secondary Outcome: Major cardiovascular, renal, or hepatic disease.

6.3 *Results*

Primary Outcome: Patients in the intermittent ART group had a 2.6-fold increased risk of AIDS-related events or death compared to the continuous ART group (HR 2.6, [95% CI, 1.9–3.7; $p < 0.001$]).

Secondary Outcome:

- The intermittent ART group experienced a 1.7-fold higher rate of major cardiovascular, renal, or hepatic disease (HR 1.2, [95% CI, 1.1–2.5; p = 0.009]).
- These complications were attributed to increased immune activation and inflammation caused by frequent ART interruptions and restarts.

6.4 Key Takeaways

- Continuous antiretroviral therapy (ART) is superior to episodic ART guided by CD4+ count thresholds in HIV-infected patients.
- The drug conservation strategy (interruption until CD4+ <250) led to significantly higher rates of opportunistic infections, death from any cause, and major cardiovascular, renal, or hepatic events.
- Stopping ART resulted in rapid declines in CD4+ count and rises in HIV viral load, contributing to immunosuppression and increased clinical risk.
- The trial was stopped early due to harm in the drug conservation group, including unexpected increases in non-opportunistic causes of death.
- Findings support the importance of maintaining continuous viral suppression, even in patients with relatively preserved CD4+ counts.

6.5 Clinical Application

- Do not stop ART based on CD4 count alone. ART should be lifelong to prevent both AIDS and non-AIDS complications.
- Avoid episodic or CD4-guided ART interruptions, as they increase the risk of opportunistic infections, non-AIDS-related illnesses, and all-cause mortality.
- Emphasize adherence to ART in HIV-positive patients, even if CD4+ counts are above 350 cells/mm^3.
- Monitor CD4+ and viral load regularly, but use this information to assess immune status, not to guide treatment interruption.
- Use SMART trial findings to reinforce early and sustained ART initiation and maintenance as a cornerstone of HIV management.

6.6 When to Discuss on Rounds

Discuss this trial on rounds with the following scenarios:

- When discussing why HIV therapy should be continuous.
- When explaining why HIV patients on ART have lower heart disease and kidney failure rates.
- When discussing chronic inflammation in untreated HIV.
- When justifying why even stable patients should remain on ART.

6.7 *Relevant Guidelines*

The **Department of Health and Human Services** HIV guidelines incorporated findings from the SMART trial, recommending against CD4-guided interruptions of antiretroviral therapy (ART) and affirming that ART should be continued indefinitely. The **International AIDS Society-USA Guidelines** reinforced this stance, citing SMART as key evidence that ART interruptions increase mortality and cardiovascular risk. Building on these findings, the **World Health Organization (WHO)** HIV treatment guidelines recommended that all HIV patients remain on lifelong ART regardless of CD4 count, marking a significant global shift in HIV management strategy.

7 SUPPORT Trial Summary (Palliative Care) [8]

Full Title: A Controlled Trial to Improve Care for Seriously Ill Hospitalized Patients: The Study to Understand Prognoses and Preferences for Outcomes and Risks of Treatments
Publication Year: 1995
Journal: Journal of the American Medical Association

7.1 *Background*

The SUPPORT trial aimed at improving the care of seriously ill patients by understanding their preferences for medical treatment and ensuring that care was aligned with these preferences. At the time of this study there was significant concern about aggressive treatments for terminally ill patients that did not align with their desires.

7.2 *Study Design*

Type: Multicenter, randomized controlled trial.
Population: 9,105 patients with serious illness (cancer, COPD, heart failure, etc.).
Intervention:

- **Palliative Care Intervention:** Focused on discussions about goals of care, patient preferences, and advanced directives. The intervention included a care plan that emphasized comfort and quality of life rather than aggressive treatment.
- **Usual Care Group:** Standard care with minimal discussion about end-of-life decisions or patient preferences.

Primary Outcome: Composite of earlier DNR (Do Not Resuscitate) orders, fewer days in an undesired state, better pain control, fewer hospital resource use, and improved patient-physician communication and decision-making.

Secondary Outcomes:

- Median time to DNR order
- Pain control near death
- Undesirable states
- Resource utilization
- Communication and satisfaction

7.3 *Results*

Primary Outcome: The intervention failed to significantly improve any of the five targeted outcomes. Despite robust implementation, there was no difference between the intervention and control group.

7.4 *Key Takeaways*

- End-of-life care was often inadequate with nearly half of DNR orders were written in the last 2 days of life, and many patients spent their final days in undesirable states (e.g., ICU, on a ventilator, comatose).
- Pain was undertreated with 50% of communicative patients experienced moderate to severe pain in their final days.
- The SUPPORT intervention failed to improve key outcomes, including timing of DNR orders, patient pain, or time spent in the ICU, despite intensive nurse-led support and provision of prognostic information.
- The trial exposed systemic inertia in serious illness care—existing patterns of care persisted, and physicians, patients, and families may have been resistant to change.
- The study highlighted the need for deeper cultural and systemic reform to achieve meaningful improvement in palliative and end-of-life care.

7.5 *Clinical Application*

- Do not rely on communication interventions alone to improve end-of-life care; systemic, cultural, and institutional changes are likely required.
- Proactively initiate goals-of-care conversations early in the hospitalization, especially for patients with serious, life-limiting illnesses.

- Avoid delays in DNR discussions. Waiting until the final days of life often leads to prolonged suffering and unwanted aggressive interventions.
- Routinely assess and manage pain in seriously ill patients; untreated pain remains common even in the hospital setting.
- Recognize the limitations of relying solely on prognosis tools. Physician behavior and patient experiences are shaped by more than just clinical data.
- Use SUPPORT findings to advocate for stronger palliative care integration, earlier hospice referral, and structured decision-making frameworks within hospitals.

7.6 When to Discuss on Rounds

Discuss this case on rounds with the following scenarios:

- When discussing end-of-life care and the importance of aligning treatment with patients preferences.
- When encouraging early conversations with terminally ill patients about their goals and treatment preferences.
- When discussing appropriate use of life-sustaining treatments in terminally ill patients.
- When talking about family support and decision-making during end-of-life care discussions.

7.7 Relevant Guidelines

The **Institute of Medicine** report on end-of-life care incorporated findings from the SUPPORT study, calling for a greater role of palliative care in managing terminal illness. Building on this, the **National Consensus Project for Quality Palliative Care** emphasized early integration of palliative services and advance care planning for patients with serious illnesses. The **America College of Physicians (ACP)** guidelines extended this approach, recommending that palliative care begin at diagnosis of chronic, life-limiting diseases rather than waiting until the terminal phase. Similarly, the **American Academy of Hospice and Palliative Medicine (AAHPM)** guidelines reinforced the value of early palliative interventions to align care with patient preferences and enhance quality of life throughout the disease trajectory.

8 PLCO Trial Summary [9]

Full Title: Prostate, Lung, Colorectal, and Ovarian Cancer Screening Trial
Journal: Results published in multiple journals

8.1 Background

The PLCO trial was a landmark study designed to determine whether screening for prostate, lung, colorectal, and ovarian cancers reduces cancer-specific mortality in asymptomatic adults. At the time, there was significant uncertainty about the efficacy of screening tests, particularly for prostate cancer (PSA) testing) and ovarian cancer (CA-125 and transvaginal ultrasound), in improving outcomes.

8.2 Study Design

Type: Randomized controlled trial.
Population: 155,000 men and women aged 55–74 years in the U.S., enrolled between 1993 and 2001.
Intervention:

- **Prostate Cancer:** PSA testing and digital rectal examination.
- **Lung Cancer:** Chest X-rays.
- **Colorectal Cancer:** Flexible sigmoidoscopy.
- **Ovarian Cancer:** CA-125 blood test and transvaginal ultrasound.

Control Group: Usual care (no organized screening).
Primary Outcomes: Cancer-specific mortality for each cancer type.

8.3 Results

Prostate Cancer Screening:

- No significant reduction in prostate cancer mortality in the screening group compared to usual care.
- Higher rates of prostate cancer diagnosis in the screening group due to increased detection (overdiagnosis).

Lung Cancer Screening:

- Chest X-ray screening did not reduce lung cancer mortality.
- Later studies (e.g., NLST) showed that low-dose CT, not chest X-rays, is effective for lung cancer screening.

Colorectal Cancer Screening:

- Flexible sigmoidoscopy reduced colorectal cancer mortality by 21%.

Ovarian Cancer Screening:

- Screening with CA-125 and transvaginal ultrasound did not reduce ovarian cancer mortality.
- High rates of false positives led to unnecessary surgeries and associated complications.

Overall Findings:

- Screening was beneficial for colorectal cancer with flexible sigmoidoscopy.
- Screening for prostate, lung, and ovarian cancers did not reduce mortality.

8.4 Key Takeaways

- Screening for colorectal cancer with flexible sigmoidoscopy reduces mortality.
- PSA testing for prostate cancer and CA-125/transvaginal ultrasound for ovarian cancer can lead to overdiagnosis and overtreatment without improving mortality outcomes.
- Chest X-ray screening for lung cancer is ineffective; subsequent studies demonstrated the benefit of low-dose CT scans for lung cancer screening instead.
- Screening programs should balance the risks of overdiagnosis and false positives with potential mortality benefits.

8.5 Clinical Application

- Inform patients about the risks of overdiagnosis and overtreatment when considering prostate cancer screening.
- Recommended low-dose CT scans for high-risk patients (e.g., smokers).
- Flexible sigmoidoscopy or other modalities (e.g., colonoscopy) effectively reduce colorectal cancer mortality.
- Avoid routine ovarian cancer screening—Use CA-125 and transvaginal ultrasound only in high-risk populations (e.g., BRCA mutation carriers).

8.6 *When to Discuss on Rounds*

Discuss this trial on rounds with the following scenarios:

- When discussing PSA testing and the need for shared decision-making in prostate cancer screening.
- When explaining why chest X-rays are not recommended for lung cancer screening.
- When discussing ovarian cancer screening, especially in low-risk populations.
- When advocating for colorectal cancer screening options in eligible patients.

8.7 *Relevant Guidelines*

Findings from the PLCO trial influenced several major **USPSTF** recommendations. For prostate cancer, the USPSTF issued a Grade C recommendation for PSA screening in men aged 55–69, emphasizing shared decision-making due to the risks of overdiagnosis and overtreatment, and advised against PSA testing in men over 70. For colorectal cancer, the USPSTF recommends screening adults aged 45–75, with flexible sigmoidoscopy among the accepted modalities. Regarding ovarian cancer, the USPSTF recommends against routine screening with CA-125 or transvaginal ultrasound, citing no demonstrated mortality benefit and high false-positive rates.

9 LOTUS Trial Summary [10]

Full Title: Long-Term Usage of Esomeprazole vs Surgery for Treatment of Chronic GERD
Publication Year: 2011
Journal: Journal of the American Medical Association

9.1 *Background*

Chronic gastroesophageal reflux disease (GERD) is often treated with proton pump inhibitors (PPIs) as the first-line therapy. However, questions remained about the long-term efficacy and safety of PPIs compared to surgical interventions, such as laparoscopic anti-reflux surgery (LARS). The LOTUS trial was designed to compare the long-term outcomes of medical versus surgical management of GERD.

9.2 Study Design

Type: Multicenter, open-label, randomized controlled trial.
Population: 554 patients with chronic GERD requiring long-term therapy.
Intervention: Patients received titrated doses of esomeprazole (20–40 mg daily) based on symptom control (esomeprazole group) vs. patients underwent LARS (surgical group)
Primary Outcome: Time to treatment failure (for LARS, defined as need for acid suppressive therapy; for esomeprazole, inadequate symptom control after dose adjustment).
Secondary Outcomes:

- GERD-related symptoms
- Quality of life
- Adverse events
- Patient satisfaction

9.3 Results

Primary Outcome: At 5 years, remission rates were 92% in the esomeprazole group and 85% in the LARS group (95% CI: 89–96%, 81–90%; p = 0.48), indicating no significant difference in efficacy between the two approaches. Both treatment strategies were similarly effective in maintaining long-term control of GERD symptoms.
Secondary Outcomes:

- GERD symptoms: were better controlled in LARS group; however, dysphagia, bloating, and flatulence were more common after surgery.
- Quality of life: improved similarly in both groups, with no significant differences observed.
- Adverse events: rare in both groups, and no significant long-term side effects of PPIs-such as infections or osteoporosis-were observed over the 5-year follow-up period.

9.4 Key Takeaways

- Both laparoscopic antireflux surgery (LARS) and esomeprazole were effective long-term treatments for GERD in PPI-responsive patients.
- Symptom control was durable for 5 years in both groups, but side effect profiles differed substantially.

- LARS was associated with higher rates of dysphagia, bloating, and flatulence, while regurgitation was more common in the esomeprazole group.
- LARS led to fewer hiatal hernias and maintained better anatomic outcomes on endoscopy.
- Dose escalation of esomeprazole was frequently required, highlighting the need for individualized titration in medical therapy.
- Serious adverse event rates were similar between groups, and there was no perioperative mortality, suggesting both approaches are safe with appropriate patient selection.
- Trial enrolled only PPI responders, limiting generalizability to those with refractory GERD symptoms.
- Study was not designed for superiority or equivalence, but rather to estimate long-term efficacy in a pragmatic, real-world population.

9.5 *Clinical Application*

- Use LARS in patients who prefer a procedural approach or wish to avoid lifelong medication, but counsel about potential postoperative side effects like bloating and dysphagia.
- Continue PPI for patients managed medically, with regular reassessment and dose escalation as needed for symptom control.
- Recognize that anatomical benefits of LARS (e.g., reduced hiatal hernia recurrence) may be important for some patients.
- Do not generalize these findings to PPI non-responders. Further diagnostic evaluation is needed in that group.
- Reassure patients that both strategies have favorable safety profiles when performed or monitored appropriately.

9.6 *When to Discuss on Rounds*

Discuss this trial with the following scenarios:

- When debating medical versus surgical options for chronic GERD.
- When discussing post-surgical complications or counseling patients on treatment options.
- When addressing concerns about the adverse effects of prolonged PPI use.

9.7 Relevant Guidelines

American College of Gastroenterology (ACG) guidelines for GERD emphasize that PPIs are the first-line therapy for chronic GERD due to their efficacy and tolerability, while LARS is recommended as an alternative for patients who fail or do not wish to continue medical therapy.

10 MDRD Study Summary [11]

Full Title: The Effects of Dietary Protein Restriction and Blood-Pressure Control on the Progression of Chronic Renal Disease
Publication Year: 1994
Journal: New England Journal of Medicine

10.1 Background

The MDRD study was a landmark investigation examining whether dietary protein restriction and strict blood pressure control could slow the progression of chronic kidney disease (CKD). At the time, it was hypothesized that reducing dietary protein intake might decrease intraglomerular pressure and delay the decline in kidney function.

10.2 Study Design

Type: Randomized controlled trial.

Study 1
Population: 840 adults with CKD (glomerular filtration rates [GFR] of 25–55 mL/min/1.73 m2)
Intervention:

- **Dietary Protein Restriction:**
  - Usual protein diet (1.3 g/kg/day) vs. low-protein diet (0.58 g/kg/day).
- **Blood Pressure Targets:**
  - Usual blood pressure (MAP 107 mmHg) vs. low blood pressure (MAP 92 mmHg)

Study 2

- **Population:** 255 adults with CKD (GFR of 13–24 mL/min/1.73 m2)

Intervention:

- **Dietary Protein Restriction:**
  - Low-protein diet (0.58 g/kg/day) vs. very low-protein diet (0.28 g/kg/day with keto acid supplementation)
- **Blood Pressure Targets:**
  - Usual blood pressure (MAP 107 mmHg) vs. low blood pressure (MAP 92 mmHg)

Primary Outcome: Rate of decline in GFR

10.3 Results

Study 1
Primary Outcome:

- During the first 4 months, both low-protein and low-blood-pressure groups experienced a faster initial decline in GFR than the control groups (mean decline: 2.6 mL/min/1.73 m²; $p = 0.004$ for diet, $p = 0.01$ for BP).
- After the first 4 months, the rate of GFR decline slowed in the Intervention:
  - 28% slower decline in the low-protein group vs. usual-protein ($p = 0.009$).
  - 29% slower decline in the low-blood-pressure group vs. usual-pressure ($p = 0.006$).
- Average rate of decline after month 4 was 3.3 mL/min/year in all groups.

Additional Findings:

- At 3 years, no statistically significant difference in total GFR decline between diet or BP groups:
  - Low-protein vs. usual-protein: −1.2 mL ($p = 30$).
  - Low-BP vs. usual-BP: −1.6 mL ($p = 0.18$).
- Patients with proteinuria >3 g/day derived the greatest benefit from BP lowering.
- Moderate benefit was seen with 1–3 g/day proteinuria; no benefit with <1 g/day
- Black patients had a more rapid GFR decline (19 vs. 11 mL/3 years; $p = 0.02$); BP control appeared to halve decline (14 vs. 25 mL, $p = 0.11$).
- Patients with polycystic kidney disease had a faster decline (17 vs. 10 mL; $p < 0.001$) with no observed benefit from BP lowering.

Study 2
Primary Outcome:

- No statistically significant difference in the rate of GFR decline between diet groups or BP groups.
- Using a one-slope model, the overall mean rate of GFR decline was 4.0 mL/min/year.

Additional Findings:

- GFR decline in very-low-protein vs. low-protein diet:
  - 0.8 mL/min/year slower decline in very-low-protein group (95% CI: −0.1–1.8; p = 0.07)
  - Represents a 19% reduction in GFR decline.
- GFR decline in low-BP vs. usual-BP group:
  - 0.5 mL/min/year slower decline in low-BP group (95% CI: −0.4–1.4; p = 0.28)
  - Represents a 12% reduction in GFR decline.
- No significant interaction between baseline demographics and diet interventions.
- A significant interaction was observed between baseline proteinuria and blood pressure interventions (p = 0.01), suggesting greater benefit of BP control in those with higher proteinuria.

10.4 Key Takeaways

- Dietary protein restriction provided a modest benefit in CKD progression for patients with moderate kidney disease.
- Blood pressure control is critical, especially for patients with proteinuria, with stricter targets offering more benefit.
- The study laid the groundwork for future research on dietary interventions and blood pressure management in CKD.

10.5 Clinical Application

- Encourage moderate dietary protein restriction in CKD patients. Aim for 0.6–0.8 g/kg/day in patients with moderate CKD but avoid very low-protein diets unless under specialized care.
- Implement stricter blood pressure targets for proteinuric CKD patients.
- Not all patients benefit equally from dietary protein restriction or strict blood pressure targets; assess proteinuria levels and CKD severity.
- Combine dietary advice with blood pressure management and other CKD care strategies.

10.6 When to Discuss on Rounds

Discuss this trial on rounds with the following scenarios:

- When counseling patients on dietary modifications in CKD or addressing nutritional management of kidney disease.
- When discussing the management of proteinuria in CKD or the rationale for tight blood pressure control in these patients.
- When justifying stricture blood pressure goals in CKD patients, especially those with proteinuria.

10.7 Relevant Guidelines

The **ACP** endorses dietary protein restriction for patients with chronic kidney disease (CKD), though it acknowledges that the effect size is modest. In alignment with findings from the MDRD study, the **AHA** emphasizes the importance of blood pressure control as a critical strategy in slowing CKD progression and improving patient outcomes.

References

1. ALLHAT Officers and Coordinators for the ALLHAT Collaborative Research Group. The antihypertensive and lipid-lowering treatment to prevent heart attack trial. Major outcomes in high-risk hypertensive patients randomized to angiotensin-converting enzyme inhibitor or calcium channel blocker vs diuretic: the antihypertensive and lipid-lowering treatment to prevent heart attack trial (ALLHAT) [published correction appears in JAMA 2003 Jan 8;289(2):178] [published correction appears in JAMA. 2004 May 12;291(18):2196]. JAMA. 2002;288(23):2981–97. https://doi.org/10.1001/jama.288.23.2981.
2. SPRINT Research Group, Wright JT Jr, Williamson JD, et al. A randomized trial of intensive versus standard blood-pressure control [published correction appears in N Engl J Med. 2017 Dec 21;377(25):2506. https://doi.org/10.1056/NEJMx170008.]. N Engl J Med. 2015;373(22):2103–16. https://doi.org/10.1056/NEJMoa1511939.
3. Ridker PM, Danielson E, Fonseca FA, et al. Rosuvastatin to prevent vascular events in men and women with elevated C-reactive protein. N Engl J Med. 2008;359(21):2195–207. https://doi.org/10.1056/NEJMoa0807646.
4. Diabetes Control and Complications Trial Research Group, Nathan DM, Genuth S, et al. The effect of intensive treatment of diabetes on the development and progression of long-term complications in insulin-dependent diabetes mellitus. N Engl J Med. 1993;329(14):977–86. https://doi.org/10.1056/NEJM199309303291401.
5. Nathan DM, Cleary PA, Backlund JY, et al. Intensive diabetes treatment and cardiovascular disease in patients with type 1 diabetes. N Engl J Med. 2005;353(25):2643–53. https://doi.org/10.1056/NEJMoa052187.
6. Nelson HS, Weiss ST, Bleecker ER, et al. SMART Study Group. The salmeterol multicenter asthma research trial: a comparison of usual pharmacotherapy for asthma or usual pharma-

cotherapy plus salmeterol [published correction appears in Chest. 2006 May;129(5):1393]. Chest. 2006;129(1):15–26. https://doi.org/10.1378/chest.129.1.15.
7. Strategies for Management of Antiretroviral Therapy (SMART) Study Group, El-Sadr WM, Lundgren J, et al. CD4+ count-guided interruption of antiretroviral treatment. N Engl J Med. 2006;355(22):2283–96. https://doi.org/10.1056/NEJMoa062360.
8. A controlled trial to improve care for seriously ill hospitalized patients. The study to understand prognoses and preferences for outcomes and risks of treatments (SUPPORT). The SUPPORT Principal Investigators [published correction appears in JAMA 1996 Apr 24;275(16):1232]. JAMA. 1995;274(20):1591–8.
9. National Cancer Institute. Prostate, Lung, Colorectal, and Ovarian (PLCO) Cancer Screening Trial: Trial Summary. Cancer Data Access System. https://cdas.cancer.gov/learn/plco/trial-summary/.
10. Galmiche JP, Hatlebakk J, Attwood S, et al. Laparoscopic antireflux surgery vs esomeprazole treatment for chronic GERD: the LOTUS randomized clinical trial. JAMA. 2011;305(19):1969–77. https://doi.org/10.1001/jama.2011.626.
11. Klahr S, Levey AS, Beck GJ, et al. The effects of dietary protein restriction and blood-pressure control on the progression of chronic renal disease. Modification of Diet in Renal Disease Study Group. N Engl J Med. 1994;330(13):877–84. https://doi.org/10.1056/NEJM199403313301301.

Chapter 2
Cardiology

1 ASCOT-BPLA Trial Summary [1]

Full Title: Anglo-Scandinavian Cardiac Outcomes Trial—Blood Pressure Lowering Arm
Publication Year: 2005
Journal: The Lancet

1.1 *Background*

Prior to ASCOT-BPLA, the choice of antihypertensive therapy was often based on older drug classes, particularly beta-blockers and diuretics. This trial aimed to determine whether a new antihypertensive regimen, based on amlodipine with perindopril as needed, was superior to the traditional regimen of atenolol with bendroflumethiazide as needed in reducing cardiovascular events in patients with hypertension and additional cardiovascular risk factors.

1.2 *Study Design*

Type: Multicenter, randomized, controlled trial
Population: 19,257 hypertensive patients aged 40–79 years with at least three additional cardiovascular risk factors (e.g., dyslipidemia, smoking, diabetes, LVH)
Intervention: Amlodipine ± perindopril if needed for BP control (Amlodipine-based regimen) vs. atenolol ± bendroflumethiazide if needed for BP control (Atenolol-based regimen)

A. Love, *The Essential Evidence*, https://doi.org/10.1007/978-3-032-12399-2_2

Primary Outcome: Composite of nonfatal myocardial infarction and fatal coronary heart disease

Secondary Outcomes:

- Nonfatal or fatal stroke
- Total cardiovascular events
- All-cause mortality
- Development of diabetes

1.3 Results

Primary Outcome: No statistically significant difference in the composite of MI and fatal CHD between the two groups (HR 0.90; [95% CI: 0.79–1.02; p = 0.105]).

Secondary Outcomes:

- Stroke reduction: The amlodipine-based regimen significantly reduced the risk of stroke by 23% compared to the atenolol-based regimen (HR 0.77; [95% CI: 0.66–0.89; p = 0.0003]).
- Total cardiovascular events: Lower with the amlodipine-based regimen (HR 0.84; [95% CI: 0.78–0.90; p < 0.0001]).
- All-cause mortality: Reduced by 11% in the Amlodipine-based regimen (HR 0.89; [95% CI: 0.81–0.99; p = 0.025])
- New-onset diabetes: The amlodipine-based regimen was associated with a 30% lower incidence of new-onset diabetes compared to the atenolol-based regimen (HR 0.70; [95% CI: 0.63–0.78; p < 0.0001]).

1.4 Key Takeaways

- The amlodipine-based regimen led to fewer strokes, fewer total cardiovascular events, and less new-onset diabetes compared to the atenolol-based regimen.
- Beta-blockers (atenolol) were found to be inferior as first-line therapy for hypertension in preventing stroke and overall CV events.
- Calcium channel blockers (amlodipine) were reaffirmed as effective antihypertensive agents, especially in preventing stroke.
- The results contributed to a shift away from beta-blockers as first-line therapy for hypertension in patients without specific indications (e.g., CAD, heart failure).

1.5 Clinical Application

- CCBs and ACE inhibitors should be first-line for primary hypertension.
- Beta-blockers should be reserved for specific indication, using them primarily in patients with CAD, heart failure, or other compelling indications.
- Consider stroke risk when choosing antihypertensive therapy as Amlodipine-based therapy significantly reduced stroke compared to atenolol-based therapy.
- Be mindful of new-onset diabetes risk with beta-blockers.
- Reassess long-term beta-blocker use in patients without a clear indication.

1.6 When to Discuss on Rounds

Discuss this trial on rounds with the following scenarios:

- When selecting an antihypertensive regimen and justifying the preference for CCBs over beta-blockers.
- When discussing stroke prevention in hypertensive patients, particularly in those at high cerebrovascular risk.
- When discussing why beta-blockers are no longer recommended as first-line agents for hypertension (except in CAD or heart failure).
- When discussing antihypertensive choices for patients at risk of developing diabetes.
- When drawing comparisons between landmark hypertension trials.

1.7 Relevant Guidelines

In the **ACC/AHA** hypertension guidelines, while beta-blockers remained indicated for specific conditions such as heart failure and coronary artery disease, their role in primary hypertension was deemphasized. The findings of ASCOT-BPLA contributed to this shift, reinforcing CCBs and ACE inhibitors as preferred agents in most hypertensive patients.

2 ASCOT-LLA Trial Summary [2]

Full Title: Anglo-Scandinavian Cardiac Outcomes Trial—Lipid Lowering Arm
Publication Year: 2003
Journal: The Lancet

2.1 Background

The ASCOT-LLA was a sub study of the larger ASCOT trial, focusing on the benefits of lipid-lowering therapy in patients at moderate cardiovascular risk. At the time, statins were widely used for secondary prevention of cardiovascular disease, but their role in primary prevention in patients with moderate cardiovascular risk was not well defined.

2.2 Study Design

Type: Multicenter, randomized, double-blind, placebo-controlled trial
Population: 10,305 of the hypertensive patients aged 40–79 years with at least three additional cardiovascular risk factors from the ASCOT-BPLA trial with a non-fasting cholesterol concentration of 6.5 mmol/L or less.
Intervention: Atorvastatin 10 mg daily vs. placebo
Duration: Median follow-up of 3.3 years.
Primary Outcome: Combined incidence of nonfatal myocardial infarction and fatal coronary heart disease
Secondary Outcome:

- Primary endpoint excluding silent MI
- Fatal and non-fatal stroke
- All-cause mortality
- Total coronary events

2.3 Results

Primary Outcome:

- Atorvastatin reduced the risk of nonfatal myocardial infarction and fatal coronary heart disease by 36% compared to placebo (HR: 0.64; [95% CI: 0.50–0.83, p = 0.0005]).

Secondary Outcome:

- Primary endpoint excluding silent MI: was reduced by 38% in the atorvastatin group (HR: 0.62; [95% CI: 0.47–0.81; p = 0.0005])
- Stroke risk: was reduced by 27% in the atorvastatin group (HR: 0.73; [95% CI: 0.56–0.96]).
- All-cause mortality: There was no significant difference in all-cause mortality, but the trial was stopped early due to clear benefits.
- Total coronary events: There was a significant reduction in total coronary events in the atorvastatin group (HR: 0.71; [95% CI: 0.59–0.86; p = 0.0005])

2.4 *Key Takeaways*

- In hypertensive adults at moderate cardiovascular risk, adding atorvastatin to antihypertensive therapy reduced coronary events and stroke compared with placebo.
- Benefits emerged early enough that the trial was stopped for efficacy.
- Protection was seen despite average or below-average baseline cholesterol, supporting risk-based treatment rather than cholesterol thresholds alone.
- Effects were additive to blood-pressure control, underscoring dual risk-factor management.
- No clear all-cause mortality reduction was shown over the shortened follow-up.
- Findings supported broader consideration of statins in hypertensive patients without overt dyslipidemia.

2.5 *Clinical Application*

- Consider initiating statin therapy in hypertensive patients at moderate cardiovascular risk, even when baseline cholesterol levels are not elevated.
- Combine lipid-lowering therapy with optimal blood pressure control for additive cardiovascular protection.
- Use risk-based assessment rather than LDL-C thresholds alone to guide statin initiation in hypertensive patients.
- Recognize that benefits in cardiovascular event reduction may occur within the first few years of therapy.
- Reinforce medication adherence, as consistent statin use was critical to the observed benefit.
- Educate patients that cardiovascular risk reduction from statins extends beyond cholesterol lowering, including stroke prevention.

2.6 *When to Discuss on Rounds*

Discuss this trial on rounds with the following scenarios:

- When debating statin therapy in patients with moderate cardiovascular risk or hypertension.
- When discussing the role of statins in preventing cerebrovascular events.
- When discussing ethical considerations in clinical trial design or when highlighting robust evidence.

2.7 Relevant Guidelines

The ASCOT-LLA trial influenced the **ACC/AHA** guidelines on blood cholesterol, which recommend statin therapy for adults aged 40–75 with LDL-C levels ≥70 mg/dl and an estimated 10-year ASCVD risk of ≥7.5%. This supports the use of moderate-intensity statins for primary prevention in at-risk populations.

3 ASCEND Trial Summary [3]

Full Title: Effects of Aspirin for Primary Prevention in Persons with Diabetes Mellitus
Publication Year: 2018
Journal: New England Journal of Medicine

3.1 Background

Patients with diabetes are at an elevated risk of cardiovascular disease. While antiplatelet therapy with aspirin is effective in secondary prevention, its role in primary prevention remains unclear, particularly due to the risk of bleeding. The ASCEND trial aimed to determine whether the benefits of aspirin in reducing cardiovascular events outweigh the bleeding risks in patients with diabetes without known CVD.

3.2 Study Design

Type: Multicenter, randomized, double-blind, placebo-controlled trial
Population: 15,480 patients with diabetes (type 1 or type 2), aged ≥40 years, without prior cardiovascular disease.
Intervention: Aspirin 100 mg daily vs. placebo
Primary Outcome:

- Serious vascular events (composite of nonfatal myocardial infarction, nonfatal stroke or transient ischemic attack, or vascular death, excluding confirmed intracranial hemorrhage)

Primary Safety Outcome:

- Major bleeding (intracranial bleeding, sight-threatening bleeding in the eye, gastrointestinal bleeding, or other serious bleeding requiring transfusion or hospitalization).

Secondary Outcomes:

- Gastrointestinal cancer
- Composite of any serious vascular event or any arterial revascularization procedure

3.3 Results

Primary Outcome:

- Serious vascular events occurred in 8.5% of participants in the aspirin group compared to 9.6% in the placebo group. This corresponds to a relative reduction of 12% with aspirin (Rate ratio: 0.88; [95% CI: 0.79–0.97, p = 0.01])

Primary Safety Outcome:

- Major bleeding events occurred in 4.1% of participants in the aspirin group versus 3.2% in the placebo group, indicating a relative risk increase of 29% with aspirin (Rate ratio: 1.29, [95% CI: 1.09–1.52, p = 0.003]).

Secondary Outcomes:

- Gastrointestinal cancer: No difference in the risk of GI tract cancer between groups.
- Serious vascular event or any revascularization: Occurred in 10.8% of patients in the aspirin group compared to 12.1% in the placebo group (Rate ratio: 0.88; [95% CI: 0.79–0.97; p = 0.01])

3.4 Key Takeaways

- In patients with diabetes without established cardiovascular disease, low-dose aspirin reduced the risk of serious vascular events compared with placebo.
- The benefit was offset by an increased risk of major bleeding, with absolute event reductions and increases of similar magnitude.
- No reduction was seen in gastrointestinal or other cancers over 7.4 years of follow-up.
- Findings emphasize the narrow balance between benefit and harm for aspirin in primary prevention among well-treated diabetic patients.

3.5 Clinical Application

- Use low-dose aspirin selectively for primary prevention in diabetes when overall ASCVD risk is high and bleeding risk is low, with shared decision-making about the narrow net benefit.
- Do not use routinely in average-risk patients with diabetes, or in those with elevated bleeding risk (e.g., prior GI bleed, concurrent anticoagulant/dual antiplatelet therapy, thrombocytopenia, uncontrolled HTN, advanced liver disease).
- Consider GI protection (PPI) in patients with upper-GI risk factors if aspirin is chosen.
- Optimize statins and blood pressure control first; aspirin offers only modest additional benefit in well-treated patients.
- Emphasize adherence and close follow-up, as small absolute effects are sensitive to real-world use.

3.6 When to Discuss on Rounds

Discuss this trial on rounds with the following scenarios:

- When deciding whether to start aspirin in patients with diabetes for primary prevention.
- During shared decision-making discussions or when emphasizing risk-benefit analysis.
- When discontinuing aspirin therapy in patients with no strong indications.

3.7 Relevant Guidelines

The ASCEND trial influenced the **ACC/AHA** guidelines on primary prevention of cardiovascular disease, which recommend that low-dose aspirin may be considered for primary prevention in select high-risk individuals aged 40–70 years who are not at increased risk of bleeding. However, the guidelines advise against routine aspirin use in patients over 70 or those with elevated bleeding risk. Similarly, the **ADA** standards of care suggest that aspirin can be used as a primary prevention strategy in diabetic patients with high cardiovascular risk, but not in those at low risk due to the lack of net clinical benefit.

4 DASH Trial Summary [4]

Full Title: A Clinical Trial of the Effects of Dietary Patterns on Blood Pressure
Publication Year: 1997
Journal: New England Journal of Medicine

4.1 Background

Hypertension is a leading risk factor for cardiovascular disease and stroke. While pharmacological therapy is the cornerstone of hypertension management, lifestyle interventions, particularly dietary changes, are important adjuncts. The DASH trial aimed to evaluate the effects of specific dietary patterns on blood pressure reduction.

4.2 Study Design

Type: Multicenter, randomized, controlled feeding trial.
Population: 459 adults with systolic blood pressure <160 mmHg and diastolic blood pressure between 80 and 95 mmHg. About half the participants were hypertensive.
Intervention: Typical American diet low in fruits, vegetables, and dairy (control diet) vs. high in fruits and vegetables, but without increased dairy or reduced fat (fruits-and-vegetables diet) vs. rich in fruits, vegetables, and low-fat dairy products, reduced in saturated and total fat (DASH diet
Primary Outcome: Change in diastolic blood pressure at rest
Secondary Outcomes:

- Changes in systolic blood pressure
- Changes in ambulatory systolic and diastolic blood pressure

4.3 Results

Primary Outcome:

- Compared to the control diet, the DASH combination diet reduced diastolic BP by 3.0 mmHg ($p < 0.001$).
- The fruits and vegetables diet reduced diastolic BP by 2.8 mmHg ($p < 0.001$) and 1.1 mmHg greater than the control diet ($p = 0.07$).
- Compared to the fruits and vegetables diet the DASH combination diet decreased diastolic BP by 1.9 mmHg more ($p = 0.002$).

Secondary Outcomes:

- Systolic BP: Compared to the control diet the DASH combination diet decreased systolic BP by 5.5 mmHg ($p < 0.001$). Compared to the fruits and vegetables diet the DASH combination diet decreased systolic BP by 2.7 mmHg more ($p = 0.001$).
- Ambulatory systolic and diastolic BP: Combination DASH diet reduced ambulatory systolic BP by 4.5 mmHg more than the control diet and ambulatory diastolic BP by 2.7 mmHg more ($p < 0.001$).

4.4 Key Takeaways

- The DASH diet is an effective non-pharmacological approach to reduce blood pressure.
- The blood pressure reductions observed in hypertensive individuals are comparable to the effects of single antihypertensive medications.
- The DASH diet emphasizes increased intake of fruits, vegetables, and low-fat dairy while reducing saturated and total fat.

4.5 Clinical Application

- Recommend the DASH diet for patients with hypertension or prehypertension.
- Emphasize the potential for medication reduction—Some patients may achieve blood pressure control with the DASH diet alone.
- Incorporate DASH principles into patient counseling.

4.6 When to Discuss on Rounds

Discuss this trial on rounds with the following scenarios:

- When discussing lifestyle modifications for hypertension.
- When discussing patient education or lifestyle counseling.
- When discussing evidence-based approaches to non-drug interventions.

4.7 Relevant Guidelines

The DASH trial led to strong endorsement of the DASH diet in major hypertension guidelines. The **ACC/AHA** hypertension guidelines recommend the DASH diet as a foundational lifestyle intervention for all patients with hypertension or prehypertension. Similarly, the **European Society of Cardiology/European Society of Hypertension (ESC/ESH)** hypertension guidelines highlight the DASH diet as a first-line non-pharmacological approach to support medication therapy. The **AHA** dietary guidelines also promote the DASH diet as part of a heart-healthy eating pattern aimed at reducing overall cardiovascular risk.

5 ROCKET-AF Trial Summary [5]

Full Title: Rivaroxaban versus Warfarin in Nonvalvular Atrial Fibrillation
Publication Year: 2011
Journal: New England Journal of Medicine

5.1 Background

Atrial fibrillation (AF) significantly increases the risk of stroke, traditionally managed by anticoagulation with vitamin K antagonists such as warfarin. However, warfarin therapy is associated with monitoring challenges, dietary interactions, and bleeding risks. ROCKET-AF evaluated rivaroxaban, an oral factor Xa inhibitor, as an alternative anticoagulant, compared to warfarin in patients with nonvalvular AF at moderate-to-high stroke risk.

5.2 Study Design

Type: Multicenter, randomized, double-blind, non-inferiority trial
Population: 14,264 patients with nonvalvular AF and elevated stroke risk ($CHADS_2$ score ≥2)
Intervention: Rivaroxaban (20 mg daily, or 15 mg daily if renal impairment) vs. adjusted-dose warfarin (INR target: 2.0–3.0)
Primary Objective: Composite of stroke (ischemic or hemorrhagic) and systemic embolism
Secondary Outcomes:

- Composite of stroke, systemic embolism, or death from cardiovascular causes
- Composite of stroke, systemic embolism, death from cardiovascular causes, or myocardial infarction
- Individual components of the composite end points

5.3 Results

Primary Outcome: Rivaroxaban was non-inferior to warfarin (Primary endpoint occurred in 2.1% per year rivaroxaban vs. 2.4% per year warfarin; HR 0.88; [95% CI: 0.74–1.03; p < 0.001 for non-inferiority]).

Secondary Outcomes:

- Fatal bleeding: Reduced in rivaroxaban group (0.2% vs. 0.5%, p = 0.003)
- Intracranial hemorrhage: Significantly lower with rivaroxaban (0.5% rivaroxaban vs. 0.7% warfarin; p = 0.02).
- Mortality: No significant difference (1.9% rivaroxaban vs. 2.2% warfarin per year; HR: 0.85; [95% CI: 0.70–1.02; p = 0.07]).

5.4 Key Takeaways

- In patients with nonvalvular atrial fibrillation at moderate-to-high stroke risk, rivaroxaban was noninferior to warfarin for preventing stroke or systemic embolism.
- In on-treatment analysis, rivaroxaban showed superiority to warfarin, but this was not seen in the intention-to-treat analysis.
- Overall rates of major and clinically relevant nonmajor bleeding were similar between groups.
- Rivaroxaban had lower rates of intracranial and fatal bleeding compared with warfarin.
- Gastrointestinal bleeding was more common with rivaroxaban.
- Efficacy was consistent across subgroups, including centers with good INR control.

5.5 Clinical Application

- Consider rivaroxaban as a suitable alternative to warfarin in patients with nonvalvular AF, particularly those struggling with INR management or at high risk of intracranial bleeding.
- Individualize anticoagulant selection based on patient-specific factors, bleeding risk, renal function, and patient preferences.
- Use caution in patients with a history of gastrointestinal bleeding, as rates were higher with rivaroxaban.
- Renal function should be assessed before initiation and monitored periodically, with dose adjustment in renal impairment.

5.6 *When to Discuss on Rounds*

Discuss this trial on rounds with the following scenarios:

- When evaluating anticoagulant options for patients with newly diagnosed nonvalvular AF.
- When discussing anticoagulation management in patients who experience difficulty maintaining therapeutic INR levels with warfarin.
- When reviewing stroke prevention strategies in AF with medical trainees.

5.7 *Relevant Guidelines*

ACC/AHA/Heart Rhythm Society (HRS) and **ESC** guidelines strongly endorse direct oral anticoagulants (DOACs), including rivaroxaban, as first-line therapy for stroke prevention in nonvalvular AF, directly citing ROCKET-AF outcomes.

6 AFFIRM Trial Summary [6]

Full Title: A Comparison of Rate Control and Rhythm Control in Patients with Atrial Fibrillation
Publication Year: 2002
Journal: New England Journal of Medicine

6.1 *Background*

Atrial fibrillation is a common arrhythmia associated with increased risk of stroke, heart failure, and mortality. Management strategies for atrial fibrillation historically focused on rhythm control or rate control. The AFFIRM trial compared these two approaches to determine whether rhythm control offers an advantage in mortality or stroke prevention.

6.2 *Study Design*

Type: Multicenter, randomized controlled trial.
Population: 4060 patients with atrial fibrillation and risk factors for stroke or death (mean age: 69.7 years).

Intervention: Antiarrhythmic drugs with or without electrical cardioversion (rhythm control group) vs. **r**ate control drugs to maintain HR at <80 BPM at rest and <110 BPM during six-minute walk test (rate control group)
Primary Outcome: All-cause mortality
Secondary Outcomes: Composite of death, disabling stroke, disabling anoxic encephalopathy, major bleeding, and cardiac arrest

6.3 Results

Primary Outcome: No significant difference in all-cause mortality between the rhythm-control and rate-control groups, although rhythm-control group was higher (23.8% vs. 21.3%; HR: 1.15; [95% CI: 0.99–1.34; p = 0.08]).
Secondary Outcomes:

- Composite end-point: Rate of the secondary composite end-point was similar between groups (p = 0.33).
- Stroke: Rates of stroke were similar between groups, but inadequate anticoagulation was a major factor in strokes, particularly in the rhythm-control group.
- Hospitalizations: Patients in the rhythm-control group had significantly more hospitalizations and adverse drug effects compared to the rate-control group.
- Adverse drug events: More frequent in the rhythm control group.

6.4 Key Takeaways

- In patients with atrial fibrillation and risk factors for stroke, rhythm-control and rate-control strategies showed no difference in overall mortality.
- There was a nonsignificant trend toward higher mortality in the rhythm-control group.
- Stroke rates were similar between groups and mainly occurred when anticoagulation was stopped or INR was subtherapeutic.
- Rhythm control was associated with more hospitalizations and adverse drug effects compared with rate control.
- Findings support rate control as a primary management strategy, with rhythm control reserved for select patients with persistent symptoms.

6.5 *Clinical Application*

- Initiate rate control in older or asymptomatic patients.
- Prioritize anticoagulation for stroke prevention.
- Patients with persistent symptoms or those unable to tolerate rate control may benefit from rhythm-control strategies, including antiarrhythmic drugs or ablation.
- Discuss treatment options with patients to align management strategies with their preferences and quality of life.

6.6 *When to Discuss on Rounds*

Discuss this trial on rounds with the following scenarios:

- When discussing management strategies for newly diagnosed or recurrent atrial fibrillation.
- When reinforcing the need for anticoagulation in atrial fibrillation.
- When tailoring treatment plans based on patient symptoms or preferences.

6.7 *Relevant Guidelines*

The **ACC/AHA** guidelines for the management of atrial fibrillation and the **ESC** guidelines for the management of atrial fibrillation were heavily influenced by AFFIRM. Both guidelines emphasize rate control as the preferred initial strategy for most patients with atrial fibrillation, particularly older patients or those with significant comorbidities. Rhythm control is recommended for patients with persistent symptoms despite adequate rate control or for those in whom maintaining sinus rhythm is critical (e.g., younger patients or those with heart failure). The guidelines also stress the importance of anticoagulation for stroke prevention, irrespective of the chosen management strategy.

7 CURE Trial Summary [7]

Full Title: Effects of Clopidogrel in Addition to Aspirin in Patients with Acute Coronary Syndromes without ST-Segment Elevation
Publication Year: 2001
Journal: New England Journal of Medicine

7.1 Background

Patients with acute coronary syndrome without ST-segment elevation (unstable angina or NSTEMI) are at high risk for recurrent ischemic events. Standard therapy traditionally included aspirin, but the role of dual antiplatelet therapy (DAPT) with aspirin and clopidogrel was uncertain. The CURE trial evaluated whether adding clopidogrel to aspirin improves cardiovascular outcomes in this population.

7.2 Study Design

Type: Multicenter, randomized controlled trial
Population: 12,562 patients with ACS without ST-segment elevation (NSTEMI or unstable angina)
Intervention: Clopidogrel (300 mg loading dose, followed by 75 mg daily) + aspirin (clopidogrel group) vs. aspirin + placebo (placebo group)
Primary Outcome: Composite of cardiovascular death, nonfatal myocardial infarction, or stroke
Secondary Outcomes:

- Severe ischemia
- Heart failure
- Need for revascularization

7.3 Results

Primary Outcome:

- Occurred in 9.3% of patients in the clopidogrel group compared to 11.4% of the placebo group (RR: 0.80; [95% CI: 0.72–0.90; $p < 0.001$])
- Clearest difference was in rate of MI, which was 5.2% in the clopidogrel group and 6.7% in the placebo group (RR: 0.77; [95% CI: 0.67–0.89])

Secondary Outcomes:

- Severe ischemia: Less in the clopidogrel group vs. placebo group (2.8% vs. 3.8%; RR: 0.74; [95% CI: 0.61–0.90; $p = 0.003$])
- Heart failure: Fewer incidents in the clopidogrel group compared to the placebo group (3.7% vs. 4.4%; RR: 0.82 [95% CI: 0.69–0.98; $p = 0.03$])
- Need for revascularization: Fewer patients underwent revascularization in the clopidogrel group, but this was accounted for by the difference in revascularization during the initial period of hospitalization (20.8% vs. 22.7%; $p = 0.03$).

Safety Outcomes:

- Increased risk of major bleeding in the clopidogrel group (3.7% vs. 2.7%; RR: 1.38; [95% CI: 1.13–1.67: p = 0.001]).
- No significant difference in rates of life-threatening or fatal bleeding.

7.4 *Key Takeaways*

- In patients with non–ST-elevation acute coronary syndromes, adding clopidogrel to aspirin significantly reduced the risk of cardiovascular death, nonfatal myocardial infarction, or stroke.
- Benefits were seen early, within 24 h of initiation, and were maintained throughout follow-up.
- Clopidogrel reduced recurrent ischemia, severe ischemia, and the need for urgent revascularization during initial hospitalization.
- The treatment effect was consistent across a broad range of patient subgroups and concomitant therapies.
- Major and minor bleeding were more frequent with clopidogrel, but without an increase in fatal bleeding or hemorrhagic stroke.

7.5 *Clinical Application*

- Initiate clopidogrel (or other P2Y12 inhibitors) in combination with aspirin for patients presenting with unstable angina or NSTEMI.
- Use clopidogrel in patients with lower bleeding risk, or consider newer agents if appropriate.
- Ensure a full 12 months of DAPT unless contraindicated or bleeding occurs.
- Tailor the choice of antiplatelet agent and duration of therapy based on patients comorbidities and risk factors.
- Utilize DAPT in medically managed patients and as part of preparation for potential coronary intervention.

7.6 *When to Discuss on Rounds*

Discuss this trial on rounds with the following scenarios:

- When discussing initial management of NSTEMI or unstable angina.
- When addressing anticoagulation and bleeding risk in ACS patients.
- When reviewing rationale for DAPT during bedside teaching.

7.7 *Relevant Guidelines*

CURE significantly influenced the **ACC/AHA** guidelines for the management of non-st-elevation acute coronary syndromes (NSTE-ACS) and the **ESC** guidelines on the management of acs in patients without persistent st-segment elevation guidelines. Both guidelines recommend DAPT for 12 months in patients with ACS without ST-segment elevation, unless there is a high bleeding risk. Clopidogrel was initially the standard P2Y12 inhibitor, but newer agents like ticagrelor and prasugrel are now preferred due to greater efficacy. However, clopidogrel remains an option in certain patients, especially those at higher bleeding risk or with contraindications to other agents.

8 SADHART Trial Summary [8]

Full Title: Sertraline Treatment of Major Depression in Patients With Acute MI or Unstable Angina
Publication Year: 2002
Journal: Journal of the American Medical Association

8.1 *Background*

Depression is common in patients with acute coronary syndromes and is associated with increased morbidity and mortality. However, concerns existed about the cardiovascular safety of selective serotonin reuptake inhibitors (SSRIs) in this population. The SADHART trial aimed to evaluate the safety and efficacy of sertraline (an SSRI) in patients with major depressive disorder (MDD) following acute myocardial infarction or unstable angina.

8.2 *Study Design*

Type: Multicenter, randomized, double-blind, placebo-controlled trial.
Population: 369 patients with recent MI or unstable angina and MDD
Intervention: Sertraline (50–200 mg/day) vs. placebo
Primary Outcome: Change from baseline left ventricular ejection fraction (LVEF)
Secondary Outcomes:

- Cardiac adverse events
- Scores on HAM-D and Clinical Global Impression Improvement (CGI-I) scales

8.3 Results

Primary Outcome:

- Sertraline had no significant effect on mean LVEF (sertraline: baseline, 54% [10%]; week 16, 54% [11%]; placebo: baseline, 52% [13%]; week 16, 53% [13%]; $p \geq .05$)

Secondary Outcomes:

- Cardiac adverse events: Occurred less in 14.5% of patients in the sertraline group vs. 22.4% in the placebo group, although this was not statistically significant.
- Scores: Sertraline was significantly more effective than placebo on the CGI-I scale in the overall population and showed greater benefit in patients with a history of major depressive disorder, achieving superior results on both the CGI-I and HAM-D scales. Across all subgroups, a higher proportion of sertraline-treated patients met responder criteria (CGI-I score of 1 or 2), with treatment benefits becoming more pronounced as depression severity increased.

8.4 Key Takeaways

- In patients with acute coronary syndrome (ACS) and major depressive disorder, sertraline was safe with no adverse effects on left ventricular function, arrhythmias, or other cardiac parameters.
- Rates of severe cardiovascular events were numerically lower with sertraline compared with placebo, though not statistically significant.
- Sertraline was more effective than placebo in improving depressive symptoms among patients with recurrent depression, particularly those with higher baseline severity.
- No clear efficacy advantage was seen in patients experiencing their first episode of depression after ACS.
- Findings support the cardiovascular safety of SSRIs in this population and potential benefit for depression management in those with prior history of major depressive disorder.

8.5 Clinical Application

- Routine screening for depression should be considered in patients post-MI.
- Choose SSRIs over TCAs or MAOIs as these can cause arrhythmias and hypotension, making SSRIs like sertraline the preferred choice.

- Monitor patients for adherence and side effects.
- Involve cardiology, psychiatry, and primary care in the management of post-MI depression.
- Educate patients on the importance of mental health. Address the stigma of depression in cardiac patients and emphasize the role of treatment in overall recovery.

8.6 When to Discuss on Rounds

Discuss this trial on rounds with the following scenarios:

- When discussing mental health screening in cardiac patients.
- When choosing antidepressants for patients with cardiac disease.
- When discussing holistic care in patients with ACS.

8.7 Relevant Guidelines

The **AHA/ACC** guidelines for the management of patients with non-st-elevation acute coronary syndromes and the **American Psychiatric Association (APA)** guidelines on depression both acknowledge the importance of screening and managing depression in cardiovascular patients. The SADHART trial provided key evidence for recommending SSRIs, particularly sertraline, as a first-line treatment for post-MI depression due to its safety profile.

9 SAVE Trial Summary (Heart Failure) [9]

Full Title: Effect of Captopril on Mortality and Morbidity in Patients with Left Ventricular Dysfunction after Myocardial Infarction—Results of the Survival and Ventricular Enlargement Trial
Publication Year: 1992
Journal: New England Journal of Medicine

9.1 Background

Following a myocardial infarction, patients with left ventricular dysfunction are at increased risk for heart failure and death. ACE inhibitors were known to improve outcomes in heart failure, but their role in post-MI patients with asymptomatic left ventricular dysfunction was unclear. The SAVE trial investigated whether captopril, an ACE inhibitor, could improve survival and reduce morbidity in this high-risk group.

9.2 Study Design

Type: Multicenter, randomized, double-blind, placebo-controlled trial.
Population: 2231 patients with recent MI (3–16 days prior) and left ventricular ejection fraction ≤40% but without severe heart failure.
Intervention: Captopril (starting at 6.25 mg, titrated up to 50 mg three times daily) vs. placebo
Primary Outcomes:

- All-cause mortality.
- Cardiovascular mortality
- Recurrent MI

Secondary Outcome: Hospitalization to treat congestive heart failure

9.3 Results

Primary Outcomes:

- All-cause mortality: Captopril significantly reduced all-cause mortality compared to placebo (20% captopril vs. 25% placebo; [95% CI: 0.03–0.32; p = 0.019]).
- Cardiovascular mortality: Of the deaths 84% were due to cardiovascular causes. Of these deaths 234 occurred in the placebo group and 188 in the captopril group (risk reduction: 0.21; [95% CI: 0.05–0.35; p = 0.014]).
- Recurrent MI: Captopril significantly reduced recurrence of MI (risk reduction: 0.25; [95% CI: 0.05–0.40; p = 0.015]).

Secondary Outcome:

- Hospitalization to treat CHF: Significantly reduced in the captopril group 14% vs. 17% in placebo group (risk reduction: 0.22 [95% CI: 0.04–0.37; p = 0.019]).

9.4 Key Takeaways

- In post–myocardial infarction patients with asymptomatic left ventricular dysfunction (EF ≤40%), long-term captopril therapy reduced all-cause mortality by 19% and cardiovascular mortality by 21% compared with placebo.

- Captopril significantly lowered the risk of developing severe heart failure, requiring hospitalization for heart failure, and needing open-label ACE inhibitor therapy.
- The drug also reduced the incidence of recurrent myocardial infarction by 25% and the combined endpoint of death or marked decline in left ventricular ejection fraction by 15%.
- Benefits emerged with prolonged follow-up, supporting ACE inhibitor use as preventive therapy in this high-risk population even in the absence of overt heart failure.
- The therapeutic effect was consistent across subgroups, including patients receiving standard post-MI therapies such as thrombolytics, aspirin, and beta-blockers.

9.5 Clinical Application

- Start ACE inhibitor therapy early in post-MI patients with asymptomatic LV dysfunction (EF ≤40%) to reduce long-term mortality and morbidity.
- Continue ACE inhibitors indefinitely in these patients, even if they are asymptomatic, as benefits accrue over prolonged follow-up.
- Use in conjunction with standard post-MI therapies (aspirin, beta-blockers, statins, thrombolytics when indicated) for additive benefit.
- Monitor blood pressure, renal function, and potassium regularly after initiation and during titration to target doses.
- Consider in broader patient populations at high risk for ventricular remodeling, with careful selection based on EF and clinical profile.

9.6 When to Discuss on Rounds

Discuss this trial on rounds with the following scenarios:

- When discussing guideline-directed medical therapy in post-MI patients.
- When discussing strategies to prevent post-MI complications.
- When transitioning patients from acute care to outpatient management.

9.7 Relevant Guidelines

The **ACC/AHA** guidelines for the management of st-elevation myocardial infarction (STEMI) and the **AHA/ACC/Heart Failure Society of America (HFSA)** guidelines for the management of heart failure recommend ACE inhibitors in post-MI patients with LVEF ≤40% to reduce mortality and prevent heart failure. The SAVE trial was a foundational study that led to these strong recommendations. If ACE inhibitors are not tolerated, angiotensin receptor blockers are an alternative.

10 DOSE Trial Summary [10]

Full Title: Diuretic Strategies in Patients with Acute Decompensated Heart Failure
Publication Year: 2011
Journal: New England Journal of Medicine

10.1 Background

Loop diuretics like furosemide are the mainstay of treatment for acute decompensated heart failure (ADHF), but optimal dosing and mode of administration (bolus vs. continuous infusion) were unclear. The DOSE trial aimed to determine whether high-dose diuretics improve symptoms and outcomes compared to low-dose diuretics and whether continuous infusion is superior to intermittent bolus dosing.

10.2 Study Design

Type: Multicenter, randomized, double-blind trial.
Population: 308 patients hospitalized with ADHF who were already on chronic oral loop diuretics
Intervention:

- **Dosing Strategy:** High-dose (2.5× home diuretic dose) vs. low-dose (equivalent to home dose)
- **Administration Strategy:** Intermittent IV bolus every 12 h vs. continuous infusion

Primary Outcome:

- Patient's global assessment of symptoms. Patients were asked how they were feeling by marking a 10-cm vertical line with the bottom labeled "worst you ever felt" and top labeled "best you've ever felt"

Primary Safety Outcome:

- Change in serum creatinine to assess the risk of worsening renal function

Secondary Outcomes:

- Patient-reported dyspnea improvement
- Change in body weight and net fluid loss
- Worsening renal function
- Worsening persistent heart failure
- Treatment failure

10.3 Results

Primary Outcome:

- No significant difference in global symptom improvement (mean improvement 4236 ± 1440 with boluses and 4373 ± 1404 AUC with continuous infusion; p = 0.47), or between low-dose and high-dose strategies (p = 0.06).

Primary Safety Outcome:

- No significant difference in change in creatinine in bolus vs. continuous infusion (0.05 ± 0.3 mg/dl [4.4 ± 26.5 μmol/L] and 0.07 ± 0.3 mg/dl [6.2 ± 26.5 μmol/L]; p = 0.45) or with high dose vs. low dose strategy (0.08 ± 0.3 mg/dl [7.1 ± 26.5 μmol/L] vs. 0.04 ± 0.3 mg/dl [3.5 ± 26.5 μmol/L]; p = 0.21)

Secondary Outcomes:

- Patient-reported dyspnea improvement: At 72 h, there was no significant difference between bolus and continuous infusion groups (AUC 4456 ± 1468 vs. 4699 ± 1573; p = 0.36). However, high-dose therapy led to significantly greater dyspnea relief compared to low-dose therapy (AUC 4668 ± 1496 vs. 4478 ± 1550; p = 0.04).
- Change in body weight and net fluid loss: High-dose diuretics resulted in significantly greater net fluid loss and weight loss compared to low-dose strategy. Differences were statistically significant.
- Worsening renal function: Occurred more frequently in the high-dose group (23%) than in the low-dose group (14%) (p = 0.04). No significant difference between bolus and continuous infusion.
- Worsening persistent heart failure: No significant differences reported between treatment arms in clinical worsening or heart failure progression during hospitalization.
- Treatment failure: At 60 days, the composite of death, rehospitalization, or emergency visit occurred in 42% of patients overall, with no significant difference between high vs. low dose (HR 0.83; [95% CI: 0.60–1.16; p = 0.28]) or bolus vs. continuous infusion (HR 1.15; [95% CI: 0.83–1.60; p = 0.41]).

10.4 Key Takeaways

- In acute decompensated heart failure, there was no significant difference in symptom relief or change in renal function between bolus and continuous infusion of IV furosemide.
- High-dose diuretic therapy provided greater fluid loss, weight reduction, and dyspnea relief compared with low-dose therapy, but with more frequent transient worsening of renal function.
- The transient worsening of renal function with high-dose diuretics was not associated with worse 60-day clinical outcomes.
- Serious adverse events were less frequent in the high-dose group than in the low-dose group, with no difference between bolus and continuous infusion groups.
- Findings suggest either bolus or continuous infusion is reasonable, with dose selection tailored to symptom severity and volume status.

10.5 Clinical Application

- Either bolus or continuous infusion of IV loop diuretics is reasonable; choose based on logistics and nursing workflow rather than expected differences in efficacy or renal safety.
- For patients with marked congestion, favor a higher initial diuretic intensity to achieve greater decongestion and dyspnea relief, with close monitoring.
- Expect transient creatinine bumps with higher doses; don't reflexively down-titrate if the patient is clearly decongesting and hemodynamically stable.
- Reassess at ~48 h: adjust dose/intensity based on urine output, weight change, edema, and symptom trajectory.
- Track daily weights, strict I/O, BMPs, and electrolytes (especially K^+, Mg^{2+}); replace electrolytes proactively.
- Transition to oral diuretics once euvolemic/improving, ensuring a successful oral dose trial before discharge.
- No difference in short-term clinical events was seen between strategies, so individualize therapy to symptom severity, volume status, and renal tolerance.

10.6 When to Discuss on Rounds

Discuss this trial on rounds with the following scenarios:

- When discussing diuretic dosing strategies for ADHF patients.
- When evaluating diuresis vs. kidney function in heart failure management.
- When deciding how to administer IV diuretics.

10.7 Relevant Guidelines

The **AHA/ACC/HFSA** guidelines for the management of heart failure recommend IV loop diuretics as first-line therapy for ADHF but do not favor bolus vs continuous infusion. The DOSE trial provided key evidence that diuretic dosing should be individualized, with high-dose strategies used when rapid volume removal is needed despite potential transient renal impairment.

References

1. Dahlöf B, Sever PS, Poulter NR, et al. Prevention of cardiovascular events with an antihypertensive regimen of amlodipine adding perindopril as required versus atenolol adding bendroflumethiazide as required, in the Anglo-Scandinavian Cardiac Outcomes Trial-Blood Pressure Lowering Arm (ASCOT-BPLA): a multicenter randomised controlled trial. Lancet. 2005;366(9489):895–906. https://doi.org/10.1016/S0140-6736(05)67185-1.
2. Sever PS, Dahlöf B, Poulter NR, et al. Prevention of coronary and stroke events with atorvastatin in hypertensive patients who have average or lower-than-average cholesterol concentrations, in the Anglo-Scandinavian Cardiac Outcomes Trial–Lipid Lowering Arm (ASCOT-LLA): a multicenter randomised controlled trial. Lancet. 2003;361(9364):1149–58. https://doi.org/10.1016/S0140-6736(03)12948-0.
3. ASCEND Study Collaborative Group, Bowman L, Mafham M, et al. Effects of aspirin for primary prevention in persons with diabetes mellitus. N Engl J Med. 2018;379(16):1529–39. https://doi.org/10.1056/NEJMoa1804988.
4. Appel LJ, Moore TJ, Obarzanek E, et al. A clinical trial of the effects of dietary patterns on blood pressure. DASH Collaborative Research Group. N Engl J Med. 1997;336(16):1117–24. https://doi.org/10.1056/NEJM199704173361601.
5. Patel MR, Mahaffey KW, Garg J, et al. Rivaroxaban versus warfarin in nonvalvular atrial fibrillation. N Engl J Med. 2011;365(10):883–91. https://doi.org/10.1056/NEJMoa1009638.
6. Wyse DG, Waldo AL, DiMarco JP, et al. A comparison of rate control and rhythm control in patients with atrial fibrillation. N Engl J Med. 2002;347(23):1825–33. https://doi.org/10.1056/NEJMoa021328.
7. Yusuf S, Zhao F, Mehta SR, et al. Effects of clopidogrel in addition to aspirin in patients with acute coronary syndromes without ST-segment elevation [published correction appears in N Engl J Med 2001 Dec 6;345(23):1716] [published correction appears in N Engl J Med 2001 Nov 15;345(20):1506]. N Engl J Med. 2001;345(7):494–502. https://doi.org/10.1056/NEJMoa010746.
8. Glassman AH, O'Connor CM, Califf RM, et al. Sertraline treatment of major depression in patients with acute MI or unstable angina [published correction appears in JAMA 2002 Oct 9;288(14):1720]. JAMA. 2002;288(6):701–9. https://doi.org/10.1001/jama.288.6.701.
9. Pfeffer MA, Braunwald E, Moyé LA, et al. Effect of captopril on mortality and morbidity in patients with left ventricular dysfunction after myocardial infarction. Results of the survival and ventricular enlargement trial. The SAVE Investigators. N Engl J Med. 1992;327(10):669–77. https://doi.org/10.1056/NEJM199209033271001.
10. Felker GM, Lee KL, Bull DA, et al. Diuretic strategies in patients with acute decompensated heart failure. N Engl J Med. 2011;364(9):797–805. https://doi.org/10.1056/NEJMoa1005419.

Chapter 3
Pulmonology

1 BASALT Trial Summary [1]

Full Title: Comparison of Physician-, Biomarker-, and Symptom-Based Strategies for Adjustment of Inhaled Corticosteroid Therapy in Adults With Asthma
Publication Year: 2012
Journal: Journal of the American Medical Association

1.1 Background

Asthma treatment guidelines recommend inhaled corticosteroids as maintenance therapy. Traditionally, dose adjustments were made based on symptoms or scheduled provider visits. The BASALT trial aimed to compare three strategies for adjusting ICS therapy in adults with mild to moderate persistent asthma.

1.2 Study Design

Type: Multicenter, randomized, double-blind trial
Population: 342 adults with mild to moderate persistent asthma
Intervention:

- Physician-based adjustment (PABA): ICS dose adjusted every 6 weeks based on provider assessment
- Biomarker-based adjustment (BBA): ICS dose adjusted every 6 weeks based on fraction of exhaled nitric oxide (FeNO) levels
- Patient-based adjustments (SBA): Patients used ICS only as needed when they used their short-acting beta-agonist (SABA)

A. Love, *The Essential Evidence*, https://doi.org/10.1007/978-3-032-12399-2_3

Primary Outcome: Time to first asthma treatment failure
Secondary Outcomes:

- Spirometry
- Albuterol reversibility
- Methacholine responsiveness
- Sputum eosinophils
- Daytime and nighttime symptom and rescue β-agonist diaries
- Asthma Control Questionnaire (ACQ)
- Asthma Symptom Utility Index (ASUI)
- Asthma Quality-Of-Life Questionnaire (AQLQ)

1.3 Results

Primary Outcome:

- No significant difference in time to treatment failure between the three groups over 9 months (22% PABA vs. 20% BBA vs. 15% SBA).
  - PABA vs. BBA (HR 1.2; [97.5% CI: 0.6–2.3; p = 0.68]).
  - PABA vs. SBA (HR 1.6; [97.5% CI: 0.8–3.3; p = 0.18]).
  - BBA vs. SBA (HR 1.4; [97.5% CI: 0.6–2.9; p = 0.35]).

Secondary Outcomes:

- Spirometry:
  - Pre-bronchodilator FEV_1 improved in the SBA group by −0.13 L (95% CI: −0.24 to −0.02; p = 0.01).
  - FEV_1 % predicted improved similarly in all groups; SBA: −3.43%, BBA: −2.45%, PABA: −3.44% (all p < 0.001).
  - Post-bronchodilator FEV_1 also improved in all groups (all p < 0.001), with no significant difference between groups.
- Albuterol reversibility:
  - SBA group showed a significant increase in FEV_1 reversibility: +2.26% (95% CI: 0.28–4.25; p = 0.01).
  - No significant change in other groups.
- Methacholine responsiveness
  - PABA group showed significant improvement in PC_{20}: −0.63 $\log_2$ mg/mL (95% CI −1.09 to −0.17; p = 0.002).
  - BBA vs. PABA showed a significant difference: +0.83 (95% CI: 0.16–1.50; p = 0.006).
- Sputum eosinophils: No significant between-group differences.
- ACQ/ASUI/AQLQ: No significant changes or improvements in any group.

1.4 Key Takeaways

- In adults with mild to moderate persistent asthma, symptom-based adjustment (SBA) of inhaled corticosteroids (ICS), taking low-dose beclomethasone whenever albuterol is used was not superior to physician assessment–based adjustment (PABA) or biomarker-based adjustment (BBA, using exhaled nitric oxide) for preventing treatment failure over 9 months.
- Treatment failure rates were similar: 22% (PABA), 20% (BBA), 15% (SBA); none of the pairwise differences were statistically significant.
- Exacerbation rates, lung function, and asthma symptom scores did not differ significantly among groups.
- Ethnic differences were noted. Hispanic participants responded differently to SBA vs PABA compared to non-Hispanic whites, suggesting possible cultural, environmental, or pharmacogenetic influences.
- SBA offers a simpler, patient-driven approach with lower ICS exposure, which may be an appropriate alternative in most patients with mild to moderate asthma — though caution is warranted in those with poor symptom perception or adherence issues.

1.5 Clinical Application

- For adults with mild to moderate asthma who are stable, symptom-based ICS use (taking ICS with each SABA use) can maintain control while reducing cumulative steroid exposure.
- SBA is appropriate for motivated patients with good symptom recognition, reliable inhaler technique, and consistent access to both ICS and SABA inhalers; these patients should also demonstrate a history of adherence to previous regimens and an ability to promptly escalate therapy if symptoms worsen.
- SBA is not recommended for patients with poor adherence, difficulty recognizing worsening symptoms, or high exacerbation risk.
- SBA can be considered when minimizing steroid exposure is a priority (e.g., to reduce long-term adverse effects).

1.6 When to Discuss on Rounds

Discuss this trial on rounds with the following scenarios:

- When discussing step-down therapy or alternative asthma management strategies.
- When considering as-needed ICS for a patient with mild persistent asthma who is well-controlled and reluctant to use daily inhalers.
- When educating patients on self-monitoring and ICS use, especially in shared decision-making.

1.7 Relevant Guidelines

The **Global Initiative for Asthma Guidelines** incorporated findings from BASALT and other studies to recommend as-needed ICS/formoterol as an alternative to daily ICS in mild asthma. The study provided key evidence supporting patient-driven ICS use instead of strict daily dosing.

2 TORCH Trial Summary [2]

Full Title: Salmeterol and Fluticasone Propionate and Survival in Chronic Obstructive Pulmonary Disease
Publication Year: 2007
Journal: New England Journal of Medicine

2.1 Background

Chronic obstructive pulmonary disease is a leading cause of morbidity and mortality, but no pharmacologic therapy had been definitively proven to reduce mortality. The TORCH trial aimed to determine whether the combination of fluticasone (ICS) and salmeterol (LABA) could improve survival compared to placebo or monotherapy.

2.2 Study Design

Type: Multicenter, randomized, double-blind, placebo-controlled trial.
Population: 6112 patients with moderate-to-severe COPD (FEV <60% predicted)
Intervention: Fluticasone/salmeterol (ICS/LABA) combination therapy vs. salmeterol (LABA) alone vs. fluticasone (ICS) alone vs. placebo
Primary Outcome: Time to death by any cause at 3 years
Secondary Outcomes:

- Rate of COPD exacerbations
- Health status (St. George's Respiratory Questionnaire)

2.3 *Results*

Primary Outcome:

- Salmeterol/fluticasone combination therapy did not significantly reduce all-cause mortality compared to placebo over 3 years (12.6% combination vs. 15.2% placebo; HR 0.825 [95% CI: 0.68–1.00; $p = 0.052$]).

Secondary Outcomes:

- COPD exacerbations: Significantly reduced in combination therapy group compared to placebo (annual rate: 0.85 vs. 1.13; rate ratio 0.75; [95% CI: 0.69–0.81; $p < 0.001$]).
- Health Status (SGRQ): Improved quality-of-life scores with combination therapy compared to placebo (−3.1 units; $p < 0.001$).

2.4 *Key Takeaways*

- Combination therapy with salmeterol + fluticasone showed a trend toward reduced all-cause mortality in COPD, though it did not reach statistical significance
- Combination therapy significantly reduced the rate of COPD exacerbations by 25% and improved lung function and quality of life.
- Both salmeterol and fluticasone alone also reduced exacerbation rates, but combination therapy had the greatest overall benefit.
- Combination therapy improved health-related quality of life and maintained better lung function compared to placebo and either monotherapy.
- Increased risk of pneumonia was observed in groups receiving fluticasone-containing therapies, though this did not translate into increased pneumonia-related mortality.
- No significant differences were observed among groups for fractures, bone mineral density changes, cataract development, or excess cardiac events.
- Findings are generalizable due to large, international patient enrollment and high follow-up completeness.

2.5 *Clinical Application*

- Use salmeterol plus fluticasone propionate combination inhaler for patients with moderate to severe COPD (post-bronchodilator FEV_1 <60% predicted) who experience ≥1–2 exacerbations per year despite optimal long-acting bronchodilator therapy.

- Prescribe combination therapy when the goal is to reduce exacerbation frequency, improve quality of life, and maintain lung function, even if a definitive mortality benefit is not established.
- Consider combination therapy for patients with a history of COPD-related hospitalization, as it reduces admission rates compared to placebo and monotherapy.
- Monitor closely and counsel patients about pneumonia risk when using fluticasone-containing regimens, particularly in older adults, those with prior pneumonia, or those with significant comorbid lung disease.
- Avoid or discontinue inhaled corticosteroid–containing therapy in patients with recurrent pneumonia or intolerable corticosteroid side effects, and switch to a long-acting bronchodilator–only regimen when appropriate.
- Incorporate shared decision-making, weighing the benefits of exacerbation and hospitalization reduction against the increased risk of pneumonia, especially in patients with borderline ICS indications.

2.6 When to Discuss on Rounds

Discuss this trial on rounds with the following scenarios:

- When discussing the role of ICS/LABA in COPD treatment.
- When debating ICS use in COPD patients, particularly those with a high risk of pneumonia.
- When evaluating inhaled corticosteroid/long-acting beta-agonist combination therapy for patients with moderate to severe COPD and frequent exacerbations.
- When counseling patients on realistic expectations of therapy, including improvements in quality of life and lung function without a proven mortality benefit.
- When discussing step-up therapy for COPD.

2.7 Relevant Guidelines

The **Global Initiative for Chronic Obstructive Lung Disease** guidelines incorporate TORCH findings, recommending ICS/LABA for COPD patients with frequent exacerbations or high eosinophil counts (>300 cells/μL).

3 UPLIFT Trial Summary [3]

Full Title: A 4-Year Trial of Tiotropium in Chronic Obstructive Pulmonary Disease
Publication Year: 2008
Journal: New England Journal of Medicine

3.1 Background

Tiotropium, a long-acting muscarinic antagonist (LAMA), had been shown to improve symptoms and reduce exacerbations, but its long-term effects on disease progression and mortality were unknown. The UPLIFT trial aimed to assess whether tiotropium could slow the decline in lung function and improve outcomes in patients with moderate-to-severe COPD.

3.2 Study Design

Type: Multicenter, randomized, double-blind, placebo-controlled trial.
Population: 5993 patients with moderate-to-severe COPD (FEV1 <70% predicted)
Intervention: Tiotropium (LAMA) once daily vs. placebo (both groups received usual COPD therapy, except for other inhaled anticholinergics)
Primary Outcome: Yearly rate of decline in FEV1 (both pre and post-bronchodilator)
Secondary Outcomes:

- Rate of decline in mean forced vital capacity (FVC) and slow vital capacity (SVC)
- Health-related quality of life, measured by St. George's Respiratory Questionnaire (SGRQ) score (0–100 scale; ≥4-unit change considered clinically meaningful)
- COPD exacerbation frequency and related hospitalizations
- All-cause mortality

3.3 Results

Primary Outcome:

- No significant difference between tiotropium and placebo in the annual rate of decline in mean FEV1 (both pre- and post-bronchodilator) from day 30 to study completion.
- In post hoc analysis, patients who were not receiving inhaled corticosteroids or long-acting beta-agonists at baseline, tiotropium modestly slowed the decline in post-bronchodilator FEV1 compared to placebo ($p = 0.046$).

Secondary Outcome:

- Decline of FVC: No significant difference in FVC decline between groups.
- Health Status and Quality of Life (SGRQ): Significant improvement in quality-of-life scores with tiotropium ($p < 0.001$).

- Exacerbations: Significantly fewer COPD exacerbations in tiotropium-treated patients ($p < 0.001$).
- Mortality: No significant reduction in all-cause mortality with tiotropium vs. placebo (14.9% vs. 16.5%; HR: 0.89 [95% CI: 0.79–1.02; $p = 0.09$]).

3.4 Key Takeaways

- Tiotropium (18 μg daily) for up to 4 years in COPD patients did not slow the overall rate of decline in FEV_1 compared with placebo, but it consistently produced better absolute lung function throughout the study.
- Tiotropium improved both pre- and post-bronchodilator FEV_1 and FVC at all time points, with differences of roughly 87–103 mL pre-bronchodilator and 47–65 mL post-bronchodilator compared with placebo.
- Health-related quality of life, as measured by SGRQ scores, was consistently better with tiotropium, and a greater proportion of patients achieved clinically meaningful improvements each year.
- The drug reduced exacerbations by 14%, delayed the time to first exacerbation by about 4 months, and delayed exacerbation-related hospitalizations.
- Benefits occurred despite high background use of other COPD medications, indicating tiotropium's additive effect in an optimized treatment setting.
- Safety profile matched prior experience, with dry mouth and constipation as common side effects, and fewer serious respiratory events compared with placebo.

3.5 Clinical Application

- In patients with moderate-to-severe COPD (GOLD stage II–IV) who are already receiving other standard therapies such as inhaled corticosteroids and/or long-acting beta-agonists, adding tiotropium 18 μg daily can provide sustained improvements in lung function and reduce exacerbations, even if it does not slow overall FEV_1 decline.
- Appropriate for patients with frequent exacerbations or hospitalizations despite optimized inhaler regimens, as tiotropium delayed time to first exacerbation and first exacerbation-related hospitalization.
- May be especially useful in patients with significant symptom burden (e.g., dyspnea, activity limitation) where improving quality of life is a goal, since more patients on tiotropium achieved clinically meaningful SGRQ improvements compared with placebo.
- Suitable for long-term maintenance therapy, given sustained benefits in airflow and symptom control over 4 years with a safety profile consistent with prior evidence.
- Consider in patients at risk for respiratory failure or with concomitant cardiac disease, given reductions in respiratory failure events and certain cardiac adverse events in the trial.

3.6 *When to Discuss on Rounds*

Discuss this trial on rounds with the following scenarios:

- When discussing long-term COPD management, bring up that tiotropium improved lung function, quality of life, and exacerbation rates over 4 years but did not slow the decline in FEV_1.
- When reviewing inhaler regimens, ask whether tiotropium should be added in patients already on ICS and/or LABA, given UPLIFT's results.
- When seeing a COPD patient with frequent exacerbations, discuss UPLIFT's finding that tiotropium delayed time to first exacerbation and first hospitalization.
- When reviewing trial methodology, highlight that UPLIFT allowed background use of other COPD medications, making results highly generalizable to real-world practice.

3.7 *Relevant Guidelines*

The **Global Initiative for Chronic Obstructive Lung Disease** guidelines incorporate UPLIFT findings, recommending LAMA therapy (such as tiotropium) as first-line treatment for symptomatic COPD patients to reduce exacerbations and hospitalizations. The trial also supports combining LAMA with LABA for patients with persistent symptoms.

4 SAVE Trial Summary (Obstructive Sleep Apnea) [4]

Full Title: CPAP for Prevention of Cardiovascular Events in Obstructive Sleep Apnea
Publication Year: 2016
Journal: New England Journal of Medicine

4.1 *Background*

Obstructive sleep apnea (OSA) is a common condition associated with increased cardiovascular risk, including hypertension, myocardial infarction, and stroke. Continuous positive airway pressure (CPAP) is the primary treatment for OSA, improving daytime sleepiness and quality of life, but its impact on cardiovascular outcomes remained uncertain. The SAVE trial aimed to evaluate whether CPAP therapy could reduce major cardiovascular events in patients with OSA and established cardiovascular disease.

4.2 *Study Design*

Type: Multicenter, randomized, open-label trial with blinded outcome assessment.
Population: 2717 patients age 40–75 with moderate-to-severe OSA (AHI ≥15 events/hour) and established cardiovascular disease.
Intervention: CPAP therapy + usual care vs. usual care alone
Primary Outcome: Composite of death from cardiovascular causes, myocardial infarction, stroke, or hospitalization for unstable angina, heart failure, or transient ischemic attack
Secondary Outcomes:

- Other cardiovascular outcomes
- Health-related quality of life
- Daytime sleepiness
- Mood

4.3 *Results*

Primary Outcome: CPAP therapy did not significantly reduce the incidence of the composite primary endpoint or other cardiovascular events (death, MI, stroke, hospitalization for unstable angina or heart failure, or TIA) compared to usual care (17.0% CPAP vs. 15.4% usual care; HR 1.10; [95% CI: 0.91–1.32; $p = 0.34$]).
Secondary Outcome:

- Other cardiovascular outcomes: No significant differences were observed in any of the composite or individual cardiovascular endpoints. Similarly, the composite of major cardiovascular events and other cardiac or cerebral endpoints were all non-significant.
- Health-related quality of life: Small but statistically significant improvements were seen in both physical (adjusted difference: +0.9 [95% CI: 0.3–1.4; $p = 0.002$]) and mental (adjusted difference: +1.2 [95% CI: 0.6–1.8; $p < 0.001$]) components of the SF-36 score in the CPAP group.
- Daytime sleepiness: CPAP significantly improved Epworth Sleepiness Scale scores by −2.5 points compared to usual care (95% CI: −2.8 to −2.2; $p < 0.001$).
- Mood: Anxiety score decreased by −0.4 points (95% CI: −0.6 to −0.2; $p = 0.002$) and depression score by −0.8 points (95% CI: −1.0 to −0.5; $p < 0.001$) in the CPAP group vs. usual care.

4.4 Key Takeaways

- In adults with established cardiovascular disease and moderate-to-severe obstructive sleep apnea (OSA), adding continuous positive airway pressure (CPAP) to usual care did not reduce the risk of recurrent serious cardiovascular events compared with usual care alone over a mean follow-up of 3.7 years.
- CPAP use significantly reduced daytime sleepiness and improved quality of life, mood, and work attendance compared with usual care.
- In adherent patients, there was a borderline lower risk of stroke and cerebral events, though these were not adjusted for multiple comparisons.
- No significant differences in rates of road-traffic accidents, serious adverse events, fractures, or cardiac events between groups.
- Findings suggest CPAP is valuable for symptom relief and functional improvement, but its role in secondary cardiovascular prevention remains unproven.

4.5 Clinical Application

- CPAP should be prescribed for symptom relief in patients with moderate-to-severe OSA and cardiovascular disease, especially when they have excessive daytime sleepiness, impaired quality of life, or mood symptoms.
- In patients with cardiovascular disease but minimal daytime symptoms, CPAP should not be expected to reduce recurrent cardiovascular events and should not be used solely for secondary cardiovascular prevention.
- For patients who can maintain good adherence (≥4 h/night), CPAP may provide additional benefits such as possible stroke risk reduction, though this is not definitively proven.
- In patients with poor adherence, strategies such as optimizing mask fit, adding humidification, and providing behavioral support should be implemented, since cardiovascular benefit may be more likely in adherent users.
- CPAP remains useful in perioperative care or other situations where untreated OSA may worsen comorbid conditions, even if cardiovascular outcome benefit is uncertain.

4.6 When to Discuss on Rounds

Discuss this trial on rounds with the following scenarios:

- When managing a patient with cardiovascular disease and newly diagnosed moderate-to-severe OSA, to highlight that CPAP improves symptoms and quality of life but does not reduce recurrent cardiovascular events in most patients.

- When considering CPAP in an asymptomatic or minimally symptomatic patient with OSA and cardiovascular disease, to discuss that it should not be prescribed solely for secondary cardiovascular prevention.
- When evaluating causes of persistent fatigue or poor work attendance in a cardiovascular patient with OSA, to discuss CPAP's demonstrated benefits for daytime alertness, mood, and reduced sick days.
- When discussing patient counseling for OSA management, to emphasize that CPAP adherence strategies are critical to maximizing any potential cardiovascular or neurologic benefits.

4.7 Relevant Guidelines

The **American Academy of Sleep Medicine Guidelines** continue to recommend CPAP as first-line therapy for moderate-to-severe OSA to improve their sleep-related symptoms. However, they acknowledge that CPAP has not been shown to reduce cardiovascular events, as demonstrated by the SAVE trial. The **ESC** guidelines on cardiovascular disease prevention note that CPAP may be considered for blood pressure reduction in OSA patients with hypertension but is not proven to prevent cardiovascular vents.

5 PIOPED Study Summary [5]

Full Title: Value of the Ventilation/Perfusion Scan in Acute Pulmonary Embolism
Publication Year: 1990
Journal: Journal of the American Medical Association

5.1 Background

Pulmonary embolism (PE) is a life-threatening condition that requires prompt and accurate diagnosis. Before the widespread use of CT pulmonary angiography (CTPA), ventilation-perfusion (V/Q) scanning was the primary imaging modality for PE diagnosis. However, the interpretation of V/Q scans was often ambiguous, leading to uncertainty in clinical decision-making. The PIOPED study aimed to assess the accuracy of V/Q scanning for diagnosing PE and to define its diagnostic utility.

5.2 Study Design

Type: Multicenter, prospective study
Population: 933 patients with suspected PE
Gold Standard Comparison: Pulmonary angiography
Diagnostic Test Evaluated: Ventilation-perfusion scanning
Outcome Measures: Sensitivity, specificity, and predictive values of V/Q scanning for PE diagnosis

5.3 Results

Accuracy of V/Q Scanning for PE Diagnosis:

- **High-probability V/Q scan:**
  - **Sensitivity:** 41% (Detected less than half of actual PE cases).
  - **Specificity:** 97% (IF a high-probability scan was present, PE was very likely).
- **Normal/near-normal V/Q scan:** Effectively ruled out PE.
- **Low-probability V/Q scan:**
  - PE still present in 16% of cases, indicating low negative predictive value.
- **Intermediate (indeterminate) V/Q scan:**
  - Found in 40% of patients, creating diagnostic uncertainty.

5.4 Key Takeaways

- High-probability V/Q scans had a strong positive predictive value for PE (≈85–90%), particularly in patients with high clinical suspicion.
- Low-probability V/Q scans in patients with low clinical suspicion had a very low likelihood of PE (<10%).
- Most patients had nondiagnostic (intermediate-probability) scans, highlighting the limitations of V/Q scanning alone in ruling in or out PE without additional testing.
- The study emphasized the importance of integrating V/Q scan results with pre-test clinical probability (Wells criteria or Geneva score were developed later but based on similar principles).
- PIOPED findings influenced PE diagnostic algorithms by promoting combined use of imaging, clinical assessment, and, when needed, pulmonary angiography for confirmation.

5.5 Clinical Application

- CTPA is now preferred over V/Q scan for PE diagnosis due to higher accuracy and fewer inconclusive results.
- V/Q scan is still useful in select populations such as patients with chronic kidney disease or contrast allergy.
- Use V/Q scan interpretation in conjunction with pre-test clinical probability to guide PE diagnosis—high-probability scans in high clinical suspicion patients strongly support PE diagnosis and can often obviate further imaging.
- Recognize that intermediate-probability V/Q scans are common; in these cases, further diagnostic workup such as CT pulmonary angiography (now preferred) or conventional pulmonary angiography is warranted.
- Apply the study's principle that low-probability scans in low-suspicion patients make PE unlikely, potentially avoiding unnecessary anticoagulation or invasive testing.
- Integrate clinical assessment tools (e.g., Wells, Geneva) with imaging results, following the PIOPED model of combining objective data with clinical judgment for optimal diagnostic accuracy.

5.6 When to Discuss on Rounds

Discuss this trial on rounds with the following scenarios:

- When evaluating a patient with suspected PE and deciding between V/Q scan and CT pulmonary angiography.
- When interpreting a V/Q scan result in the context of the patient's pre-test probability.
- When discussing the limitations of V/Q scanning, particularly the high rate of intermediate-probability results.
- When highlighting the importance of integrating clinical probability scores (e.g., Wells, Geneva) with imaging findings to improve diagnostic accuracy.
- When teaching about the historical impact of PIOPED on modern PE diagnostic algorithms and imaging choices.

5.7 Relevant Guidelines

The **American College of Chest Physicians** guidelines on pulmonary embolism diagnosis and the **ESC** guidelines on acute PE were heavily influenced by the PIOPED study. These guidelines emphasize the use of clinical pretest probability assessment (e.g., Wells Score) in conjunction with imaging studies, primary CTPA, for the diagnosis of PE.

6 EINSTEIN Trials Summary [6, 7]

Full Titles:

1. **EINSTEIN-DVT -** Rivaroxaban vs. Warfarin for Deep Vein Thrombosis (DVT)
2. **EINSTEIN-PE -** Rivaroxaban vs. Warfarin for Pulmonary Embolism (PE)
3. **EINSTEIN-Extension -** Extended Rivaroxaban Therapy for Venous Thromboembolism (VTE) Prevention

Publication Year: 2010 (EINSTEIN-DVT), 2012 (EINSTEIN-PE), 2010 (EINSTEIN-EXTENSION)
Journal: New England Journal of Medicine

6.1 Background

Warfarin had been the standard treatment for venous thromboembolism (VTE), but it requires frequent monitoring and dose adjustments. Rivaroxaban, a direct oral anticoagulant (DOAC), offered the advantage of fixed dosing without the need for routine INR monitoring. The EINSTEIN trials assessed whether rivaroxaban is non-inferior to warfarin for treating DVT and PE while evaluating safety regarding bleeding risk.

6.2 Study Design

Type: Multicenter, randomized, open-label, non-inferiority trials.
Population:

- **EINSTEIN-DVT:** 3449 patients with symptomatic DVT (without PE).
- **EINSTEIN-PT:** 4832 patients with symptomatic PE (± DVT).
- **EINSTEIN-Extension:** 1197 patients with prior VTE who completed anticoagulation and needed secondary prevention.

Intervention: Rivaroxaban 15 mg BID × 21 days, then 20 mg daily vs. enoxaparin bridge + dose-adjusted warfarin (target INR 2.0–3.0)
Primary Outcome: Recurrent symptomatic VTE (DVT or PE)
Safety Outcome: Major and clinically relevant non-major bleeding

6.3 Results

1. **EINSTEIN-DVT (Rivaroxaban vs. Warfarin for DVT):**
   - Rivaroxaban was non-inferior to warfarin for preventing recurrent VTE (2.1% vs. 3.0%, HR 0.68, $p < 0.001$ for non-inferiority).
   - Major bleeding was similar between groups (0.8% vs. 1.2%; HR 0.65; [95% CI, 0.33–1.30; $p = 0.21$]).
2. **EINSTEIN-PE (Rivaroxaban vs. Warfarin for PE):**
   - Rivaroxaban was non-inferior to warfarin for preventing recurrent PE (2.1% vs. 1.8%, HR 1.12; [95% CI: 0.75–1.68; $p = 0.003$ for non-inferiority]).
   - Major bleeding was significantly lower with rivaroxaban (1.1% vs. 2.2%; HR 0.49; [95% CI: 0.31–0.79; $p = 0.003$]).
3. **EINSTEIN-Extension (Extended Rivaroxaban Therapy):**
   - Rivaroxaban reduced recurrent VTE risk compared to placebo (1.3% vs. 7.1%, HR 0.18; [95% CI: 0.09–0.39; $p < 0.001$]).
   - No significant increase in major bleeding (0.7% vs. 0%, $p = 0.11$).

6.4 Key Takeaways

- In patients with acute symptomatic deep vein thrombosis (EINSTEIN-DVT) and those with acute symptomatic pulmonary embolism (EINSTEIN-PE), rivaroxaban as a single oral agent (15 mg twice daily for 3 weeks, then 20 mg once daily) was non-inferior to standard therapy with enoxaparin followed by a vitamin K antagonist (warfarin or acenocoumarol) for prevention of recurrent venous thromboembolism (VTE).
- Rates of major bleeding were similar in EINSTEIN-DVT and significantly lower in EINSTEIN-PE with rivaroxaban compared to standard therapy. This established rivaroxaban as an effective and potentially safer alternative for initial and long-term anticoagulation.
- In the EINSTEIN-Extension trial, continuing rivaroxaban 20 mg daily after an initial 6–12 months of anticoagulation significantly reduced recurrent VTE compared to placebo, with a modest but notable increase in major or clinically relevant non-major bleeding risk.
- The trials supported the use of rivaroxaban as a fixed-dose, single-drug approach without the need for initial parenteral anticoagulation, simplifying VTE management.
- Benefits were consistent across subgroups, including those with provoked and unprovoked events, making rivaroxaban an attractive option for both short-term treatment and extended secondary prevention of VTE.

6.5 Clinical Application

- Use rivaroxaban as a first-line alternative to LMWH plus warfarin for treatment of acute symptomatic DVT or PE, especially in patients where simplified fixed dosing and avoidance of INR monitoring are desirable.
- Consider rivaroxaban for patients with both provoked and unprovoked VTE, given its non-inferior efficacy and similar or lower major bleeding risk compared to traditional therapy.
- In patients who have completed 6–12 months of anticoagulation and remain at high risk for recurrence (e.g., unprovoked VTE, active cancer, persistent risk factors), consider extended rivaroxaban therapy at 20 mg daily to reduce recurrence, while weighing the modestly increased bleeding risk.
- Avoid rivaroxaban in patients with significant renal impairment (CrCl <30 mL/min) or those with contraindications to DOACs; use warfarin or LMWH instead in these cases.
- Use caution in patients with high bleeding risk or those on interacting medications (e.g., strong CYP3A4/P-gp inhibitors or inducers), as these may alter rivaroxaban exposure.
- In patients transitioning from acute inpatient management, rivaroxaban's no-bridging, single-drug regimen can streamline discharge planning and improve outpatient adherence.

6.6 When to Discuss on Rounds

Discuss this trial on rounds with the following scenarios:

- When comparing rivaroxaban to the traditional LMWH-to-warfarin bridge for acute VTE treatment, particularly in terms of non-inferior efficacy and reduced need for monitoring.
- When discussing the advantages of a single-drug oral regimen for both initial and long-term VTE therapy, especially for facilitating discharge planning.
- When weighing extended anticoagulation for patients at high risk of recurrence, and considering rivaroxaban's benefit in reducing recurrence versus its bleeding risk profile.
- When reviewing DOAC safety considerations in renal impairment, drug-drug interactions, or patients with elevated bleeding risk.
- When considering guideline-concordant therapy for both provoked and unprovoked DVT or PE, and whether rivaroxaban may be preferable to warfarin.

6.7 Relevant Guidelines

The **American College of Chest Physicians** guidelines on antithrombotic therapy for VTE and the **ESC guidelines** for pulmonary embolism recommend DOACs as first-line therapy for most DVT and PE patients due to their similar efficacy to warfarin with lower bleeding risk and greater convenience. Extended therapy should be considered for patients at high risk of recurrent VTE based on the EINSTEIN-Extension trial.

7 REVEAL Registry Summary [8]

Full Title: Registry to Evaluate Early and Long-term Pulmonary Arterial Hypertension Disease Management
Publication Year: Initial findings (2010), updates in subsequent years
Journal: Circulation (2010, 2012, 2017)

7.1 Background

Pulmonary arterial hypertension (PAH) is a progressive and life-threatening disease characterized by increased pulmonary vascular resistance, leading to right heart failure, Before the REVEAL registry, data on PAH were limited to clinical trial populations, which often excluded real-world patients with comorbidities and milder disease. The REVEAL registry was the largest U.S.-based prospective observational study designed to provide real-world data on PAH, including its natural history, treatment patterns, and prognostic factors.

7.2 Study Design

Type: Prospective, multicenter, observational registry
Population:

- 3515 patients diagnosed with WHO Group 1 PAH
- Enrolled from 55 U.S. centers

Primary Objectives:

1. Characterize demographics, clinical presentations, and hemodynamics of PAH patients.
2. Assess treatment patterns and outcomes in a real-world setting.
3. Develop risk stratification tools for PAH prognosis.

7.3 Key Findings

1. **PAH Demographics and Risk Factors:**
   - Mean age: 53 years (older than previously reported in clinical trials).
   - Female predominance: 79% of patients.
   - Most common PAH subtype: Idiopathic PAH (46%) followed by connective tissue disease-associated PAH (25%).
   - Comorbidities were common, including obesity, hypertension, and diabetes, which were previously underrepresented in PAH clinical trials.
2. **Clinical and Hemodynamic Characteristics:**
   - Mean 6-min walk distance (6MWD): ~340 meters.
   - Mean pulmonary artery pressure (mPAP): ~50 mmHg.
   - Right atrial pressure (RAP) and cardiac index were strong predictors of mortality.
3. **PAH Treatment Patterns:**
   - 52% of patients were on combination therapy (most commonly PDE-5 inhibitors and endothelin receptor antagonists).
   - Only 10% of patients were on IV prostacyclin therapy, despite evidence of its benefits in severe PAH.
4. **Prognostic Risk Score (REVEAL Risk Score):**
   - A risk stratification model was developed to predict 1-year mortality based on factors including:
     - Age, functional class, 6MWD, NT-proBNP levels, RAP, mPAP, and pericardial effusion.
   - High-risk patients (REVEAL score ≥10) had a 1-year mortality of ~25%

7.4 Key Takeaways

- The REVEAL registry offered detailed patient demographic and clinical profiling, revealing a marked shift toward older age at diagnosis and a stronger female predominance compared to earlier cohorts.
- Data showed that over half of patients experienced more than a year's delay from symptom onset to PAH diagnosis, highlighting a significant diagnostic lag.
- Researchers derived and validated a comprehensive REVEAL risk score, incorporating variables such as age, sex, PAH subtype, functional class, hemodynamics, biomarkers, 6-min walk distance, BP, and heart rate, to stratify 1-year survival risk effectively.
- Serial assessments demonstrated that changes in REVEAL risk scores over 12 months were strongly predictive of survival, reinforcing their role in dynamic risk monitoring.

7.5 Clinical Application

- Use the REVEAL risk score to assess PAH prognosis.
- Monitor changes in REVEAL scores over time to assess disease progression or treatment response, adjusting therapy when scores worsen.
- Incorporate registry insights into earlier screening and referral for PAH in patients with unexplained dyspnea to address the frequent diagnostic delays identified in REVEAL.
- Apply risk score–based stratification to select patients for advanced PAH therapies, combination regimens, or referral to specialized centers.
- Use the registry's demographic and clinical trends to educate clinicians on the evolving profile of PAH patients, including older age at diagnosis and the predominance of women.

7.6 When to Discuss on Rounds

Discuss this trial on rounds with the following scenarios:

- When evaluating a patient with pulmonary arterial hypertension (PAH) and deciding how to risk stratify them for prognosis and treatment planning.
- When following a PAH patient over time and needing to determine whether changes in clinical status warrant therapy escalation, using REVEAL scores as objective markers.
- When discussing the importance of early referral to specialized PAH centers, particularly in the context of REVEAL findings showing diagnostic delays and their impact on outcomes.
- When considering combination PAH therapy in higher-risk patients, referencing REVEAL data linking risk category to mortality.

7.7 Relevant Guidelines

The **ESC and European Respiratory Society Guidelines** on pulmonary hypertension and the **CHEST** guidelines integrate REVEAL findings into PAH risk stratification and management. The REVEAL risk score is recommended as a validated tool for predicting PAH prognosis and guiding treatment decisions. Patients classified as high-risk (REVEAL score $\geq$10) should receive aggressive treatment, including early initiation of IV prostacyclin therapy. The Guidelines also emphasize the importance of upfront combination therapy, as REVEAL demonstrated that many PAH patients in clinical practice were undertreated despite their high mortality risk.

8 AMBITION Trial Summary [9]

Full Title: Initial Use of Ambrisentan plus Tadalafil in Pulmonary Arterial Hypertension
Publication Year: 2015
Journal: New England Journal of Medicine

8.1 *Background*

Traditionally, PAH treatment began with monotherapy, adding a second agent only if symptoms worsened. However, prior studies suggested that early combination therapy might improve outcomes. The AMBITION trial aimed to compare initial combination therapy (tadalafil + ambrisentan) versus monotherapy (either drug alone) in treatment-naive PAH patients, testing whether upfront combination therapy could provide superior clinical outcomes.

8.2 *Study Design*

Type: Multicenter, randomized, double-blind, controlled trial
Population: 500 treatment-naive PAH patients
Intervention: Combination therapy with ambrisentan (10 mg) + tadalafil (40 mg) vs. monotherapy with either ambrisentan (10 mg) or tadalafil (40 mg) alone
Primary Outcome: Time to first clinical failure event (defined as death, hospitalization for PAH, disease progression, or worsening functional status)
Secondary Outcomes:

- Change in pro-brain natriuretic peptide (NT-proBNP)
- 6-min walk test distance
- WHO functional class

8.3 *Results*

Primary Outcome:

- Clinical failure occurred in 18% of the combination-therapy group vs. 31% of the pooled-monotherapy group (34% ambrisentan, 28% tadalafil).
- Combination vs. pooled monotherapy: HR 0.50 (95% CI: 0.35–0.72; $p < 0.001$)
- Combination vs. ambrisentan: HR 0.48 (95% CI: 0.31–0.72; $p < 0.001$)

- Combination vs. tadalafil: HR 0.53 (95% CI: 0.34–0.83; p = 0.005)
- Most significant component difference: hospitalization for worsening PAH (4% combo vs. 12% pooled monotherapy)

Secondary Outcomes:

- Change in NT-proBNP: Greater reduction in NT-proBNP in the combination group (−67.2%) compared to pooled monotherapy (−50.4%); p < 0.001.
- 6-min walk distance: Median improvement of 48.98 m in the combination group vs. 23.80 m in pooled monotherapy; p < 0.001.
- WHO functional class: At week 24, 37% of the combination group improved vs. 33% in pooled monotherapy; no significant difference (p = 0.24).

8.4 Key Takeaways

- Combination therapy (ambrisentan + tadalafil) is superior to monotherapy in treatment-naive PAH patients.
- Significantly reduces clinical worsening, PAH-related hospitalizations, and improves functional status.
- Now considered first-line treatment for most newly diagnosed PAH patients.
- Improves surrogate markers such as NT-proBNP levels and 6-min walk distance, supporting enhanced cardiopulmonary function.

8.5 Clinical Application

- Start PAH patients on combination therapy.
- Recognize that monotherapy is no longer first-line. PAH guidelines now recommend dual therapy as the standard of care.
- Be aware of side effects as combination therapy increases risk of peripheral edema, hypotension, and headache, requiring careful monitoring.
- Use AMBITION findings to support early, aggressive treatment and to educate patients on the rationale for dual therapy.

8.6 When to Discuss on Rounds

Discuss this trial on rounds with the following scenarios:

- When discussing the standard of care for newly diagnosed PAH patients.
- When considering strategies to prevent PAH-related hospital admissions.
- When explaining why combination therapy

8.7 *Relevant Guidelines*

The **ESC/ERS** guidelines on pulmonary hypertension and the **CHEST** guidelines fully incorporate AMBITION's findings. These guidelines recommend initial combination therapy with an endothelin receptor antagonist and a phosphodiesterase-5 inhibitor for most newly diagnosed PAH patients.

9 ASCEND & CAPACITY Trial Summary [10, 11]

Full Titles:

- Assessment of Pirfenidone to Confirm Efficacy and Safety in Idiopathic Pulmonary Fibrosis
- Clinical Studies Assessing Pirfenidone in Idiopathic Pulmonary Fibrosis: Research of Efficacy and Safety)

Publication Year: 2011 (CAPACITY), 2014 (ASCEND)
Journal: The Lancet, New England Journal of Medicine

9.1 *Background*

Idiopathic pulmonary fibrosis (IPF) is a progressive, fatal lung disease characterized by fibrosis and declining lung function. Before these trials, there was no proven pharmacologic treatment to slow disease progression. Pirfenidone, an antifibrotic and anti-inflammatory agent, had shown promise in early studies. The CAPACITY trials (two parallel phase 3 studies) and the ASCEND trial (a confirmatory phase 3 study) aimed to determine whether pirfenidone could slow lung function decline in IPF patients.

9.2 *Study Design*

CAPACITY:

- **Type:** Two parallel, phase 3, randomized, double-blind, placebo-controlled trials (studies 004 & 006).
- **Length:** Conducted over 72 weeks

ASCEND:

- **Type:** A confirmatory, phase 3, multicenter, randomized, double-blind, placebo-controlled trial.
- **Length:** Conducted over 52 weeks

Participants: Over 1200 patients across both trials with mild-to-moderate IPF
Intervention: Pirfenidone (2403 mg daily) vs. placebo
Primary Outcome: Change in forced vital capacity (FVC) over the study period.
Secondary Outcomes:

- Progression-Free Survival (PFS)
- All-cause mortality

9.3 *Results*

Primary Outcome:

- **ASCEND:** 47.9% of pirfenidone patients had an FVC decline of ≥10% vs 31.4% in placebo ($p < 0.001$).
- **CAPACITY:** Pirfenidone slowed the decline in FVC compared to placebo.

Secondary Outcomes:

- Reduced risk of disease progression
  - 48% relative reduction in FVC decline in ASCEND.
- All-cause mortality
  - AT 52 weeks was significantly lower in patients treated with pirfenidone compared with placebo (HR 0.52; [95% CI: 0.31–0.87; $p = 0.0107$]).

Safety:

- Most common side effects: GI upset, rash, and photosensitivity.
- Generally well tolerated, but some patients discontinued due to side effects.

9.4 *Key Takeaways*

- Pirfenidone slows FVC decline and disease progression in IPF.
- Pirfenidone significantly reduced all-cause mortality at 52 weeks compared to placebo
- Mortality benefit persisted up to 120 weeks for treatment-emergent and IPF-related deaths.
- These findings indicate pirfenidone offers both disease-modifying and survival benefits in idiopathic pulmonary fibrosis.

9.5 Clinical Application

- Use pirfenidone in patients with idiopathic pulmonary fibrosis (IPF) who meet diagnostic criteria and have mild-to-moderate disease, as it not only slows functional decline but also reduces all-cause and IPF-related mortality.
- Consider early initiation of therapy, given that survival benefits were seen within one year and persisted with longer follow-up.
- Counsel patients on the mortality benefit in addition to symptom and lung function preservation when discussing treatment options, especially for those hesitant about starting antifibrotic therapy.
- Reinforce adherence, as consistent therapy is key to maximizing both functional and survival outcomes.
- Integrate routine monitoring of liver function and adverse effects while maintaining treatment to ensure safety without compromising the mortality benefit.

9.6 When to Discuss on Rounds

Discuss this trial on rounds with the following scenarios:

- When discussing antifibrotic therapy options for idiopathic pulmonary fibrosis and the evidence for mortality benefit with pirfenidone.
- When considering early initiation of treatment in newly diagnosed IPF patients, especially those with preserved lung function.
- When addressing patient concerns about the long-term value of therapy, particularly its impact on both disease progression and survival.

9.7 Relevant Guidelines

The **American Thoracic Society/European Respiratory Society/Japanese Respiratory Society/American Thoracic Association (ATS/ERS/JRS/ALAT)** guidelines for idiopathic pulmonary fibrosis and the **CHEST** guidelines recommend pirfenidone (or nintedanib) as first-line therapy for patients with mild-to-moderate IPF based on the ASCEND and CAPACITY trials. The guidelines emphasize that antifibrotic therapy should be initiated early to preserve lung function and slow disease progression, as delaying treatment may lead to worse outcomes.

10 Lung Health Study (LHS) Summary [12]

Full Title: Effects of Smoking Intervention and the Use of an Inhaled Anticholinergic Bronchodilator on the Rate of Decline of FEV1: The Lung Health Study
Publication Year: 1994
Journal: Journal of the American Medical Association

10.1 Background

The Lung Health Study investigated whether smoking cessation and inhaled ipratropium could slow lung function decline in middle-aged smokers with mild-to-moderate COPD. AT the time, there was limited prospective evidence linking quitting smoking to long-term preservation of lung function, making this a pivotal trial in shaping COPD prevention and management.

10.2 Study Design

Type: Multicenter randomized controlled trial
Population: 5887 middle-aged current smokers, aged 35–60 years who had mild-to-moderate airflow obstruction based on spirometry (FEV_1 55–90% of predicted and $FEV_1/FVC < 0.70$)
Intervention: Smoking intervention plus bronchodilator vs. smoking intervention plus placebo vs. no intervention
Primary Outcome: Rate of change and cumulative change in FEV_1

10.3 Results

Primary Outcome:

- Participants in the two smoking-Intervention (with or without ipratropium) experienced significantly smaller declines in FEV_1 over five years compared to the control group, mainly driven by sustained smoking cessation. Most of the benefit occurred in the first year, attributable to quitting smoking.
- Use of inhaled ipratropium bromide resulted in a small, non-cumulative improvement in FEV_1, but this benefit disappeared once the bronchodilator was discontinued, and it did not influence the long-term rate of FEV_1 decline.

10.4 Key Takeaways

- Intensive smoking cessation intervention significantly reduced the rate of FEV_1 decline in middle-aged smokers with mild-to-moderate COPD.
- The greatest improvement in lung function occurred within the first year after quitting smoking, highlighting the immediate benefits of cessation.
- Inhaled ipratropium provided only a modest, reversible improvement in FEV_1 while in use, with no long-term effect on the rate of lung function decline.
- Sustained smoking cessation, not chronic inhaled anticholinergic use, was the key factor in slowing COPD progression.
- Results reinforced smoking cessation as the most effective intervention for preserving lung function in early COPD.

10.5 Clinical Application

- Use intensive, structured smoking cessation programs for all patients with early COPD, as quitting smoking has the strongest evidence for slowing disease progression.
- Consider inhaled ipratropium for symptomatic relief in mild-to-moderate COPD, but counsel that it does not alter long-term decline in lung function.
- Prioritize smoking cessation counseling and pharmacotherapy (e.g., nicotine replacement, bupropion, varenicline) over maintenance inhalers in newly diagnosed, mild COPD patients without significant symptoms.
- Use these findings to reinforce the importance of early intervention—cessation is most effective before advanced airflow limitation develops.

10.6 When to Discuss on Rounds

Discuss this trial on rounds with the following scenarios:

- When seeing a patient with mild-to-moderate COPD who still smokes, bring up the evidence that intensive smoking cessation programs significantly slow the decline in FEV1.
- When counseling a patient early after diagnosis of COPD, highlight that the largest benefit in lung function occurs in the first year after quitting.
- When discussing prognosis with a patient who is still smoking, use the study to illustrate that continued smoking accelerates lung function loss and worsens outcomes.

10.7 Relevant Guidelines

The Lung Health Study was pivotal in shaping COPD management guidelines, particularly those from the **Global Initiative for Chronic Obstructive Lung Disease (GOLD)** and the **American Thoracic Society.** These guidelines emphasize smoking cessation as the most effective intervention for slowing disease progression in patients with mild-to-moderate COPD, directly reflecting the study's findings that quitting smoking significantly reduced the rate of FEV1 decline.

References

1. Calhoun WJ, Ameredes BT, King TS, et al. Comparison of physician-, biomarker-, and symptom-based strategies for adjustment of inhaled corticosteroid therapy in adults with asthma: the BASALT randomized controlled trial. JAMA. 2012;308(10):987–97. https://doi.org/10.1001/2012.jama.10893.
2. Calverley PM, Anderson JA, Celli B, et al. Salmeterol and fluticasone propionate and survival in chronic obstructive pulmonary disease. N Engl J Med. 2007;356(8):775–89. https://doi.org/10.1056/NEJMoa063070.
3. Tashkin DP, Celli B, Senn S, et al. A 4-year trial of tiotropium in chronic obstructive pulmonary disease. N Engl J Med. 2008;359(15):1543–54. https://doi.org/10.1056/NEJMoa0805800.
4. McEvoy RD, Antic NA, Heeley E, et al. CPAP for prevention of cardiovascular events in obstructive sleep apnea. N Engl J Med. 2016;375(10):919–31. https://doi.org/10.1056/NEJMoa1606599.
5. PIOPED Investigators. Value of the ventilation/perfusion scan in acute pulmonary embolism. Results of the prospective investigation of pulmonary embolism diagnosis (PIOPED). JAMA. 1990;263(20):2753–9. https://doi.org/10.1001/jama.1990.03440200057023.
6. EINSTEIN Investigators, Bauersachs R, Berkowitz SD, et al. Oral rivaroxaban for symptomatic venous thromboembolism. N Engl J Med. 2010;363(26):2499–510. https://doi.org/10.1056/NEJMoa1007903.
7. EINSTEIN–PE Investigators, Büller HR, Prins MH, et al. Oral rivaroxaban for the treatment of symptomatic pulmonary embolism. N Engl J Med. 2012;366(14):1287–97. https://doi.org/10.1056/NEJMoa1113572.
8. Benza RL, Miller DP, Gomberg-Maitland M, et al. Predicting survival in pulmonary arterial hypertension: insights from the registry to evaluate early and long-term pulmonary arterial hypertension disease management (REVEAL). Circulation. 2010;122(2):164–72. https://doi.org/10.1161/CIRCULATIONAHA.109.898122.
9. Galiè N, Barberà JA, Frost AE, et al. Initial use of ambrisentan plus tadalafil in pulmonary arterial hypertension. N Engl J Med. 2015;373(9):834–44. https://doi.org/10.1056/NEJMoa1413687.
10. King TE Jr, Bradford WZ, Castro-Bernardini S, et al. A phase 3 trial of pirfenidone in patients with idiopathic pulmonary fibrosis [published correction appears in N Engl J Med. 2014 Sep 18;371(12):1172]. N Engl J Med. 2014;370(22):2083–92. https://doi.org/10.1056/NEJMoa1402582.
11. Noble PW, Albera C, Bradford WZ, et al. Pirfenidone in patients with idiopathic pulmonary fibrosis (CAPACITY): two randomised trials. Lancet. 2011;377(9779):1760–9. https://doi.org/10.1016/S0140-6736(11)60405-4.
12. Anthonisen NR, Connett JE, Kiley JP, et al. Effects of smoking intervention and the use of an inhaled anticholinergic bronchodilator on the rate of decline of FEV1. The Lung Health Study. JAMA. 1994;272(19):1497–505.

Chapter 4
Critical Care

1 ARDSNet Trial Summary [1]

Full Title: Ventilation with Lower Tidal Volumes as Compared with Traditional Tidal Volumes for Acute Lung Injury and the Acute Respiratory Distress Syndrome
Publication Year: 2000
Journal: New England Journal of Medicine

1.1 Background

Acute Respiratory Distress Syndrome (ARDS) is characterized by diffuse lung injury and severe hypoxemia. Traditional mechanical ventilation often utilized higher tidal volumes to improve oxygenation but increased the risk of ventilator-induced lung injury (VILI). Before the ARDSNet trial, there was no clear consensus on optimal ventilatory strategies. This landmark trial sought to determine if low tidal volume ventilation could decrease mortality and reduce complications in ARDS patients.

1.2 Study Design

Type: Randomized, controlled trial
Population: 861 patients with ARDS
Intervention: Low tidal volume (6 mL/kg IBW) vs. traditional tidal volume (12 mL/kg IBW)

A. Love, *The Essential Evidence*, https://doi.org/10.1007/978-3-032-12399-2_4

Primary Outcomes:

- Death before a patient was discharged home and was breathing without assistance
- Number of days without ventilator use from day 1 to 28

Secondary Outcomes:

- Incidence of barotrauma
- Incidence of multi-organ failure
- Breathing without assistance by day 28

1.3 Results

Primary Outcomes:

- Significantly lower 60-day mortality with low tidal volume (31% in low tidal volume vs. 39.8% in traditional tidal volume; 95% CI: 2.4–15.3; $p = 0.007$).
- 12 ± 11 days without ventilator use in the first 28 days in the low tidal volume group vs. 10 ± 11 in the traditional tidal volume group ($p = 0.007$).

Secondary Outcomes:

- Incidence of barotrauma was similar between the groups (10% low vs. 11% traditional, $p = 0.43$).
- Decreased incidence of multi-organ failure with low tidal volume ($p = .006$).
- More patients were breathing without assistance by day 28 in the low tidal volume group vs. the traditional group (65.7 vs. 55.0; $p < 0.001$)

1.4 Key Takeaways

- Low tidal volume ventilation (6 mL/kg ideal body weight) significantly reduced mortality in patients with ARDS.
- The mortality benefit was independent of baseline lung compliance, supporting low tidal volume use regardless of lung mechanics.
- Barotrauma rates were similar between groups, indicating low tidal volume did not increase this risk.
- Prior trials may have failed to show benefit due to smaller tidal volume differences, insufficient power, or acidosis-related confounders.
- Slightly higher PEEP was required early in the low tidal volume group to maintain oxygenation but was not the primary driver of benefit.

1.5 Clinical Application

- Use low tidal volume ventilation (6 mL/kg ideal body weight) as first-line strategy in ARDS.
- Monitor plateau pressures regularly and maintain ≤30 cm H_2O to minimize ventilator-induced lung injury.
- Avoid traditional high tidal volumes, as they increase mortality and barotrauma risk.
- Monitor for permissive hypercapnia and manage pH carefully; mild acidosis is acceptable if needed to maintain lung-protective strategy.
- Prioritize ventilator strategies that minimize lung inflammation and systemic injury to improve survival and ventilator-free days.

1.6 When to Discuss on Rounds

Discuss this trial on rounds with the following scenarios:

- When managing a patient with acute respiratory distress syndrome and deciding on initial ventilator settings.
- When explaining the rationale for targeting tidal volumes of approximately 6 mL/kg predicted body weight in ARDS patients.
- When discussing the trade-offs of permissive hypercapnia and higher respiratory rates to achieve lower tidal volumes.
- When reviewing the physiologic benefits of limiting plateau pressures (≤30 cm H_2O) to reduce stretch-induced lung injury.
- When counseling ICU staff that mortality reduction with low tidal volumes is independent of baseline lung compliance.

1.7 Relevant Guidelines

The **Surviving Sepsis Campaign Guidelines** and the **ATS/ERS Guidelines** recommend low tidal volume ventilation (6 mL/kg IBW) and plateau pressures ≤30 cm H_2O in all ARDS patients to reduce mortality and lung injury.

2 PROVESA Trial Summary [2]

Full Title: Prone Positioning in Severe Acute Respiratory Distress Syndrome
Publication Year: 2013
Journal: New England Journal of Medicine

2.1 Background

Prone positioning has been suggested as a method to improve oxygenation in ARDS patients by improving ventilation-perfusion matching and reducing VILI. Prior studies demonstrated physiological improvement but provided inconclusive results regarding mortality. The PROVESA trial was designed to definitively evaluate the affect of prolonged prone positioning on survival in severe ARDS.

2.2 Study Design

Type: Randomized, controlled trial
Population: 466 patients with severe ARDS (PaO_2/FiO_2 <150 mmHg)
Intervention: Prone positioning ≥16 h/day vs. supine positioning
Primary Outcome: 28-day mortality
Secondary Outcomes:

- 90-day mortality
- Successful extubation at day 90
- Ventilation-free days

2.3 Results

Primary Outcome: Significantly lower 28-day mortality in prone group (16% vs. 32.8%; HR: 0.39; [95% CI: 0.25–0.63; $p < 0.001$]).
Secondary Outcomes:

- Reduced 90-day mortality (23.6% vs. 41%; HR: 0.44; [95% CI: 0.29–0.67; $p < 0.001$]).
- Greater successful extubation in the prone positioning group at 90 days (186/231 vs. 145/223, HR: 0.45; [95% CI: 0.29–0.70; $p < 0.001$]).
- More ventilator-free days in the prone positioning group at both 28 and 90 days (14 ± 9 and 57 ± 34 vs. 10 ± 10 and 43 ± 38, $p < 0.001$).

2.4 Key Takeaways

- In patients with severe ARDS (PaO_2/FiO_2 <150 mm Hg, FiO_2 ≥0.6, and PEEP ≥5 cm H_2O), early application of prolonged prone positioning significantly reduced 28-day mortality and 90-day mortality compared to supine positioning.

- The survival benefit persisted after adjustment for baseline SOFA score, vasopressor use, and neuromuscular blocker use.
- Prone positioning improved oxygenation (higher PaO_2/FiO_2 ratios at days 3 and 5) and allowed for lower PEEP, FiO_2, and plateau pressures by day 3.
- Rates of successful extubation were significantly higher in the prone group, with no significant increase in major complications aside from fewer cardiac arrests compared to supine positioning.
- Long daily prone sessions (average 17 h) over a concentrated period and adherence to lung-protective ventilation (tidal volume <6 mL/kg predicted body weight, plateau pressure <30 cm H_2O) likely contributed to the survival benefit.
- The benefit was observed in a setting where staff were experienced in performing prone positioning safely, underscoring the importance of training and team coordination for implementation.

2.5 *Clinical Application*

- Use prone positioning early in patients with moderate-to-severe ARDS (PaO_2/FiO_2 <150 on FiO_2 ≥0.6 and PEEP ≥5), ideally within 36 h of intubation to improve oxygenation and reduce mortality.
- Use prone positioning in conjunction with lung-protective ventilation (tidal volume ~6 mL/kg predicted body weight, plateau pressure <30 cm H_2O) to minimize ventilator-induced lung injury.
- Ensure prone sessions last at least 16 consecutive hours per day to achieve the mortality benefit seen in PROSEVA.
- Coordinate multidisciplinary support—including trained nursing, respiratory therapy, and sedation teams—to safely implement prone ventilation.
- Monitor for potential complications of proning, such as pressure injuries, tube dislodgement, and facial edema, but recognize that these risks are manageable and outweighed by survival benefit.

2.6 *When to Discuss on Rounds*

Discuss this trial on rounds with the following scenarios:

- When managing a patient with severe ARDS and debating initiation of prone positioning.
- When discussing strategies to reduce mortality in ARDS beyond lung-protective ventilation alone.
- When emphasizing the need for a trained ICU team to safely perform prone positioning and avoid complications.

- When considering rescue therapies for severe hypoxemia and comparing prone positioning to ECMO or inhaled nitric oxide.
- When explaining to learners how prone positioning improves oxygenation and potentially reduces ventilator-induced lung injury by promoting more uniform lung inflation.

2.7 Relevant Guidelines

The **ATS/ERS ARDS Guidelines** and the **Surviving Sepsis Campaign** strongly recommend early prone positioning (≥16 h/day) for patients with severe ARDS to significantly improve outcomes and survival.

3 SEPSISPAM Trial Summary [3]

Full Title: High versus Low Blood-Pressure Target in Patients with Septic Shock
Publication Year: 2014
Journal: New England Journal of Medicine

3.1 Background

Optimal mean arterial pressure (MAP) targets in septic shock were previously unclear. Higher MAP targets could theoretically enhance perfusion and prevent organ failure but may require higher vasopressor doses, increasing potential side effects. The SEPSISPAM trial assessed whether a higher MAP target improved patient outcomes compared to the standard target.

3.2 Study Design

Type: Randomized, controlled trial
Population: 776 patients with septic shock
Intervention: MAP target of 65–70 mmHg (low target) vs. 80–85 mmHg (high target)
Primary Outcome: All-cause mortality at day 28
Secondary Outcomes:

- 90-day mortality
- Survival at day 28 without organ support

- Doubling of plasma creatinine
- Need for renal replacement therapy (RRT)

3.3 Results

Primary Outcome: No significant difference in 28-day mortality 34% (low target) vs. 36.6% (high target) (HR (in high target group) 1.07; [95% CI: 0.84–1.38; p = 0.57]).

Secondary Outcomes:

- 90-day mortality: No significant difference between groups 43.7% vs. 42.3% (HR: 1.04; [95% CI: 0.83–1.30; p = 0.74]).
- No significant difference in survival at day 28 without organ support.
- Doubling of plasma creatinine: In those with chronic hypertension significantly higher in the low target group 52% vs. the high target group 38.9 (p = 0.02)
- Need for RRT: Significantly higher in those with chronic hypertension in the low target group 42.2% vs. those in the high target group 31.7% (p = 0.046)

3.4 Key Takeaways

- No mortality benefit was observed with targeting a higher MAP (80–85 mm Hg) compared to standard MAP (65–70 mm Hg) in septic shock.
- Patients with chronic hypertension had improved renal outcomes (less doubling of creatinine and less need for renal replacement therapy) with higher MAP targets.
- Higher MAP targets increased atrial fibrillation risk, likely due to higher and longer vasopressor use.
- The study was underpowered to detect smaller mortality differences due to lower-than-expected death rates.
- Surviving Sepsis Campaign MAP target of ≥65 mm Hg remains appropriate for most patients, with potential individualized benefit in chronic hypertensives.

3.5 Clinical Application

- Target MAP ≥65 mmHg in most patients with septic shock, consistent with current Surviving Sepsis Campaign guidelines.
- Consider higher MAP targets (80–85 mmHg) in patients with chronic hypertension to potentially preserve renal function.

- Avoid unnecessary escalation of vasopressors in normotensive patients, as higher doses may increase the risk of atrial fibrillation without mortality benefit.
- Tailor vasopressor goals based on individual patient profiles, weighing renal perfusion needs against cardiovascular risks.

3.6 When to Discuss on Rounds

Discuss this trial on rounds with the following scenarios:

- When establishing blood pressure targets for newly diagnosed septic shock patients.
- When individualizing MAP goals for patients with chronic hypertension.
- When evaluating the risk-benefit ratio of higher vasopressor doses.
- When counseling about study limitations (open-label, underpowered for smaller differences, narrow enrollment window) and how that affects confidence in subgroup signals.
- When contrasting MAP escalation with alternative strategies for renal protection (optimize volume status, minimize nephrotoxins) rather than reflexively increasing vasopressors.

3.7 Relevant Guidelines

The **Surviving Sepsis Campaign Guidelines** advocate a MAP target of 65 mmHg for septic shock patients but emphasizer individualized targets in patients with chronic hypertension, with careful monitoring for adverse effects.

4 VASST Trial Summary [4]

Full Title: Vasopressin Versus Norepinephrine Infusion in Patients with Septic Shock
Publication Year: 2008
Journal: New England Journal of Medicine

4.1 Background

Septic shock is characterized by profound hypotension unresponsive to fluid resuscitation, often requiring vasopressor support. Norepinephrine is commonly used, but escalating doses are associated with adverse effects. Vasopressin, a naturally occurring hormone, emerged as a potential alternative or adjunct to norepinephrine, theoretically allowing lower norepinephrine doses and potentially reducing related complications. The VASST trial evaluated whether adding vasopressin to norepinephrine therapy could improve outcomes compared to norepinephrine alone in septic shock.

4.2 *Study Design*

Type: Randomized, controlled trial
Population: 778 patients with septic shock requiring vasopressors
Intervention: Patients already receiving a minimum of 5 μg norepinephrine a minute received either low-dose vasopressin (0.01–0.03 U per minute) vs. norepinephrine (5–15 μg per minute) in addition to open label vasopressors.
Primary Outcome: 28-day mortality
Secondary Outcomes:

- 90-day mortality
- Organ dysfunction scores (Brussels criteria)
- Incidence of adverse events (e.g., cardiac ischemia, arrhythmias)

4.3 *Results*

Primary Outcome: No significant difference in 28-day mortality (35.4% vasopressin group vs. 39.3% norepinephrine group, ARR: 3.9; [95% CI: −2.9 to 10.7; $p = 0.26$]). However, there was a lower mortality in less severe shock subgroup receiving vasopressin (26.5% vs. 35.7%, $p = 0.05$).
Secondary Outcomes:

- No significant difference in 90-day mortality (43.9% vs. 49.6%, $p = 0.11$), but in subgroup analysis there was a significant difference in 90-day mortality in those with less severe septic shock in the vasopressin group vs. norepinephrine group (35.8% vs. 46.1%, $p = 0.04$).
- No significant difference in days free from organ dysfunction.
- No significant difference in rates of adverse events.

4.4 *Key Takeaways*

- Low-dose vasopressin (0.03 U/min) did not reduce 28-day or 90-day mortality compared to norepinephrine in patients with septic shock.

- Vasopressin was effective as a catecholamine-sparing agent, allowing for lower norepinephrine requirements while maintaining MAP.
- No significant difference in rates of organ dysfunction or serious adverse events between groups.
- Subgroup analysis suggested possible benefit in less severe septic shock, but this was hypothesis-generating only.
- Vasopressin was associated with more digital ischemia, though overall safety profile was similar to norepinephrine.
- The trial was underpowered to detect small mortality differences due to lower-than-expected event rates.

4.5 Clinical Application

- Consider low-dose vasopressin (0.03 U/min) as an adjunct to norepinephrine in septic shock patients to reduce catecholamine requirements.
- Avoid vasopressin in patients with risk factors for ischemia, such as peripheral vascular disease or existing digital ischemia.
- Monitor for complications like digital ischemia and hyponatremia during vasopressin use.
- May consider vasopressin earlier in septic shock when MAP is still responsive to vasopressors, but evidence for timing benefit is limited.

4.6 When to Discuss on Rounds

Discuss this trial on rounds with the following scenarios:

- When deciding whether to add vasopressin or simply escalate norepinephrine in septic shock patients already requiring vasopressors.
- When evaluating risks of vasopressors, noting trends toward fewer cardiac arrests with vasopressin but more digital ischemia.
- When teaching about physiologic vasopressin deficiency in septic shock and why replacement was considered as a therapeutic strategy.
- When comparing vasopressin to other adjunctive agents for refractory septic shock.
- When reinforcing guideline recommendations that norepinephrine remains the first-line vasopressor, with vasopressin considered an adjunct in catecholamine-refractory cases.

4.7 *Relevant Guidelines*

The **Surviving Sepsis Campaign Guidelines** support norepinephrine as first-line vasopressor therapy and recommend considering vasopressin as an adjunct, particularly in patients requiring escalating doses of norepinephrine.

5 HYPRESS Trial Summary [5]

Full Title: Effect of Hydrocortisone on Development of Shock Among Patients with Severe Sepsis
Publication Year: 2016
Journal: Journal of the American Medical Association

5.1 *Background*

Corticosteroids have been used in septic shock to attenuate systemic inflammation and improve vascular responsiveness to catecholamines. However, the role of corticosteroids in preventing progression from severe sepsis to septic shock remained uncertain. The HYPRESS trial aimed to evaluate whether early administration of hydrocortisone could prevent the progression of severe sepsis to septic shock.

5.2 *Study Design*

Type: Randomized, double-blind, placebo-controlled trial
Population: 380 patients with severe sepsis but without shock
Intervention: Hydrocortisone (200 mg/day) vs. placebo
Primary Outcome: Development of septic shock within 14 days
Secondary Outcomes:

- Time until septic shock
- Mortality in ICU or hospital
- 180-day survival

Adverse Effects:

- Secondary infections
- Weaning failure
- Muscle weakness
- Hyperglycemia

5.3 Results

Primary Outcome: No significant reduction in progression to septic shock (21.2% hydrocortisone vs. 22.9% placebo, $p = 0.70$)

Secondary Outcomes: No significant difference observed between groups in any of the secondary outcomes.

Adverse Effects:

- No significant different between groups with secondary infections, weaning failure, or muscle weakness.
- Hyperglycemia: Greater hyperglycemia found in the hydrocortisone group vs. placebo (90.9% vs. 81.5%; $p = 0.009$)

5.4 Key Takeaways

- In patients with severe sepsis not yet in septic shock, low-dose hydrocortisone did not reduce the progression to septic shock within 14 days compared with placebo
- An exploratory finding was that delirium was less frequent in the hydrocortisone group (8.5% vs 19.2%; $p = 0.01$), though this was a post hoc result and hypothesis-generating only.
- Subgroup analysis of patients with critical illness–related corticosteroid insufficiency (CIRCI) showed higher risk of septic shock overall, but no treatment benefit from hydrocortisone in this subgroup.
- The trial's results do not support the use of hydrocortisone in severe sepsis without shock, aligning with guideline recommendations to reserve steroids for vasopressor-refractory septic shock rather than as prophylaxis in early sepsis.

5.5 Clinical Application

- Do not start hydrocortisone in adults with severe sepsis who are not in septic shock; it does not prevent progression to shock, shorten LOS, or improve survival.
- Reserve hydrocortisone for septic shock with persistent vasopressor requirement after adequate fluid resuscitation (e.g., MAP <65 mm Hg despite norepinephrine), not as prophylaxis in early sepsis.
- Avoid initiating hydrocortisone solely because of suspected CIRCI in severe sepsis without shock; HYPRESS showed no benefit in that subgroup.
- If the patient later develops shock and you start hydrocortisone, reassess daily; plan to taper off once vasopressors are discontinued (no prolonged taper needed if $\leq$7 days of therapy).

- Anticipate hyperglycemia with any steroid exposure: implement q4–6h glucose checks and insulin protocol; warn nursing and set thresholds for escalation.
- Monitor for steroid-associated adverse effects (hypernatremia, myopathy, secondary infection), even though rates were similar overall.
- Continue a patient's chronic outpatient steroids (stress-dose if shock develops) but avoid adding hydrocortisone "just in case" in stable, non-shock sepsis.

5.6 When to Discuss on Rounds

Discuss this trial on rounds with the following scenarios:

- When deciding whether to start hydrocortisone in a patient with severe sepsis but no septic shock.
- When reviewing why guidelines restrict steroid use to patients with vasopressor-refractory septic shock rather than early sepsis.
- When clarifying for the team that hydrocortisone should not be used as "prophylaxis" to prevent progression to shock.
- When teaching about potential harms of unnecessary steroids (hyperglycemia, infection risk, myopathy) despite lack of demonstrated benefit in this population.

5.7 Relevant Guidelines

The **Surviving Sepsis Campaign Guidelines** recommend against routine use of corticosteroids in patients with severe sepsis who do not have septic shock, based on the findings of the HYPRESS trial.

6 CRASH-2 Trial Summary [6]

Full Title: Effects of Tranexamic Acid on Death, Vascular Occlusive Events, and Blood Transfusion in Trauma Patients with Significant Haemorrhage: a Randomised, Placebo-Controlled Trial
Publication Year: 2010
Journal: Lancet

6.1 Background

Trauma is a leading cause of mortality worldwide, often exacerbated by significant hemorrhage. Tranexamic acid (TXA), an antifibrinolytic medication, reduces bleeding by inhibiting clot breakdown. However, prior to the CRASH-2 trial, the effectiveness and safety of TXA in trauma patients with substantial hemorrhage were uncertain. The CRASH-2 trial aimed to assess whether early administration of TXA could reduce mortality in trauma patients.

6.2 Study Design

Type: Randomized, placebo-controlled trial
Population: 20,211 trauma patients with significant bleeding
Intervention: TXA (1 g loading dose followed by 1 g infusion over 8 h) vs. placebo
Primary Outcome: All-cause mortality within 4 weeks
Secondary Outcomes:

- Vascular occlusive events
- Surgical intervention
- Receipt of blood transfusion
- Units of blood products transfused

6.3 Results

Primary Outcome: Significantly lower all-cause mortality in the TXA group (14.5% vs. 16%, RR 0.91, $p = 0.0035$)
Secondary Outcomes: No significant difference was observed between groups in any of the secondary outcomes.

6.4 Key Takeaways

- Tranexamic acid (TXA) reduced all-cause mortality in bleeding trauma patients.
- Death specifically due to bleeding was significantly reduced.
- The benefit was strongly time-dependent with greatest benefit being when TXA was given within 3 h of injury, especially if within the first hour.
- No significant increase in thromboembolic events (MI, stroke, PE, DVT) was observed.
- Findings support early administration of TXA in trauma patients at risk of significant hemorrhage.

6.5 Clinical Application

- Administer TXA early (within 3 h of injury) to trauma patients with significant hemorrhage.
- Ensure correct dosing regimen (1 g initial bolus followed by 1 g infusion over 8 h).
- Incorporate TXA into massive transfusion protocols and trauma resuscitation bundles.
- Do not delay administration for labs, imaging, or transfer—the benefit is time-dependent.
- Consider TXA even before arrival to definitive care (prehospital or ED setting) if severe bleeding is suspected.
- No need to withhold TXA out of concern for increased clotting risk as large trial data showed no rise in thromboembolic events.

6.6 When to Discuss on Rounds

Discuss this trial on rounds with the following scenarios:

- When managing a trauma patient with significant hemorrhage and considering early administration of tranexamic acid.
- When emphasizing the importance of giving TXA within 3 h, and ideally within the first hour, to maximize survival benefit.
- When discussing why TXA is part of modern trauma protocols and massive transfusion pathways.
- When clarifying that CRASH-2 showed no increase in thromboembolic complications with TXA use.

6.7 Relevant Guidelines

The **American College of Surgeons Advanced Trauma Life Support (ATLS)** guidelines and the **WHO** guidelines recommend the early administration of TXA for trauma patients with significant bleeding, based largely on findings from the CRASH-2 trial.

7 ALBIOS Trial Summary [7]

Full Title: Albumin Replacement in Patients with Severe Sepsis or Septic Shock
Publication Year: 2014
Journal: New England Journal of Medicine

7.1 Background

Fluid resuscitation in severe sepsis and septic shock commonly uses crystalloids, but colloids such as albumin have been proposed as potentially beneficial alternatives due to their capacity to maintain intravascular volume. Prior trials evaluating albumin provided inconsistent results regarding mortality benefit. The ALBIOS trial sought to determine whether albumin administration improved survival outcomes compared to crystalloids alone in patients with severe sepsis or septic shock.

7.2 Study Design

Type: Randomized, controlled trial
Population: 1818 patients with severe sepsis or septic shock
Intervention: Albumin plus crystalloids vs. crystalloids alone
Primary Outcome: 28-day mortality
Secondary Outcomes:

- 90-day mortality
- Incidence of organ dysfunction
- Length of stay in the ICU and hospital

7.3 Results

Primary Outcome: No significant difference in 28-day mortality (31.8% albumin vs. 32% crystalloids, RR 1.00; [95% CI: 0.87–1.14; p = 0.94])
Secondary Outcomes:

- No significant difference in 90-day mortality (41.1% albumin vs. 43.6% crystalloids, RR 0.95; [95% CI: 0.85–1.05; p = 0.29]).
- Incidence of organ dysfunction: No significant difference observed between groups.
- Length of stay in ICU and hospital: No significant difference observed between groups.

7.4 Key Takeaways

- Albumin plus crystalloids did not reduce 28-day or 90-day mortality compared to crystalloids alone in patients with severe sepsis or septic shock.
- Albumin therapy produced small hemodynamic benefits, including higher mean arterial pressure, lower heart rate, and lower cumulative fluid balance.
- Time to discontinuation of vasopressors was shorter in the albumin group, reflecting improved hemodynamic stability.
- Albumin administration was safe overall, though slight increases in bilirubin and decreases in platelet count were noted.
- Results do not support routine albumin supplementation in all sepsis patients but raise the possibility of targeted benefit in septic shock.

7.5 Clinical Application

- Albumin should not be used routinely for all patients with severe sepsis, as it did not improve overall mortality compared with crystalloids.
- In patients with septic shock who remain hypotensive despite adequate fluid resuscitation with crystalloids, albumin may be considered as an adjunct to help achieve hemodynamic stability.
- Albumin may be useful for patients with persistent hypoalbuminemia (<30 g/L) where correction could improve oncotic pressure and intravascular fluid balance.
- When using albumin, anticipate modest benefits such as earlier discontinuation of vasopressors, lower heart rate, and improved mean arterial pressure.
- Be aware of potential downsides, including mild increases in bilirubin and lower platelet counts, which should be monitored during therapy.

7.6 When to Discuss on Rounds

Discuss this trial on rounds with the following scenarios:

- When discussing fluid resuscitation strategies in patients with severe sepsis or septic shock.
- When considering whether to add albumin to crystalloids in a patient with persistent hypotension despite adequate fluid administration.
- When reviewing the hemodynamic benefits of albumin, such as earlier discontinuation of vasopressors and improved mean arterial pressure.
- When teaching about the physiologic effects of albumin beyond volume expansion (oncotic pressure, nitric oxide scavenging, anti-inflammatory properties).

7.7 *Relevant Guidelines*

The **Surviving Sepsis Campaign Guidelines** recommend crystalloids as the first-line fluid for resuscitation in sepsis, highlighting selective use of albumin in specific patient populations based on clinical judgement, consistent with findings from the ALBIOS trial.

8 FACTT Trial Summary [8]

Full Title: Comparison of Two Fluid-Management Strategies in Acute Lung Injury
Publication Year: 2006
Journal: New England Journal of Medicine

8.1 *Background*

Optimal fluid management strategies in Acute Respiratory Distress Syndrome (ARDS) were unclear prior to this trial. Excessive fluid administration could exacerbate pulmonary edema and prolong mechanical ventilation, while overly restrictive fluid management might impair perfusion and organ function. The FACTT trial evaluated whether a conservative fluid management strategy could improve clinical outcomes in ARDS patients compared to a liberal fluid strategy.

8.2 *Study Design*

Type: Randomized, controlled trial
Population: 1000 patients with ARDS
Intervention: Conservative fluid strategy vs. liberal fluid strategy
Primary Outcome: 60-day mortality
Secondary Outcomes:

- Ventilator-free days
- Organ-failure-free days
- Measures of lung physiology

8.3 Results

Primary Outcome: No significant difference in 60-day mortality between groups (25.5% conservative vs. 28.4% liberal, p = 0.30)

Secondary Outcome:

- Increased ventilator-free days in the conservative group (14.6 ± 0.5 vs. 12.1 ± 0.5, p < 0.001)
- Organ-failure-free days: Conservative strategy group had more days free of CNS failure compared to the liberal group (18.8 ± 0.5 vs. 17.2 ± 0.5; p = 0.03). Although, there was a slight increase in the number of cardiovascular-failure-free days during the first 7 days in the liberal group compared to conservative (4.2 ± 0.01 vs. 3.9 ± 0.1; p = 0.04).
- Measures of lung physiology: Conservative group overall had better lung injury scores, oxygenation indexes, lower plateau pressures, and positive end-expiratory pressures.

8.4 Key Takeaways

- A conservative fluid management strategy in patients with acute lung injury (ALI)/ARDS significantly reduced net fluid balance compared to a liberal strategy.
- Conservative fluid management improved lung physiology: better lung injury scores, lower plateau pressures, improved oxygenation indices, and more ventilator-free days.
- Conservative strategy shortened ICU stays.
- No significant mortality difference was observed at 60 days.
- Renal outcomes were similar between groups; rates of renal replacement therapy did not significantly differ.
- Safety concerns: conservative strategy was associated with more metabolic alkalosis and electrolyte disturbances (hyponatremia, hypokalemia, etc.), but no excess in arrhythmias or severe adverse outcomes.
- Subgroup findings: Black and Hispanic patients had higher overall mortality than white patients, though treatment effect was consistent across racial/ethnic subgroups.
- Overall, conservative fluid management provided substantial non-mortality benefits such as better lung function, shorter ventilation, and reduced ICU time, without increasing mortality or major organ dysfunction.

8.5 *Clinical Application*

- Use a conservative fluid management strategy (guided diuresis, lower filling pressures) in patients with ARDS/acute lung injury once shock has resolved, as it improves lung function and decreases ventilator and ICU days.
- Recognize that mortality is not reduced, but the conservative strategy provides important morbidity benefits (earlier liberation from mechanical ventilation, less ICU time).
- Monitor closely for electrolyte disturbances and metabolic alkalosis with diuresis; correct proactively to avoid complications.
- Apply this strategy in practice by aiming for neutral or slightly negative fluid balance after initial resuscitation, provided the patient is hemodynamically stable.
- Understand that renal outcomes were not worsened by a conservative approach, supporting its safety in critically ill patients without ongoing shock.

8.6 *When to Discuss on Rounds*

Discuss this trial on rounds with the following scenarios:

- When discussing ventilator management in a patient with ARDS, bring up FACTT as evidence that conservative fluid management can shorten ventilator days.
- When asked about fluid balance in critically ill patients, note that targeting a neutral or slightly negative balance after initial resuscitation improves lung function without harming the kidneys.
- When teaching about ARDS outcomes, emphasize that mortality was not improved, but morbidity (ventilator-free days, ICU-free days) was significantly better with conservative fluids.
- When reviewing potential risks of diuresis in the ICU, cite FACTT to highlight the need for close monitoring of electrolytes and metabolic alkalosis.
- When considering liberal versus conservative strategies for fluid management, explain that FACTT shows conservative management is safe and beneficial once shock has resolved.

8.7 *Relevant Guidelines*

The **ATS/ERS ARDS** guidelines and **Surviving Sepsis Campaign** guidelines recommend a conservative fluid management approach for ARDS patients, emphasizing reduced fluid administration to limit pulmonary complications, consistent with FACTT trial findings.

9 AKIKI Trial Summary [9]

Full Title: Initiation Strategies for Renal-Replacement Therapy in the Intensive Care Unit
Publication Year: 2016
Journal: New England Journal of Medicine

9.1 Background

Optimal timing for initiation of renal replacement therapy (RRT) in critically ill patients with acute kidney injury (AKI) was uncertain prior to the AKIKI trial. Early initiation might prevent complications from fluid overload and metabolic disturbances, but it also might expose patients unnecessarily to potential complications of dialysis. Conversely, delayed initiation could limit unnecessary treatment but risk progression of AKI and associated complications. The AKIKI trial evaluated early versus delayed initiation of RRT in critically ill patients with severe AKI.

9.2 Study Design

Type: Randomized, controlled trial
Population: 620 critically ill patients with severe AKI
Intervention: Early initiation of RRT vs. delayed initiation (based on predefined criteria)
Primary Outcome: 60-day mortality
Secondary Outcomes:

- Receipt of RRT at least once
- Numbers of RRT-free days
- Mechanical ventilation-free days
- Vasopressor therapy-free days

9.3 Results

Primary Outcome: No significant difference in 60-day mortality (48.5% early vs. 49.7% delayed; [95% CI: 42.6–53.8; p = 0.79]).
Secondary Outcomes:

  - Receipt of RRT at least once: Delayed strategy had significantly less patients initiated on RRT compared to the early strategy group (51% vs. 98%, $p < 0.001$).
  - RRT-free days: Significantly more RRT-free days in the delayed strategy group vs. early strategy (19 vs. 17, $p < 0.001$).
  - No significant difference observed between either groups in mechanical ventilation and vasopressor-free days.

9.4 Key Takeaways

- Early initiation of renal replacement therapy (RRT) in critically ill patients with severe AKI did not reduce 60-day mortality compared with a delayed initiation strategy.
- Nearly half of patients in the delayed group never required RRT, avoiding unnecessary dialysis exposure.
- Delayed initiation was associated with more RRT-free days and fewer catheter-related bloodstream infections.
- Complication rates (e.g., bleeding, electrolyte disturbances) were overall similar between groups, though hypophosphatemia occurred more often with early initiation.
- Findings support a monitored "watchful waiting" approach, initiating RRT only when clear clinical or biochemical indications arise, rather than routinely starting early.

9.5 Clinical Application

- In critically ill patients with severe AKI, clinicians can consider delaying RRT until clear indications arise (persistent anuria/oliguria, refractory hyperkalemia, severe acidosis, or very high BUN), as many will recover renal function without dialysis.
- A delayed strategy can reduce unnecessary RRT exposure, sparing patients the risks of catheter placement, infection, and electrolyte disturbances.
- Early initiation should still be used when urgent complications of AKI (e.g., life-threatening hyperkalemia, refractory metabolic acidosis, fluid overload with hypoxia) are present.
- The trial supports close monitoring of urine output, electrolytes, and acid–base status in patients managed with a delayed approach, ensuring RRT is initiated without harmful delay when required.
- In ICU practice, AKIKI provides evidence to individualize RRT timing based on patient trajectory rather than reflexively initiating early.

9.6 *When to Discuss on Rounds*

Discuss this trial on rounds with the following scenarios:

- When a patient has KDIGO stage 3 AKI but no emergent indication (no refractory hyperkalemia, acidosis, or pulmonary edema), consider citing AKIKI to support a delayed RRT strategy with close monitoring.
- When urine output remains low, discuss AKIKI's trigger thresholds (e.g., persistent anuria/oliguria >72 h, BUN >112 mg/dL) as objective cues for starting RRT.
- When catheter-related infection risk is high, note that delaying RRT in AKIKI reduced dialysis catheter bloodstream infections and increased RRT-free days.
- When a patient has hyperkalemia with ECG changes, severe acidosis, or refractory fluid overload appear, emphasize that AKIKI supports immediate RRT despite the general "delay" strategy.

9.7 *Relevant Guidelines*

The **KDIGO guidelines** and critical care consensus statements now support delayed initiation of dialysis in critically ill AKI patients unless severe complications develop, reflecting the findings from the AKIKI trial.

10 NICE-SUGAR Trial Summary [10]

Full Title: Intensive versus Conventional Glucose Control in Critically Ill Patients
Publication Year: 2009
Journal: New England Journal of Medicine

10.1 *Background*

Prior single-center studies suggested that strict glucose control (target 80–110 mg/dL) reduced mortality in critically ill patients. This led many ICUs to adopt intensive insulin protocols. NICE-SUGAR was designed to test whether intensive glucose control improved survival compared to a more conventional glucose target.

10.2 Study Design

Type: Multicenter, randomized controlled trial
Population: 6104 critically ill patients in the ICU
Intervention: Intensive glucose control (target BGL of 81–108 mg/dl) vs. conventional glucose control (target BGL of 180 mg/dl or less)
Primary Outcome: 90-day all-cause mortality
Secondary Outcomes:

- Survival time during first 90 days
- Cause-specific death
- Durations of mechanical ventilation, renal replacement therapy, and stays in the ICU and hospital

10.3 Results

Primary Outcome: Significantly more patients in the intensive group had died than the conventional group (27.5% vs. 24.9%, OR 1.14; [95% CI: 1.02–1.28; p = 0.02]).
Secondary Outcomes:

- Survival time during first 90 days: Significantly lower in the intensive group than in the conventional group (HR 1.11; [95% CI: 1.01–1.23; p = 0.03]).
- Cause-specific death: A higher proportion of deaths in the intensive group were from cardiovascular causes, with 41.6% compared with 35.8% in the conventional group (p = 0.02).
- No significant difference was observed between groups in duration of mechanical ventilation, RRT, and days stayed in the ICU and hospital.

10.4 Key Takeaways

- Intensive glucose control with a target of 81–108 mg/dL increased 90-day mortality compared with conventional control (<180 mg/dL).
- Severe hypoglycemia occurred far more often in the intensive group, with 6.8% affected compared with 0.5% in the conventional group.
- There were no significant differences in ICU or hospital length of stay, organ failure, duration of mechanical ventilation, renal replacement therapy, or infection rates between the groups.
- The results challenged earlier single-center studies suggesting benefit from intensive glucose control and showed instead that it caused harm in critically ill patients.
- The findings established the practice standard of aiming for glucose levels between 140 and 180 mg/dL in the ICU rather than striving for normoglycemia.

10.5 Clinical Application

- Glucose management in the ICU should aim for a moderate target of 140–180 mg/dL rather than tight control to 81–108 mg/dL.
- Intensive glucose lowering with insulin should be avoided in most critically ill patients, as it increases mortality and markedly raises the risk of severe hypoglycemia.
- This trial supports prioritizing safety over normoglycemia, highlighting that "normal" physiologic values may not always translate to better outcomes in the critically ill.
- The results emphasize the importance of tailoring metabolic management to evidence-based mortality outcomes rather than surrogate markers such as glucose normalization.

10.6 When to Discuss on Rounds

Discuss this trial on rounds with the following scenarios:

- When discussing glucose targets in the ICU.
- When evaluating a patient with recurrent hypoglycemia in the ICU, highlight that the trial showed a nearly 15-fold increase in severe hypoglycemia with intensive control.
- When caring for a patient on steroids or with septic shock, use NICE-SUGAR as an example that subgroup outcomes did not show benefit from tight glucose control.
- When a colleague suggests pursuing "normal" blood glucose in critical illness, mention NICE-SUGAR as evidence that striving for physiologic norms can sometimes cause harm.

10.7 Relevant Guidelines

The NICE-SUGAR trial directly shaped international critical care practice guidelines. The **Society of Critical Care Medicine** and **ADA** consensus statements, along with the **Surviving Sepsis Campaign guidelines**, revised glucose management targets upward to recommend a blood glucose range of 140–180 mg/dL for most critically ill patients, rather than pursuing near-normal glycemia. The **ADA** standards of medical care in diabetes continue to cite NICE-SUGAR as pivotal evidence against intensive control in the ICU. Similarly, the **European Society of Intensive Care Medicine** and the **ESC** have aligned with this moderate target, emphasizing the avoidance of hypoglycemia.

References

1. Acute Respiratory Distress Syndrome Network, Brower RG, Matthay MA, et al. Ventilation with lower tidal volumes as compared with traditional tidal volumes for acute lung injury and the acute respiratory distress syndrome. N Engl J Med. 2000;342(18):1301–8. https://doi.org/10.1056/NEJM200005043421801.
2. Guérin C, Reignier J, Richard JC, et al. Prone positioning in severe acute respiratory distress syndrome. N Engl J Med. 2013;368(23):2159–68. https://doi.org/10.1056/NEJMoa1214103.
3. Asfar P, Meziani F, Hamel JF, et al. High versus low blood-pressure target in patients with septic shock. N Engl J Med. 2014;370(17):1583–93. https://doi.org/10.1056/NEJMoa1312173.
4. Russell JA, Walley KR, Singer J, et al. Vasopressin versus norepinephrine infusion in patients with septic shock. N Engl J Med. 2008;358(9):877–87. https://doi.org/10.1056/NEJMoa067373.
5. Keh D, Trips E, Marx G, et al. Effect of hydrocortisone on development of shock among patients with severe sepsis: the HYPRESS randomized clinical trial. JAMA. 2016;316(17):1775–85. https://doi.org/10.1001/jama.2016.14799.
6. CRASH-2 trial collaborators, Shakur H, Roberts I, et al. Effects of tranexamic acid on death, vascular occlusive events, and blood transfusion in trauma patients with significant haemorrhage (CRASH-2): a randomised, placebo-controlled trial. Lancet. 2010;376(9734):23–32. https://doi.org/10.1016/S0140-6736(10)60835-5.
7. Caironi P, Tognoni G, Masson S, et al. Albumin replacement in patients with severe sepsis or septic shock. N Engl J Med. 2014;370(15):1412–21. https://doi.org/10.1056/NEJMoa1305727.
8. National Heart, Lung, and Blood Institute Acute Respiratory Distress Syndrome (ARDS) Clinical Trials Network, Wiedemann HP, Wheeler AP, et al. Comparison of two fluid-management strategies in acute lung injury. N Engl J Med. 2006;354(24):2564–75. https://doi.org/10.1056/NEJMoa062200.
9. Gaudry S, Hajage D, Schortgen F, et al. Initiation strategies for renal-replacement therapy in the intensive care unit. N Engl J Med. 2016;375(2):122–33. https://doi.org/10.1056/NEJMoa1603017.
10. NICE-SUGAR Study Investigators, Finfer S, Chittock DR, et al. Intensive versus conventional glucose control in critically ill patients. N Engl J Med. 2009;360(13):1283–97. https://doi.org/10.1056/NEJMoa0810625.

Chapter 5
Endocrinology

1 UKPDS Trial Summary [1]

Full Title: United Kingdom Prospective Diabetes Study
Publication Year: 1998
Journal: The Lancet

1.1 *Background*

Prior to the UKPDS trial, there was limited evidence regarding the long-term impact of intensive glycemic control on diabetes-related complications in type 2 diabetes. Clinicians largely relied on expert consensus rather than robust trial data. The UKPDS trial was designed to determine whether tight blood glucose control, achieved through diet, oral hypoglycemic agents, or insulin, could reduce the incidence of microvascular and macrovascular complications in patients newly diagnosed with type 2 diabetes.

1.2 *Study Design*

Type: Randomized, controlled trial
Population: 3,867 newly diagnosed type 2 diabetes patients
Intervention: Intensive glucose control (target fasting glucose <108 mg/dL) using insulin, sulfonylureas, or metformin vs. conventional management (dietary modification alone)

A. Love, *The Essential Evidence*, https://doi.org/10.1007/978-3-032-12399-2_5

Primary Outcomes

- Any diabetes-related endpoint
- Diabetes-related death
- All-cause mortality

1.3 Results

Primary Outcomes

- Any diabetes-related endpoint: Intensive glucose control significantly reduced the risk of any diabetes-related endpoint compared with conventional treatment (Risk Reduction 12%; [95% CI: 0.79–0.99; p = 0.029]).
- Diabetes-related death: There was no stastically significant reduction in diabetes-related deaths with intensive glucose control (HR 0.91; [95% CI: 0.76–1.09; p = 0.27]).
- All-cause mortality: No significant reduction in all-cause mortality (HR 0.94; [95% CI: 0.80–1.10; p = 0.44]).

1.4 Key Takeaways

- Intensive glycemic control significantly reduces microvascular complications in patients with type 2 diabetes.
- Intensive therapy did not significantly reduce diabetes-related mortality or all-cause mortality
- Metformin demonstrates significant cardiovascular benefits in overweight patients.
- These findings established glycemic control as a cornerstone of diabetes management for preventing microvascular complications, though not sufficient alone to reduce mortality or macrovascular events.

1.5 Clinical Application

- Target tight glycemic control early in newly diagnosed type 2 diabetes patients to minimize microvascular complications.
- HbA1c targets should be individualized, but a general approach of tighter glucose control is appropriate early in the disease course to reduce long-term microvascular risk.
- Clinicians should recognize that glycemic control alone is not sufficient to reduce macrovascular outcomes or mortality, so additional strategies (blood pressure management, statins, antiplatelet therapy) are necessary for comprehensive risk reduction.

- Patient counseling should emphasize that while good glucose control may not change heart attack or stroke risk directly, it is critical for preventing blindness, kidney disease, and neuropathy.
- This trial supports early initiation of structured glycemic control strategies at diagnosis of type 2 diabetes, forming the foundation for long-term care.

1.6 When to Discuss on Rounds

Discuss this trial on rounds with the following scenarios:

- When managing a newly diagnosed patient with type 2 diabetes and choosing initial pharmacotherapy.
- When you want to highlight that microvascular complications such as retinopathy and nephropathy can be significantly reduced by tighter glucose control.
- When teaching that macrovascular complications (MI, stroke) were not significantly improved by intensive glucose control alone, underscoring the need for multifactorial risk reduction.
- When emphasizing that HbA1c is a meaningful target for guiding therapy and long-term risk reduction.

1.7 Relevant Guidelines

The **ADA** guidelines and the **EASD** guidelines recommend intensive glycemic control early in type 2 diabetes, with metformin as the preferred initial agent, largely based on findings from the UKPDS trial.

2 ACCORD Trial Summary [2]

Full Title: Effects of Intensive Glucose Lowering in Type 2 Diabetes
Publication Year: 2008
Journal: New England Journal of Medicine

2.1 Background

Prior to the ACCORD trial, the optimal glycemic target in type 2 diabetes, particularly for high-risk cardiovascular patients, was uncertain. While intensive glucose control had been shown to reduce microvascular complications in previous studies, its impact on macrovascular outcomes and mortality in high-risk individuals was unclear. The ACCORD trial was specifically designed to determine if targeting intensive glycemic control (HbA1c <6.0%) in type 2 diabetes patients with existing cardiovascular risk could reduce cardiovascular events or mortality compared to standard control.

2.2 Study Design

Type: Randomized, controlled trial
Population: 10,251 patients with type 2 diabetes and high cardiovascular risk
Intervention: Intensive glycemic control (target HbA1c <6.0%) vs. standard glycemic control (HbA1c 7.0–7.9%)
Primary Outcome: Composite of nonfatal myocardial infarction, nonfatal stroke, or cardiovascular death
Secondary Outcomes:

- All-cause mortality
- Cardiovascular death
- Nonfatal MI

2.3 Results

Primary Outcome: No significant reduction in composite cardiovascular events with intensive control (HR 0.90; [95% CI: 0.78–1.04; p = 0.16]).
Secondary Outcome:

- All-cause mortality: Greater all-cause mortality was observed in the intensive therapy group vs. the standard therapy group (HR 1.22; [95% CI: 1.01–1.46; p = 0.04]).
- Cardiovascular death: More deaths were found to be by cardiovascular causes in the intensive therapy group vs. the standard therapy group (HR 1.35; [95% CI: 1.04–1.76; p = 0.02]).
- Nonfatal MI: There were more episodes of nonfatal MI observed in the standard therapy group (HR 0.76; [95% CI: 0.62–0.92; p = 0.004]) .

2.4 Key Takeaways

- Intensive glycemic control targeting HbA1c <6.0% in high-risk type 2 diabetes patients does not reduce major cardiovascular events and is associated with increased mortality.

- Increased mortality risk appears related to hypoglycemia and potential cardiovascular stress from aggressive glucose lowering.
- The trial was stopped early at 3.5 years due to increased mortality in the intensive-therapy group.
- Benefits of fewer nonfatal MIs were outweighed by excess mortality, raising concerns about rapid and aggressive HbA1c reduction in high-risk type 2 diabetics with cardiovascular disease or risk factors.

2.5 Clinical Application

- Intensive glucose lowering to a target HbA1c <6.0% should not be routinely pursued in high-risk type 2 diabetics with cardiovascular disease or multiple risk factors because it was associated with increased mortality.
- Standard therapy with a target HbA1c of ~7.0–7.9% remains safer and is supported for most patients with type 2 diabetes.
- Intensive therapy may reduce nonfatal myocardial infarction, but this benefit is outweighed by increased cardiovascular and all-cause mortality.
- Rapid reductions in HbA1c, polypharmacy, and increased hypoglycemia risk likely contributed to adverse outcomes and should caution clinicians against aggressive short-term lowering.
- Patients at lower cardiovascular risk or with lower baseline HbA1c may derive some benefit from tighter glycemic control, but this remains hypothesis-generating rather than practice-changing.
- Long-term diabetes management should balance glycemic control with avoidance of hypoglycemia, weight gain, and drug toxicity, emphasizing individualized therapy.

2.6 When to Discuss on Rounds

Discuss this trial on rounds with the following scenarios:

- When setting A1c goals for a high-risk patient with established ASCVD or multiple risk factors, explain why a moderate target (~7–8%) is safer than aiming <6.0% per ACCORD.
- When a patient has recurrent hypoglycemia or wide glucose variability on multi-drug regimens, use ACCORD to justify de-intensifying therapy to reduce mortality risk.
- When deciding how fast to lower an elevated A1c, caution the team that rapid early drops with complex polypharmacy were part of the intensive strategy associated with harm.

- When choosing agents for escalation, emphasize minimizing hypoglycemia (e.g., prefer metformin, GLP-1 RA, SGLT2i over high-dose sulfonylurea/insulin where appropriate) in light of ACCORD's hypoglycemia signal.
- When managing an older, comorbid patient with limited life expectancy, argue for relaxed glycemic targets and symptom-focused care to avoid treatment-related harm.

2.7 Relevant Guidelines

The **ADA** and the **ACP** guidelines emphasize individualized glycemic control goals and caution on against overly aggressive targets in high-risk populations, citing the findings of the ACCORD trial to support less stringent HbA1c goals in these groups.

3 ADVANCE Trial Summary [3]

Full Title: Intensive Blood Glucose Control and Vascular Outcomes in Patients with Type 2 Diabetes
Publication Year: 2008
Journal: New England Journal of Medicine

3.1 Background

Prior to the ADVANCE trial, uncertainty persisted regarding the impact of intensive glycemic control combined with blood pressure management on macrovascular and microvascular outcomes in type 2 diabetes. While previous trials had demonstrated clear benefits on microvascular complications, evidence regarding macrovascular benefits remained inconsistent. ADVANCE specifically aimed to evaluate whether intensive glucose control and strict blood pressure management could reduce the risk of cardiovascular disease and microvascular complications among type 2 diabetes patients.

3.2 Study Design

Type: Randomized, controlled trial
Population: 11,140 type 2 diabetes patients aged 55 or older with cardiovascular risk factors

Intervention:

- Intensive glucose control (gliclazide MR plus other agents, HbA1c ≤6.5%) vs. standard control
- Intensive blood pressure control using perindopril and indapamide combination vs. placebo

Primary Outcome: Composite of major macrovascular (cardiovascular death, nonfatal MI, nonfatal stroke) and microvascular events (new or worsening nephropathy or retinopathy)

Secondary Outcomes:

- All-cause mortality
- Cardiovascular death
- New or worsening nephropathy
- Visual deterioration
- Hospitalizations
- Severe hypoglycemia

3.3 *Results*

Primary Outcome: Intensive glucose control led to significant reduction in the composite endpoint, primarily due to the fewer microvascular complications (HR 0.90; [95% CI: 0.82–0.98; $p = 0.01$]).

Secondary Outcomes:

- No significant difference observed in all-cause mortality or cardiovascular death between the groups.
- New or worsening nephropathy: Significantly reduced in the intensive control group (HR 0.79; [95% CI: 0.66–0.93, $p = 0.006$]).
- Hospitalizations: Greater amount of hospitalizations due to any cause was observed in the intensive control group (44.9% vs. 42.8%, HR 1.07; [95% CI: 1.01–1.13; $p = 0.03$]).
- Severe hypoglycemia: Occurred more frequently in the intensive control group (HR 1.86; [95% CI: 1.14–2.40; $p < 0.001$]).

3.4 *Key Takeaways*

- Intensive glucose control with gliclazide MR lowered HbA1c to a mean of 6.5% compared to 7.3% in standard therapy.
- There was no significant reduction in major macrovascular events or all-cause mortality.

- The renal protective effect highlights glucose control as an important factor in preventing microvascular complications in type 2 diabetes.
- The trial underscored that macrovascular risk reduction requires a multifactorial approach beyond glycemic control, including aggressive management of blood pressure and lipids.

3.5 Clinical Application

- Intensive glucose lowering should be balanced against the increased risk of severe hypoglycemia and higher hospitalization rates, so it is best applied in motivated patients who can adhere to frequent monitoring and follow-up.
- In patients with high cardiovascular risk, intensive glycemic control alone should not be expected to reduce macrovascular outcomes, and additional aggressive management of blood pressure and lipids is required.
- The trial supports tailoring glycemic targets to individual patient profiles, using lower targets for those who can tolerate intensive therapy without excessive hypoglycemia risk.

3.6 When to Discuss on Rounds

Discuss this trial on rounds with the following scenarios:

- When establishing glycemic and blood pressure targets for older patients with type 2 diabetes and cardiovascular risk factors.
- When evaluating the impact of intensive glycemic control on nephropathy progression and kidney outcomes.
- When balancing the benefits of intensive management against potential side effects, particularly in older adults.

3.7 Relevant Guidelines

The **American Diabetes Association (ADA)** and the **European Society of Cardiology (ESC)** guidelines recommend tight glycemic control primarily to reduce microvascular complications, particularly nephropathy, while also emphasizing aggressive blood pressure control based on the results of the ADVANCE trial.

4 DPP Trial Summary [4]

Full Title: Reduction in the Incidence of Type 2 Diabetes with Lifestyle Intervention or Metformin
Publication Year: 2002
Journal: New England Journal of Medicine

4.1 *Background*

Prior to the DPP trial, there was uncertainty regarding the most effective strategies for preventing type 2 diabetes in individuals at high risk (impaired glucose tolerance or prediabetes). While lifestyle interventions and pharmacotherapy showed promise, high-quality evidence was lacking to guide clinical practice. The DPP trial evaluated the effectiveness of intensive lifestyle intervention, metformin, and placebo in preventing or delaying progression from impaired glucose tolerance to type 2 diabetes.

4.2 *Study Design*

Type: Randomized, controlled trial
Population: 3,234 patients with impaired glucose tolerance (prediabetes)
Intervention: Intensive lifestyle intervention (weight reduction ≥7%, ≥150 min/week physical activity) vs. metformin (850 mg twice daily) vs. placebo
Primary Outcome: Progression from prediabetes to type 2 diabetes

4.3 *Results*

Primary Outcome:

- Intensive lifestyle intervention reduced diabetes incidence by 58% compared to placebo (4.8 vs. 11.0 cases per 100 person-years; 95% CI: 0.48–0.66).
- Metformin reduced diabetes incidence by 31% compared to placebo (7.8 vs. 11.0 cases per 100 person-years; 95% CI: 0.17–0.43).
- Intensive lifestyle intervention reduced diabetes incidence by 39% compared to Metformin (4.8 vs. 7.8 cases per 100 person-years; 95% CI: 0.24–0.51).

4.4 *Key Takeaways*

- Intensive lifestyle modification is highly effective in preventing or delaying type 2 diabetes in high-risk individuals.
- Metformin also significantly reduces diabetes risk, though less effectively than lifestyle changes.
- Lifestyle modification provides additional cardiovascular and metabolic benefits beyond diabetes prevention.
- The lifestyle intervention was effective across all sex, racial, and ethnic subgroups, including older adults, demonstrating broad applicability.
- Weight loss and increased physical activity were key drivers of diabetes prevention in the lifestyle group.
- Metformin was less effective in participants with lower BMI or lower fasting glucose at baseline, suggesting patient-specific differences in benefit.
- Both interventions were safe, with only minor increases in gastrointestinal symptoms with metformin and musculoskeletal symptoms with lifestyle intervention.

4.5 *Clinical Application*

- Intensive lifestyle modification with structured weight loss and physical activity programs should be offered as first-line therapy to patients with impaired glucose tolerance or prediabetes.
- Metformin can be considered for patients at high risk of developing diabetes, particularly those who are younger, have higher BMI, or have elevated fasting glucose levels.
- Counseling patients that even modest weight loss (5–7% of body weight) and at least 150 minutes of physical activity per week can significantly lower their risk of progression to diabetes.
- The trial supports offering culturally adaptable, structured lifestyle programs in diverse populations, including older adults, given the broad effectiveness observed.

4.6 *When to Discuss on Rounds*

Discuss this trial on rounds with the following scenarios:

- When discussing strategies to prevent the progression from prediabetes to type 2 diabetes in high-risk patients.
- When highlighting the superiority of lifestyle interventions over pharmacologic therapy (metformin) for diabetes prevention.

- When considering metformin use in younger, obese patients with impaired glucose tolerance as a preventive measure.
- When reviewing the impact of modest weight loss (5–7%) and regular exercise on reducing diabetes incidence.

4.7 Relevant Guidelines

The **ADA** guidelines recommend intensive lifestyle interventions for all patients with prediabetes and support considering metformin in high-risk individuals (especially younger patients, BMI ≥35 kg/m², or history of gestational diabetes) based largely on findings from the DPP trial.

5 VADT Trial Summary [5]

Full Title: Glucose Control and Vascular Complications in Veterans with Type 2 Diabetes
Publication Year: 2009
Journal: New England Journal of Medicine

5.1 Background

Before the VADT, previous trials like UKPDS and ACCORD had produced mixed results regarding the cardiovascular benefits of intensive glucose control in type 2 diabetes. VADT aimed specifically to clarify whether intensive glycemic control could reduce cardiovascular events in a veteran population characterized by older age, long diabetes duration, and established cardiovascular risk factors.

5.2 Study Design

Type: Randomized, controlled trial
Population: 1,791 veterans with type 2 diabetes, mean duration of diabetes ~11.5 years
Intervention: Intensive glucose control (HbA1c <6.0%) vs. standard glucose control (HbA1c target ~8–9%)
Primary Outcomes:

- Time from randomization to the first occurrence of a major cardiovascular event

- Composite of major cardiovascular events (MI, stroke, cardiovascular death, heart failure, surgery for vascular disease, inoperable coronary disease, and amputation for ischemic gangrene)

Secondary Outcome:

- New or worsening angina
- New TIA
- New intermittent claudication
- New critical limb ischemia
- All-cause mortality
- Microvascular complications (nephropathy, retinopathy, neuropathy)

Adverse Effects:

- Hypoglycemic episodes

5.3 *Results*

Primary Outcome:

- No significant difference was observed in time to first cardiovascular event in the intensive-therapy group (HR 0.88; [95% CI: 0.74–1.05; $p = 0.14$]).
- No significant difference in any of the individual components of the outcomes.

Secondary Outcomes:

- No significant differences between groups was observed in the individual secondary outcomes.

Adverse Effects:

- Hypoglycemic episodes: Significantly more events was observed in the intensive therapy group than in the standard therapy group ($p < 0.001$).

5.4 *Key Takeaways*

- Intensive glucose control in patients with longstanding type 2 diabetes (mean duration ~11.5 years, baseline HbA1c 9.4%) achieved a sustained HbA1c difference (6.9% vs 8.4%) compared to standard therapy.
- Despite lowering HbA1c, intensive therapy did not significantly reduce the risk of cardiovascular events.
- All-cause mortality was similar between groups.

- Hypoglycemia was significantly more frequent in the intensive-therapy group, and weight gain was greater.
- Microvascular outcomes showed no significant benefit except for a reduced progression of albuminuria.
- Retinopathy and neuropathy outcomes were not significantly improved, though a nonsignificant trend toward less retinopathy progression was observed

5.5 *Clinical Application*

- In patients with long-standing type 2 diabetes (mean duration >10 years, baseline HbA1c ~9.4%) who are already at high cardiovascular risk, pursuing intensive glucose control to a target HbA1c <7% does not meaningfully reduce cardiovascular events and should not be prioritized over blood pressure, lipid, and lifestyle interventions.
- Clinicians should individualize HbA1c targets in older patients, those with long-standing disease, and those at risk of hypoglycemia—aiming for a reasonable target (e.g., <8%) rather than aggressive lowering that carries more harm than benefit.
- In patients with diabetic nephropathy, intensive glucose control may be considered for reducing progression of albuminuria, but this must be weighed against the increased risk of hypoglycemia and weight gain.
- For patients on insulin or with frequent hypoglycemia, tight control should be avoided; management should focus instead on comprehensive risk reduction with statins, antihypertensives, and antiplatelet therapy.

5.6 *When to Discuss on Rounds*

Discuss this trial on rounds with the following scenarios:

- When managing an older patient with long-standing type 2 diabetes and high cardiovascular risk, bring up the VADT trial to highlight that intensive glucose control did not reduce cardiovascular events despite lowering HbA1c.
- When discussing targets for HbA1c in clinic or inpatient diabetes management, reference VADT as evidence for tailoring less aggressive glycemic goals in patients with advanced disease to avoid hypoglycemia and weight gain.
- When caring for a patient with diabetic nephropathy, mention that VADT found modest benefit in slowing albuminuria progression with intensive glucose control, though this came at the cost of more hypoglycemia.
- When explaining the importance of comprehensive risk reduction, use VADT to emphasize that controlling blood pressure, lipids, and using statins and antiplate-

lets has a stronger impact on cardiovascular outcomes than intensive glucose lowering alone.

5.7 *Relevant Guidelines*

The **ADA** and **American Geriatrics Society (AGS)** guidelines advise less stringent glycemic targets in older adults or patients with long-standing diabetes, multiple comorbidities, or limited life expectancy, reflecting findings from the VADT.

6 EMPA-REG OUTCOME Trial Summary [6]

Full Title: Empagliflozin, Cardiovascular Outcomes, and Mortality in Type 2 Diabetes
Publication Year: 2015
Journal: New England Journal of Medicine

6.1 *Background*

Before the EMPA-REG OUTCOME trial, most diabetes medications were evaluated primarily or glucose-lowering efficacy and microvascular complications, with limited evidence on cardiovascular safety or benefit. The FDA required cardiovascular outcome trials for diabetes drugs, prompting this trial to assess empagliflozin, an SGLT2 inhibitor, specifically for cardiovascular outcomes in patients with type 2 diabetes and established cardiovascular disease.

6.2 *Study Design*

Type: Randomized, placebo-controlled trial
Population: 7,020 patients with type 2 diabetes and established cardiovascular disease
Intervention: Empagliflozin (10 mg or 25 mg daily) vs. placebo
Primary Outcome: Composite of cardiovascular death, nonfatal myocardial infarction, and nonfatal stroke
Secondary Outcomes:

- Primary outcome plus hospitalization for unstable angina

6.3 Results

Primary Outcome: Significant reduction in the composite primary outcome (10.5% in pooled empagliflozin group vs. 12.1% in placebo group, HR 0.86; [95% CI: 0.74–0.99; p = 0.04 for superiority])

Secondary Outcomes:

- Primary outcome plus hospitalization for unstable angina: No significant difference in secondary outcome (p = 0.08).
- Significantly lower rates of cardiovascular death in the empagliflozin group (HR 0.68; [95% CI: 0.49–0.77; p < 0.001]), as well as lower rates of death from any cause (HR 0.68; [95% CI: 0.57–0.82, p < 0.001])..
- Lower rates of hospitalization for heart failure in the empagliflozin group vs. placebo (HR 0.65; [95% CI: 0.50–0.85; p = 0.002])

6.4 Key Takeaways

- Empagliflozin significantly reduced the primary composite outcome of cardiovascular death, nonfatal MI, or nonfatal stroke compared with placebo.
- The benefit was driven primarily by a marked reduction in cardiovascular death, which was lowered by 38% with empagliflozin.
- All-cause mortality was reduced by 32% in the empagliflozin group, representing one of the first diabetes trials to show a clear survival benefit.
- There was no significant difference between empagliflozin and placebo in the risk of myocardial infarction or stroke.
- Benefits emerged early during the trial and were sustained throughout the 3-year follow-up.
- Modest improvements in HbA1c, weight, blood pressure, and uric acid were seen, but the magnitude of cardiovascular benefit suggests mechanisms beyond glycemic control.
- Safety was generally comparable to placebo, with genital infections more frequent in the empagliflozin group but no excess in ketoacidosis, renal injury, or fracture.
- The trial established empagliflozin and SGLT2 inhibitors as cornerstone therapies for type 2 diabetes patients with established cardiovascular disease.

6.5 Clinical Application

- Strongly consider empagliflozin (or other SGLT2 inhibitors with proven cardiovascular benefits) in type 2 diabetes patients with cardiovascular disease.

- Recognize empagliflozin's significant benefit in heart failure prevention and renal protection, beyond glycemic control.
- SGLT2 inhibitors such as empagliflozin are now preferred agents in diabetic patients with high cardiovascular risk, independent of baseline HbA1c or background therapy.
- Benefits are additive to standard cardioprotective therapies such as statins, ACE inhibitors/ARBs, and antiplatelet agents.
- Genital mycotic infections should be anticipated and discussed with patients, but overall safety is comparable to placebo, and risk of serious adverse events is low.
- The magnitude and rapid onset of cardiovascular benefit suggest empagliflozin should be prioritized for patients with diabetes who have already experienced cardiovascular events.

6.6 When to Discuss on Rounds

Discuss this trial on rounds with the following scenarios:

- When presenting a patient with type 2 diabetes and established cardiovascular disease, mention EMPA-REG as evidence that empagliflozin significantly reduces cardiovascular and all-cause mortality.
- When deciding between glucose-lowering agents for a patient with diabetes and prior myocardial infarction or stroke, highlight EMPA-REG as justification for selecting an SGLT2 inhibitor over other oral agents.
- When reviewing diabetic patients already on optimal cardioprotective therapies (statins, ACE inhibitors/ARBs, aspirin), emphasize EMPA-REG as showing additive mortality benefit with empagliflozin.
- When counseling patients about side effects of SGLT2 inhibitors, note that EMPA-REG found a higher rate of genital infections but no increase in hypoglycemia, renal injury, or fractures compared to placebo.

6.7 Relevant Guidelines

The **ADA, ESC,** and **KDIGO** guidelines now recommend SGLT2 inhibitors (including empagliflozin) as preferred medications in patients with type 2 diabetes and cardiovascular or renal disease, heavily influenced by findings from EMPA-REG OUTCOME.

7 LEADER Trial Summary [7]

Full Title: Liraglutide and Cardiovascular Outcomes in Type 2 Diabetes
Publication Year: 2016
Journal: New England Journal of Medicine

7.1 *Background*

Prior to the LEADER trial, there was uncertainty regarding the cardiovascular effects of GLP-1 receptor agonists, such as liraglutide, in patients with type 2 diabetes. Following the FDA's directive requiring cardiovascular safety data for diabetes medications, LEADER was conducted to assess whether liraglutide could reduce major cardiovascular events in high-risk patients with type 2 diabetes.

7.2 *Study Design*

Type: Randomized, double-blind, placebo-controlled trial
Population: 9,340 patients with type 2 diabetes and high cardiovascular risk (≥50 years with established cardiovascular disease or ≥ 60 years with cardiovascular risk factors)
Intervention: Liraglutide (1.8 mg/day) vs. placebo
Primary Outcome: Composite of cardiovascular death, nonfatal myocardial infarction, and nonfatal stroke
Secondary Outcomes:

- Cardiovascular death
- All-cause mortality
- Composite of renal or retinal microvascular events
- Adverse events (hypoglycemia, pancreatitis)

7.3 *Results*

Primary Outcome: Significant reduction in the primary outcome with liraglutide 13% vs placebo 14.9% (HR 0.87; [95% CI: 0.78–0.97; $p < 0.001$ for noninferiority; $p = 0.01$).
Secondary Outcome:

- Cardiovascular death: Significant reduction in cardiovascular death (HR 0.78; [95% CI: 0.66–0.93; $p = 0.007$]).

- All-cause mortality: Reduction in all-cause mortality (HR 0.85; [95% CI: 0.74–0.97; p = 0.02]).
- Composite microvascular events: Reduced incidence of composite renal or retinal microvascular events (HR 0.84; [95% CI: 0.73–0.97; p = 0.02]).
- No significant difference in rates of pancreatitis or severe hypoglycemia compared to placebo.

7.4 Key Takeaways

- Liraglutide significantly reduced the primary composite outcome (CV death, nonfatal MI, or nonfatal stroke) compared to placebo
- Nonfatal MI and nonfatal stroke were numerically lower with liraglutide, but not statistically significant.
- Liraglutide reduced microvascular complications, driven primarily by fewer renal events (notably macroalbuminuria); effect on retinopathy was nonsignificant.
- Benefits were more pronounced in patients with established cardiovascular disease and those with impaired renal function (eGFR <60 mL/min/1.73 m^2).
- Liraglutide produced modest improvements in glycemic control (HbA1c −0.40%), weight (−2.3 kg), and systolic blood pressure (−1.2 mmHg), with a slight increase in heart rate (+3 bpm).
- Safety profile: lower risk of severe hypoglycemia versus placebo, but higher rates of gastrointestinal side effects and gallstone disease. Pancreatic and thyroid cancer signals were monitored but not statistically significant.

7.5 Clinical Application

- Consider liraglutide as an add-on therapy in patients with type 2 diabetes and established cardiovascular disease to reduce cardiovascular mortality and overall mortality.
- Use liraglutide in patients with type 2 diabetes and chronic kidney disease (eGFR <60 mL/min/1.73 m^2), where benefits appear more pronounced, particularly for renal protection.
- Recognize liraglutide as a preferred GLP-1 receptor agonist for patients needing both glycemic control and cardiovascular risk reduction.
- Choose liraglutide in overweight or obese patients with diabetes, given its weight-lowering effects compared with insulin or sulfonylureas.
- Consider liraglutide in patients at risk of hypoglycemia who require additional glucose-lowering therapy, as it carries a lower risk of severe hypoglycemia than insulin or sulfonylureas.

- Monitor for gastrointestinal side effects (nausea, vomiting, diarrhea) and for gallstone disease, as these were more common with liraglutide use.

7.6 When to Discuss on Rounds

Discuss this trial on rounds with the following scenarios:

- When discussing glucose-lowering therapy in a patient with type 2 diabetes and established cardiovascular disease, mention that liraglutide reduced major adverse cardiovascular events and cardiovascular mortality.
- When reviewing treatment options for a patient with type 2 diabetes and CKD (eGFR <60), highlight that liraglutide provided greater benefit in this subgroup, especially with respect to renal outcomes.
- When discussing multifactorial risk reduction in diabetes, emphasize that liraglutide is one of the few glucose-lowering drugs with proven mortality benefit beyond glycemic control.

7.7 Relevant Guidelines

The **American Diabetes Association (ADA), European Society of Cardiology (ESC),** and other major diabetes societies strongly recommend GLP-1 receptor agonists (such as liraglutide) for patients with type 2 diabetes and established cardiovascular or chronic kidney disease, largely influenced by LEADER trial outcomes.

8 WHI Trial Summary [8]

Full Title: Women's Health Initiative Randomized Controlled Trial
Publication Year: 2002
Journal: Journal of the American Medical Association

8.1 Background

Before the WHI trial, hormone replacement therapy (HRT), specifically estrogen plus progestin, was commonly prescribed to postmenopausal women, believed to protect against cardiovascular disease, osteoporosis, and menopausal symptoms. However, long-term safety data were limited. The WHI trial was initiated to evaluate risks and benefits of combined estrogen plus progestin therapy in healthy postmenopausal women.

8.2 *Study Design*

Type: Randomized, controlled trial
Population: 16,608 healthy postmenopausal women aged 50–79 years
Intervention: Combined estrogen plus progestin (conjugated equine estrogen 0.625 mg/day plus medroxyprogesterone acetate 2.5 mg/day) vs. placebo
Primary Outcome: Coronary heart disease (nonfatal myocardial infarction and coronary death)
Secondary Outcomes:

- Invasive breast cancer
- Stroke
- Pulmonary embolism
- Hip fracture
- Colorectal cancer
- Endometrial cancer

8.3 *Results*

Primary Outcome: Increased risk of coronary heart disease with combined HRT by 29% relative to placebo (HR 1.29; [95% CI: 1.02–1.63; p = 0.05]).
Secondary Outcomes:

- Invasive breast cancer: Increased risk of invasive breast cancer (HR 1.26; [95% CI: 1.00–1.59]).
- Stroke: Increased risk of stroke (HR 1.41; [95% CI: 1.07–1.85]).
- Pulmonary embolism: Increased pulmonary embolism (HR 2.13; [95% CI: 1.39–3.25]).
- Hip fracture: Decreased incidence was observed in the HRT group (HR 0.66; [95% CI: 0.45–0.98]).
- Colorectal cancer: Significantly reduced risk of colorectal cancer by 37% (HR 0.63; [95% CI: 0.43–0.92]).
- Endometrial cancer: No significant difference was observed between groups.

8.4 Key Takeaways

- Combined estrogen plus progestin therapy increased the risk of coronary heart disease, with most of the excess due to nonfatal myocardial infarctions.
- Despite benefits for bone health and colorectal cancer, the global index showed overall harm, with ~19 excess adverse events per 10,000 women per year on therapy.
- There was no difference in all-cause mortality between estrogen plus progestin and placebo groups over 5.2 years of follow-up.
- The WHI trial provided definitive evidence that combined hormone replacement therapy should not be used for the primary prevention of chronic disease in postmenopausal women with an intact uterus.

8.5 Clinical Application

- Avoid routine long-term combined hormone replacement therapy in healthy postmenopausal women for cardiovascular disease prevention.
- Discuss risks of HRT: highlighting the increased risk of CHD, stroke, VTE, and breast cancer, which outweighed benefits for fractures and colorectal cancer.
- Regarding osteoporosis management discussions: while HRT reduces fracture risk, alternative agents (bisphosphonates, denosumab, SERMs) are safer for bone health.
- Inform decision-making in women with family history of breast cancer or personal risk factors, as HRT further elevates invasive breast cancer risk.
- Use in multidisciplinary care (e.g., gynecology, primary care, cardiology) when aligning therapy plans, reinforcing that short-term HRT may still be considered for severe menopausal symptoms, but not for disease prevention.

8.6 When to Discuss on Rounds

Discuss this trial on rounds with the following scenarios:

- When counseling postmenopausal patients considering hormone replacement therapy.
- When educating trainees about weighing risk and benefits of HRT, especially in relation to cardiovascular health and cancer risk.
- When reviewing alternatives to HRT for cardiovascular and osteoporosis risk management in postmenopausal patients.
- When managing a patient already on combined HRT, discuss WHI evidence to guide shared decision-making about discontinuation, especially in those with elevated CV or breast cancer risk.

8.7 *Relevant Guidelines*

The **USPSTF, AHA,** and **North American Menopause Society (NAMS)** guidelines recommend against routine use of combined estrogen-progestin therapy for prevention of chronic conditions in postmenopausal women, primarily due to WHI trial results.

9 SUSTAIN-6 Trial [9]

Full Title: Semaglutide and Cardiovascular Outcomes in Patients with Type 2 Diabetes
Publication Year: 2016
Journal: New England Journal of Medicine

9.1 *Background*

Prior to the SUSTAIN-6 trial, the cardiovascular safety and efficacy of GLP-1 receptor agonists beyond liraglutide were uncertain. Semaglutide, a once-weekly GLP-1 receptor agonist, was hypothesized to provide cardiovascular protection in patients with type 2 diabetes. SUSTAIN-6 aimed specifically to assess the cardiovascular safety and potential benefits of semaglutide among patients at high cardiovascular risk.

9.2 *Study Design*

Type: Randomized, double-blind, placebo-controlled trial
Population: 3,297 patients with type 2 diabetes at high cardiovascular risk
Intervention: Semaglutide (0.5 mg or 1 mg once-weekly) vs. placebo
Primary Outcome: Composite of first occurrence of cardiovascular death, nonfatal myocardial infarction, or nonfatal stroke
Secondary Outcomes:

- Individual cardiovascular endpoints (cardiovascular death, MI, stroke)
- Individual components of the composite outcomes
- Retinopathy complications
- New or worsening nephropathy

9.3 Results

Primary Outcome: Significant reduction in major cardiovascular events with semaglutide compared to placebo (6.6% vs. 8.9%, HR 0.74; [95% CI: 0.58–0.95; $p < 0.001$ for noninferiority]).

Secondary Outcomes:

- Individual cardiovascular endpoints:
  - No significant difference was observed in nonfatal MI between groups.
  - Nonfatal stroke occurred in 1.6% of patients in the semaglutide group vs. 2.7% in the placebo group (HR 0.61; [95% CI: 0.38–0.99; $p = 0.04$]).
  - Rates of cardiovascular death was similar between both groups.
- Retinopathy complications: rates of retinopathy complications were significantly higher in the semaglutide group vs. placebo (HR 1.76; [95% CI: 1.11–2.78; $p = 0.02$]).
- New or worsening nephropathy: Lower in the semaglutide group (HR 0.64; [95% CI: 0.46–0.88; $p = 0.005$]).

9.4 Key Takeaways

- In patients with type 2 diabetes and established cardiovascular disease or risk factors, semaglutide significantly reduced the risk of the composite outcome of CV death, nonfatal MI, or nonfatal stroke compared with placebo.
- Semaglutide improved glycemic control (A1c reduction of ~1.0% more than placebo), promoted meaningful weight loss (3–5 kg), and modestly reduced systolic blood pressure.
- semaglutide was linked to an increased risk of diabetic retinopathy complications, particularly in those with preexisting retinopathy, possibly related to rapid glucose lowering.
- Gastrointestinal side effects were common and led to more discontinuations, though overall serious adverse events were not increased.
- The trial confirmed noninferiority for cardiovascular safety and showed superiority in reducing major adverse cardiovascular events, despite being designed primarily as a safety trial.
- SUSTAIN-6 positioned semaglutide as one of the first GLP-1 receptor agonists to demonstrate cardiovascular risk reduction, influencing its adoption in diabetes care for patients with high CV risk.

9.5 Clinical Application

- Strongly consider semaglutide as a preferred GLP-1 receptor agonist in patients with type 2 diabetes and high cardiovascular or renal risk.
- Consider semaglutide for patients with type 2 diabetes who are overweight or obese, as it produces meaningful weight loss.
- Select semaglutide for patients with diabetic kidney disease, as it lowers risk of new or worsening nephropathy.
- Monitor for retinopathy, particularly in patients with rapid glycemic improvement, and perform appropriate ophthalmologic screening.
- Reduce insulin or sulfonylurea doses when starting semaglutide to minimize hypoglycemia risk.

9.6 When to Discuss on Rounds

Discuss this trial on rounds with the following scenarios:

- When selecting diabetes medications for patients with type 2 diabetes at increased cardiovascular or renal risk.
- When discussing GLP-1 receptor agonists, highlight that semaglutide reduced major adverse cardiovascular events in high-risk patients with T2DM.
- When covering adverse effects, emphasize the unexpected increase in diabetic retinopathy complications, especially in those with preexisting disease.
- When discussing safety, mention that GI side effects were common but usually manageable, while hypoglycemia risk was not increased.

9.7 Relevant Guidelines

The **ADA** and **ESC** guidelines strongly recommend GLP-1 receptor agonists like semaglutide for type 2 diabetes patients with established cardiovascular disease or high cardiovascular risk, informed by outcomes of SUSTAIN-6

10 FIT Trial Summary [10]

Full Title: Randomized Trial of Effect of Alendronate on Risk of Fracture in Women with Existing Vertebral Fractures
Publication Year: 1996
Journal: The Lancet

10.1 Background

Osteoporotic fractures are a leading cause of disability and death in postmenopausal women, but before the 1990s, there was little randomized trial evidence that medications could prevent them. Alendronate, a bisphosphonate, had been shown to increase bone mineral density, but its effect on actual fracture risk was unknown. The FIT trial was designed to test whether alendronate could reduce vertebral, hip, and other fractures in women with low bone density, making it the first large study to establish bisphosphonates as effective fracture-preventing therapy.

10.2 Study Design

Type: Large, multicenter, randomized controlled trial
Population: 2027 women aged 55–81 with low femoral-neck bone mineral density (BMD)
Intervention: Alendronate (5 mg daily initially and then increased to 10 mg at 24 months) vs. placebo
Primary Outcome: New vertebral fractures (defined as decrease of 20% (and at least 4 mm) in at least one vertebral height between the baseline and latest follow-up radiograph)
Secondary Outcome: Cumulative proportion of woman with any clinical fracture

10.3 Results

Primary Outcome: Risk of new vertebral fracture was significantly lower in the alendronate group vs. placebo ($p < 0.001$)
Secondary Outcome: Significantly lower in the alendronate group vs. placebo (13.6% vs. 18.2%, HR 0.72; [95% CI: 0.58–0.90])

10.4 Key Takeaways

- Alendronate significantly increased bone mineral density (BMD) at multiple skeletal sites, including the femoral neck (+4.1%), total hip (+4.7%), and lumbar spine (+6.2%) compared with placebo.
- The risk of multiple vertebral fractures was dramatically lower with alendronate.
- Other non-vertebral fracture sites (shoulder, ribs, pelvis, ankle, foot, etc.) showed no significant difference between groups.

- Alendronate slowed height loss, suggesting protection against vertebral compression.
- Adverse events, including gastrointestinal side effects, were similar between alendronate and placebo groups, with no excess risk of esophagitis or ulceration under careful dosing instructions.
- Overall, alendronate substantially reduced vertebral, hip, and wrist fractures in postmenopausal women with prior vertebral fractures, with a favorable safety profile.

10.5 Clinical Application

- Use alendronate in postmenopausal women with low bone mass and prior vertebral fractures to reduce risk of future fractures.
- Consider alendronate as first-line therapy in women at high risk for vertebral, hip, and wrist fractures.
- Recognize that alendronate not only improves bone mineral density but also meaningfully reduces clinically relevant fracture outcomes.
- Counsel patients that adherence to proper administration (taking with water, remaining upright) minimizes gastrointestinal side effects.
- Apply FIT results when deciding between lifestyle measures alone versus pharmacologic therapy in patients with established osteoporosis.

10.6 When to Discuss on Rounds

- When presenting a patient with osteoporosis and prior vertebral fracture, mention that the FIT trial showed alendronate reduces new vertebral fractures by nearly 50%.
- When discussing hip fracture prevention, highlight that alendronate lowered hip fracture risk by about half in this trial.
- When comparing treatment options, emphasize that alendronate reduced wrist fractures in addition to vertebral and hip fractures.
- When evaluating side effects, note that FIT showed no significant increase in upper GI adverse events when patients were counseled properly on medication use.

10.7 Relevant Guidelines

The results of the Fracture Intervention Trial (FIT) were pivotal in shaping osteoporosis guidelines worldwide. The **National Osteoporosis Foundation (NOF)**, the **Endocrine Society**, and the **American Association of Clinical Endocrinologists (AACE)** incorporated FIT findings as the foundation for recommending bisphosphonates, particularly alendronate, as first-line therapy in postmenopausal women at high fracture risk. Internationally, the **WHO** and **National Institute for Health and Care Excellence (NICE)** guidelines also cited FIT as critical evidence supporting bisphosphonate use to prevent vertebral and hip fractures.

References

1. Intensive blood-glucose control with sulphonylureas or insulin compared with conventional treatment and risk of complications in patients with type 2 diabetes (UKPDS 33). UK Prospective Diabetes Study (UKPDS) Group [published correction appears in Lancet 1999 Aug 14;354(9178):602]. Lancet. 1998;352(9131):837–53.
2. Action to Control Cardiovascular Risk in Diabetes Study Group, Gerstein HC, Miller ME, et al. Effects of intensive glucose lowering in type 2 diabetes. N Engl J Med. 2008;358(24):2545–59. https://doi.org/10.1056/NEJMoa0802743
3. ADVANCE Collaborative Group, Patel A, MacMahon S, et al. Intensive blood glucose control and vascular outcomes in patients with type 2 diabetes. N Engl J Med 2008;358(24):2560–2572. doi:https://doi.org/10.1056/NEJMoa0802987
4. Knowler WC, Barrett-Connor E, Fowler SE, et al. Reduction in the incidence of type 2 diabetes with lifestyle intervention or metformin. N Engl J Med. 2002;346(6):393–403. https://doi.org/10.1056/NEJMoa012512.
5. Duckworth W, Abraira C, Moritz T, et al. Glucose control and vascular complications in veterans with type 2 diabetes [published correction appears in N Engl J Med. 2009 Sep 3;361(10):1028] [published correction appears in N Engl J Med. 2009 Sep 3;361(10):1024-5. Doi: 10.1056/NEJMc096250.]. N Engl J Med. 2009;360(2):129–39. https://doi.org/10.1056/NEJMoa0808431.
6. Zinman B, Wanner C, Lachin JM, et al. Empagliflozin, cardiovascular outcomes, and mortality in type 2 diabetes. N Engl J Med. 2015;373(22):2117–28. https://doi.org/10.1056/NEJMoa1504720.
7. Marso SP, Daniels GH, Brown-Frandsen K, et al. Liraglutide and cardiovascular outcomes in type 2 diabetes. N Engl J Med. 2016;375(4):311–22. https://doi.org/10.1056/NEJMoa1603827.
8. Rossouw JE, Anderson GL, Prentice RL, et al. Risks and benefits of estrogen plus progestin in healthy postmenopausal women: principal results from the Women's Health Initiative randomized controlled trial. JAMA. 2002;288(3):321–33. https://doi.org/10.1001/jama.288.3.321.
9. Marso SP, Bain SC, Consoli A, et al. Semaglutide and cardiovascular outcomes in patients with type 2 diabetes. N Engl J Med. 2016;375(19):1834–44. https://doi.org/10.1056/NEJMoa1607141.
10. Black DM, Cummings SR, Karpf DB, et al. Randomised trial of effect of alendronate on risk of fracture in women with existing vertebral fractures. Fracture Intervention Trial Research Group. Lancet. 1996;348(9041):1535–41. https://doi.org/10.1016/s0140-6736(96)07088-2.

Chapter 6
Nephrology

1 RENAAL Trial Summary [1]

Full Title: Effects of Losartan on Renal and Cardiovascular Outcomes in Patients with Type 2 Diabetes and Nephropathy
Publication Year: 2001
Journal: New England Journal of Medicine

1.1 Background

Before the RENAAL trial, progression of diabetic nephropathy to ESRD was common, and treatment options to slow renal decline were limited primarily to tight glucose and blood pressure control. Angiotensin-converting enzyme inhibitors (ACEIs) were known to reduce nephropathy progression, but the benefit of angiotensin receptor blockers (ARBs) in type 2 diabetic nephropathy was not clearly established. RENAAL evaluated whether losartan could slow kidney disease progression and reduce associated morbidity and mortality in patients with type 2 diabetes and nephropathy.

1.2 Study Design

Type: Randomized, placebo-controlled trial
Population: 1,513 patients with type 2 diabetes, hypertension, and nephropathy (proteinuria and elevated serum creatinine)

A. Love, *The Essential Evidence*, https://doi.org/10.1007/978-3-032-12399-2_6

Intervention: Losartan (50–100 mg daily) vs. placebo (both groups also received conventional antihypertensive therapy excluding ACEIs and ARBs)

Primary Outcome: Composite of doubling of serum creatinine, progression to ESRD, or death

Secondary Outcomes:

- Composite of cardiovascular morbidity and mortality, proteinuria, and the rate of progression of renal disease

1.3 Results

Primary Outcome: Significant reduction in composite endpoint with losartan (16% RRR; $p = 0.02$).

Secondary Outcomes:

- Morbidity and mortality: No significant difference observed in the composite endpoint of morbidity and mortality.
- Cardiovascular endpoints: No significant difference observed between groups.
  - Exception was first hospitalization with heart failure with less patients being hospitalized in the Losartan group vs. placebo (11.9% vs. 16.7%, $p = 0.005$).
- Greater reduction in the level of proteinuria was observed in the losartan group. Placebo group tended to have an increase in urinary albumin-to-creatinine ratio ($p < 0.001$).

1.4 Key Takeaways

- Losartan reduced the risk of the primary composite endpoint.
- Losartan lowered the risk of end-stage renal disease by 28%, delaying the need for dialysis or transplant.
- There was no difference in overall mortality between losartan and placebo.
- Cardiovascular event rates were similar between groups.
- Losartan was well tolerated, with adverse events comparable to placebo.

1.5 Clinical Application

- Preferentially use ARBs (such as losartan) in hypertensive type 2 diabetic patients with nephropathy to slow renal progression and reduce proteinuria.
- Consider losartan for patients at risk of heart failure hospitalization with diabetic kidney disease.

- Recognize that mortality benefit was not demonstrated, so therapy should be combined with other risk-reducing strategies.
- Monitor for hyperkalemia and rises in serum creatinine when initiating losartan.

1.6 When to Discuss on Rounds

Discuss this trial on rounds with the following scenarios:

- When managing hypertension and proteinuria in diabetic patients with established kidney disease.
- When teaching trainees about mechanisms and evidence supporting ARBs for renal protection.
- When emphasizing early initiation of RAAS inhibition therapy in diabetic nephropathy.
- When evaluating CV outcomes with losartan, note that mortality was not improved, but heart failure hospitalizations were reduced.

1.7 Relevant Guidelines

The **ADA** and **KDIGO** guidelines strongly recommend the use of ARBs or ACE inhibitors as first-line therapy in diabetic kidney disease patients, heavily influenced by outcomes of the RENAAL trial.

2 TEMP 3:4 Trial Summary [2]

Full Title: Tolvaptan in Patients with Autosomal Dominant Polycystic Kidney Disease
Publication Year: 2012
Journal: New England Journal of Medicine

2.1 Background

Before TEMP 3:4, there was no specific treatment proven to slow cyst growth or renal function decline in patients with autosomal dominant polycystic kidney disease (ADPK). ADPKD is a common genetic cause of ESRD, characterized by progressive cyst enlargement, Kidney growth, and renal impairment. Tolvaptan, a vasopressin V2 receptor antagonist, was hypothesized to slow cyst growth and delay kidney function decline through inhibition of cAMP-mediated cyst formation.

2.2 *Study Design*

Type: Randomized, double-blind, placebo-controlled trial
Population: 1,445 patients with ADPKD and relatively preserved kidney function
Intervention: Tolvaptan vs. placebo
Primary Outcome: Annual rate of change in total kidney volume (TKV)
Secondary Outcomes:

- Composite of time to clinical progression and rate of kidney-function

2.3 *Results*

Primary Outcome: Tolvaptan significantly slowed kidney enlargement (annual growth rate 2.8% with tolvaptan vs. 5.5% with placebo; [95% CI: 2.5–3.1; $p < 0.001$]).
Secondary Outcomes:

- The secondary composite outcome was observed less in the tolvaptan group compared to placebo (44 vs. 50 events, HR 0.87; [95% CI: 0.78–0.97; $p = 0.01$]).
  - This was driven by the rate of kidney decline which was significantly lower in the tolvaptan group at 2 events per 100 persons compared to 5 events per 100 persons in the placebo group (HR 0.39; [95% CI: 0.26–0.57; $p < 0.001$]).
  - Less kidney pain in the tolvaptan group (5 vs. 7 events per 100 persons, HR 0.64; [95% CI: 0.47–0.89; $p = 0.007$])

2.4 *Key Takeaways*

- Tolvaptan significantly slowed the annual rate of kidney volume growth compared to placebo.
- Tolvaptan reduced the rate of eGFR decline by about 1 mL/min/1.73 m^2 per year compared with placebo.
- The risk of the composite endpoint of ADPKD progression events was lower with tolvaptan.
- No significant benefit was seen for hypertension or albuminuria progression.

- Adverse events were common in both groups, but tolvaptan was associated with more aquaresis-related symptoms (thirst, polyuria, nocturia) and higher rates of liver enzyme elevations.
- About 23% of patients on tolvaptan discontinued therapy, most often due to aquaresis or liver enzyme abnormalities.
- Overall, tolvaptan provided clinically meaningful slowing of disease progression in ADPKD, though tolerability and safety monitoring remain important limitations.

2.5 Clinical Application

- Consider tolvaptan therapy for adult patients with ADPKD, especially younger patients with preserved kidney function but rapidly growing cysts.
- Monitor closely for adverse effects related to increased urinary output and liver function abnormalities during treatment.
- Apply tolvaptan to reduce risk of kidney pain episodes and delay progression to end-stage renal disease, potentially deferring need for dialysis or transplant.
- Recognize that tolerability is a major limiting factor, with nearly one in four patients discontinuing therapy, so patient selection and counseling are critical.

2.6 When to Discuss on Rounds

Discuss this trial on rounds with the following scenarios:

- When evaluating a patient with autosomal dominant polycystic kidney disease and preserved kidney function, discuss how tolvaptan slowed total kidney volume growth and delayed decline in renal function.
- When reviewing long-term management options for ADPKD, mention that tolvaptan reduced clinically meaningful endpoints such as kidney pain and risk of progression to end-stage renal disease.
- When discussing potential side effects of tolvaptan, highlight that aquaresis-related symptoms (thirst, polyuria, nocturia) are common and often lead to discontinuation.
- When discussing monitoring strategies, emphasize the need for regular liver function testing due to risk of hepatotoxicity with tolvaptan.
- When discussing timing of therapy, note that benefit was greater in patients with larger kidneys or more advanced disease, supporting earlier identification of rapid progressors.

2.7 Relevant Guidelines

The **KDIGO** and **European Renal Association-European Dialysis and Transplant Association (ERA-EDTA)** guidelines support using tolvaptan in carefully selected ADPKD patients with rapidly progressing disease, largely based on TEMP 3:4 findings.

3 SHARP Trial Summary [3]

Full Title: The Effects of Lowering LDL Cholesterol with Simvastatin Plus Ezetimibe in Patients with Chronic Kidney Disease: a Randomised Placebo-Controlled Trial
Publication Year: 2011
Journal: The Lancet

3.1 Background

Patients with chronic kidney disease (CKD) are at elevated risk for cardiovascular disease, yet prior to the SHARP trial, evidence on benefits of lipid-lowering therapy in CKD was limited, particularly in patients not yet on dialysis. Statins had shown clear benefits in the general population, but their efficacy and safety in CKD patients remained uncertain. The SHARP trial aimed to determine if lowering cholesterol with simvastatin plus ezetimibe could reduce cardiovascular events in patients with CKD, including those on dialysis.

3.2 Study Design

Type: Randomized, double-blind, placebo-controlled trial
Population: 9,270 patients with CKD (approximately two-thirds pre-dialysis, one-third on dialysis)
Intervention: Simvastatin 20 mg plus ezetimibe 10 mg daily vs. placebo
Primary Outcome: Major atherosclerotic cardiovascular events (nonfatal MI, coronary death, ischemic stroke, revascularization procedures)
Secondary Outcomes: Individual cardiovascular endpoints

3.3 Results

Primary Outcome: Significant reduction in first major cardiovascular events with simvastatin-ezetimibe compared to placebo with a17% proportional reduction (RR 0.83; [95% CI: 0.74–0.94; p = 0.0021]).

Secondary Outcomes:

- Cardiovascular endpoints:
  - Significant reduction in major vascular events (RR 0.85; [95% CI: 0.77–0.94; p = 0.0012]).
  - No significant difference was observed in coronary mortality.
  - There was a significant reduction observed in ischemic stroke (RR 0.75; [95% CI: 0.60–0.94; p = 0.01]).
  - Simvastatin plus ezetimibe led to a significant reduction in the incidence of any arterial revascularization (RR 0.79; [95% CI: 0.68–0.93; p = 0.0036]).

3.4 Key Takeaways

- SHARP was the largest trial to evaluate lipid-lowering therapy in patients with chronic kidney disease, enrolling more than 9,000 patients across dialysis and non-dialysis populations.
- The study demonstrated that simvastatin plus ezetimibe reduced major atherosclerotic events in CKD, resolving longstanding uncertainty from smaller, inconclusive trials.
- The magnitude of benefit in CKD patients was consistent with what has been observed in the general population for LDL reduction.
- The trial established that LDL lowering is safe in CKD patients, showing no increase in cancer, hepatic toxicity, or severe myopathy.
- SHARP confirmed that vascular risk reduction in CKD is achievable with combination lipid-lowering therapy, shifting practice toward routine statin or statin–ezetimibe use in this high-risk group.

3.5 Clinical Application

- Use simvastatin plus ezetimibe in patients with chronic kidney disease to lower the risk of major atherosclerotic events.
- Recognize that benefit applies to both dialysis and non-dialysis patients, consistent with the general population's response to LDL lowering.
- Reassure patients that statin plus ezetimibe therapy in CKD does not increase risk of cancer, severe liver toxicity, or myopathy.

3.6 When to Discuss on Rounds

Discuss this trial on rounds with the following scenarios:

- When managing a patient with chronic kidney disease and deciding on lipid-lowering therapy, mention SHARP as evidence that statin plus ezetimibe reduces major atherosclerotic events.
- When discussing cardiovascular prevention in CKD, emphasize SHARP demonstrated safety of simvastatin plus ezetimibe without excess cancer, liver injury, or myopathy.
- When explaining treatment thresholds, use SHARP to highlight that benefit occurred regardless of baseline cholesterol level.

3.7 Relevant Guidelines

The **KDIGO** lipid management guidelines recommend statin or statin-ezetimibe combination therapy for cardiovascular risk reduction in adult patients with CKD not requiring dialysis, strongly influenced by SHARP trial outcomes.

4 AURORA Trial [4]

Full Title: Rosuvastatin and Cardiovascular Events in Patients Undergoing Hemodialysis
Publication Year: 2009
Journal: New England Journal of Medicine

4.1 Background

Patients undergoing hemodialysis have a significantly elevated cardiovascular mortality risk. While statins effectively reduce cardiovascular events in the general population, their benefit in patients on dialysis was unclear. The AURORA trial aimed to determine if rosuvastatin would reduce cardiovascular events in patients with ESRD receiving chronic hemodialysis.

4.2 Study Design

Type: Randomized, double-blind, placebo-controlled trial
Population: 2,776 adults aged 50–80 years with ESRD undergoing hemodialysis

Intervention: Rosuvastatin (10 mg daily) vs. placebo
Primary Outcome: Composite of cardiovascular death, nonfatal myocardial infarction, or nonfatal stroke
Secondary Outcomes:

- Vascular events
- All-cause mortality

4.3 *Results*

Primary Outcome:

- Rosuvastatin did not significantly reduce the composite primary outcome compared to placebo (396 events rosuvastatin [9.2 per 100 patient-years] vs. 408 events placebo [9.5 per 100 patient-years]; HR 0.96; [95% CI: 0.84–1.11; p = 0.59]).

Secondary Outcomes:

- Individual components: No effect on the individual components of the primary end point was observed.
- All-cause mortality: No significant difference was observed between groups.
- Adverse events: Similar frequency in both groups; rosuvastatin generally well tolerated.

4.4 *Key Takeaways*

- Rosuvastatin reduced LDL cholesterol by about 43% and lowered hs-CRP by 11.5% at 3 months, demonstrating effective lipid and inflammatory marker reduction.
- Despite significant lipid lowering, there was no reduction in the primary composite outcome of cardiovascular death, nonfatal myocardial infarction, or nonfatal stroke.
- Rosuvastatin did not reduce all-cause mortality or secondary cardiovascular outcomes, with results consistent across all prespecified subgroups (including diabetes, CVD, hypertension, and baseline LDL levels).
- Findings reinforced that statins may not provide cardiovascular benefit in patients on maintenance dialysis despite effective lipid lowering.
- Results raised the possibility that advanced CKD alters cardiovascular disease pathophysiology, making atherosclerosis less modifiable by statins compared to earlier CKD stages or the general population.

4.5 Clinical Application

- Consider individualizing statin use based on other indications (e.g., existing cardiovascular disease, diabetes) rather than dialysis status alone.
- Watch for drug burden and tolerability in dialysis (myalgias, interactions), and deprescribe statins if symptomatic with no clear secondary-prevention indication.

4.6 When to Discuss on Rounds

Discuss this trial on rounds with the following scenarios:

- When evaluating the role of statins for cardiovascular risk reduction in ESRD patients on dialysis.
- When addressing cardiovascular risk management and medication optimization in dialysis patients.
- When reviewing treatment strategies for reducing cardiovascular risk specifically in the dialysis population.

4.7 Relevant Guidelines

The **KDIGO** clinical practice guidelines for lipid management in chronic kidney disease incorporate findings from the AURORA trial, recommending against routine statin initiation in patients already on dialysis without specific cardiovascular indications.

5 CHOIR Trial Summary [5]

Full Title: Correction of Anemia with Epoetin Alfa in Chronic Kidney Disease
Publication Year: 2006
Journal: New England Journal of Medicine

5.1 Background

Before the CHOIR trial, treating anemia in chronic kidney disease with erythropoiesis-stimulating agents (ESAs) was common practice to reduce transfusion requirements and improve quality of life. However, the optimal hemoglobin (Hb) target was uncertain, with some evidence suggesting that targeting higher Hb levels could increase cardiovascular risk. The CHOIR trial was conducted to determine if higher hemoglobin targets improved clinical outcomes or conversely increased adverse events in CKD patients.

5.2 Study Design

Type: Randomized, controlled trial
Population: 1,432 patients with CKD not on dialysis
Intervention: High hemoglobin target (13.5 g/dL) vs. lower hemoglobin target (11.3 g/dL) using epoetin alfa
Primary Outcome: Composite of death, myocardial infarction, hospitalization for heart failure, and stroke
Secondary Outcomes:

- Time to renal replacement therapy (RRT)
- Hospitalization
- Quality of life (QOL)

5.3 Results

Primary Outcome: Higher Hb target group had a significantly higher incidence of the primary composite outcome compared to low Hb. A total of 222 composite events occurred. (17.5% vs. 13.5%; HR 1.34; [95% CI: 1.03–1.74; p = 0.03]).
Secondary Outcomes:

- Time to RRT: No significant difference was observed in the percentage of patients who required RRT (p = 0.15).
- Hospitalization: There was a greater amount of hospitalizations for cardiovascular, as well as for any cause observed in the higher Hb group compared to low (p = 0.03 for both).
- QOL: No significant difference was observed between groups in regard to quality of life.

5.4 Key Takeaways

- The trial was stopped early after interim analysis due to evidence of harm in the high-hemoglobin group and low likelihood of showing benefit.
- The excess events were mainly driven by death and hospitalizations for heart failure, which together accounted for nearly 75% of the composite events.

- Quality-of-life improvements were similar between the two groups, showing no additional benefit from higher hemoglobin targets.
- Patients in the high-hemoglobin group required almost double the dose of epoetin alfa compared to the low-hemoglobin group.
- Serious adverse events, particularly heart failure, were more common in the high-hemoglobin group.
- The trial reinforced that observational data suggesting benefit from higher hemoglobin correction do not align with randomized trial evidence.

5.5 *Clinical Application*

- Avoid aggressive anemia correction in CKD patients; aim for moderate hemoglobin targets (~10–11.5 g/dL) to minimize cardiovascular risks.
- Regularly monitor hemoglobin and adjust ESA doses cautiously, considering the potential risks.

5.6 *When to Discuss on Rounds*

Discuss this trial on rounds with the following scenarios:

- When determining hemoglobin targets and ESA dosing for anemia management in CKD patients.
- When evaluating cardiovascular risks associated with different hemoglobin targets in renal insufficiency.
- When discussing quality of life benefits of higher hemoglobin targets, emphasize that no additional improvement was observed in the high-hemoglobin group.

5.7 *Relevant Guidelines*

The **KDIGO** guidelines recommend a conservative hemoglobin target (typically 10–11.5 g/dL) in CKD patients receiving ESA therapy, largely based on outcomes from the CHOIR trial.

6 EVOLVE Trial Summary [6]

Full Title: Effect of Cinacalcet on Cardiovascular Disease in Patients Undergoing Dialysis
Publication Year: 2012
Journal: New England Journal of Medicine

6.1 Background

Before the EVOLVE trial, elevated parathyroid hormone (PTH) levels associated with secondary hyperparathyroidism were common in patients with chronic kidney disease (CKD) on dialysis, potentially increasing cardiovascular risk. Cinacalcet, a calcimimetic agent, effectively lowers PTH levels, but its impact on cardiovascular outcomes was uncertain. EVOLVE aimed to determine whether treatment with cinacalcet could reduce cardiovascular morbidity and mortality in dialysis patients with secondary hyperparathyroidism.

6.2 Study Design

Type: Randomized, double-blind, placebo-controlled trial
Population: 3,883 hemodialysis patients with moderate-to-severe secondary hyperparathyroidism
Intervention: Cinacalcet vs. placebo
Primary Outcome: Composite of death, myocardial infarction, hospitalization for unstable angina, heart failure, or peripheral vascular events
Secondary Outcomes:

- Individual components of the primary composite end point
- Cardiovascular death
- Stroke
- Bone fracture
- Parathyroidectomy

6.3 Results

Primary Outcome: No statistically significant reduction was observed in the primary composite endpoint with cinacalcet compared to placebo ($p = 0.11$).
Secondary Outcomes:

- Significantly reduced rate of parathyroidectomy (HR 0.44, $p < 0.001$).
- Reduced incidence of severe hypercalcemia and bone fractures in cinacalcet group.
- Increased risk of hypocalcemia and gastrointestinal adverse events with cinacalcet.

6.4 Key Takeaways

- The trial did not show a statistically significant reduction in the primary composite endpoint with cinacalcet in the intention-to-treat analysis.
- Cinacalcet significantly reduces the need for surgical parathyroidectomy and decreased hypercalcemia and fracture rates, but at a risk of increased hypocalcemia.
- Hypocalcemia and gastrointestinal side effects were more common in the cinacalcet group.
- Overall, EVOLVE was considered nondefinitive but provided evidence that cinacalcet may modestly improve survival and cardiovascular outcomes in patients on dialysis with secondary hyperparathyroidism.

6.5 Clinical Application

- Do not routinely use cinacalcet solely for cardiovascular risk reduction in dialysis patients.
- Consider cinacalcet in patients with severe secondary hyperparathyroidism inadequately controlled by conventional therapy or to prevent surgical parathyroidectomy.
- Monitor closely for hypocalcemia and gastrointestinal intolerance, which are common adverse effects.

6.6 When to Discuss on Rounds

Discuss this trial on rounds with the following scenarios:

- When managing hyperparathyroidism in dialysis patients and evaluating treatment goals.
- When weighing medical therapy with cinacalcet versus surgical parathyroidectomy.
- When considering benefits vs. risks of calcimimetics in dialysis-dependent patients.

6.7 *Relevant Guidelines*

The **KDIGO** and **CKD-MBD (Mineral and Bone Disorder)** guidelines recommend calcimimetics therapy such as cinacalcet selectively in dialysis patients with significant secondary hyperparathyroidism, reflecting findings from the EVOLVE trial.

7 PIVOTAL Trial Summary [7]

Full Title: Intravenous Iron in Patients Undergoing Maintenance Hemodialysis
Publication Year: 2018
Journal: New England Journal of Medicine

7.1 *Background*

Before the PIVOTAL trial, optimal intravenous (IV) iron dosing strategies in hemodialysis patients were uncertain. Many clinicians used a conservative approach to avoid risks associated with high-dose IV iron therapy, such as infections, cardiovascular events, or oxidative stress. The PIVOTAL trial sought to determine whether a proactive, high-dose IV regimen could improve clinical outcomes compared to a conservative, lower-dose approach in chronic hemodialysis patients.

7.2 *Study Design*

Type: Randomized, controlled, open-label trial
Population: 2,141 patients on maintenance hemodialysis
Intervention: Proactive IV iron therapy (monthly iron sucrose 400 mg unless ferritin >700 μg/L or transferrin saturation ≥ 40%) vs. conservative IV iron therapy (iron administered only if ferritin <200 μg/L or transferrin saturation < 20%)
Primary Outcome: Composite of death, nonfatal myocardial infarction, nonfatal stroke, or hospitalization for heart failure
Secondary Outcomes:

- Death
- Infection rates
- Erythropoiesis-stimulating agent (ESA) dose requirements

7.3 Results

Primary Outcome: Proactive IV iron significantly reduced primary composite endpoint compared to conservative iron dosing (HR 0.85; [95% CI: 0.73–1.00; p = 0.04 for superiority]).

Secondary Outcomes:

- Death: There were deaths in 22.5% in the high dose group compared to 25.7% in the low dose group (HR 0.84; [95% CI: 0.71–1.00]).
- Infection rates: No significant difference observed between groups.
- ESA dose requirements: Higher ESA dose requirements in the low dose group compared to the high dose regimen.

7.4 Key Takeaways

- High-dose intravenous iron given proactively was superior to low-dose reactive dosing in hemodialysis patients.
- The high-dose group had a lower risk of death or major adverse cardiovascular events.
- High-dose iron reduced the need for blood transfusions and lowered erythropoiesis-stimulating agent requirements.
- Hemoglobin rose more rapidly and was maintained with less ESA support in the high-dose group.
- Vascular access thrombosis occurred more often with high-dose iron, though overall safety outcomes were similar between groups.
- The trial challenged concerns from observational studies about high monthly iron dosing and supported proactive iron replacement in dialysis patients.

7.5 Clinical Application

- Consider proactive IV iron strategies in hemodialysis patients to improve cardiovascular outcomes and reduce ESA use.
- Monitor ferritin and transferrin saturation regularly, adjusting iron dosing according to safety thresholds.
- Monitor for vascular access thrombosis, which was slightly more frequent with high-dosc iron.
- Apply proactive iron replacement as a safer and more effective approach compared to reactive, low-dose dosing strategies in dialysis populations.

7.6 *When to Discuss on Rounds*

Discuss this trial on rounds with the following scenarios:

- When managing anemia and iron supplementation in chronic hemodialysis patients.
- When teaching trainees about benefits and safety of proactive vs. conservative iron dosing.
- When evaluating strategies to minimize ESA use and transfusions in dialysis populations.

7.7 *Relevant Guidelines*

The **KDIGO** anemia management guidelines advocate for proactive IV iron therapy in patients undergoing dialysis, influenced strongly by results from the PIVOTAL trial.

8 IDEAL Trial Summary [8]

Full Title: A Randomized, Controlled Trial of Early versus Late Initiation of Dialysis
Publication Year: 2010
Journal: New England Journal of Medicine

8.1 *Background*

Before the IDEAL trial, the optimal timing of dialysis initiation in patients with advanced chronic kidney disease (CKD) was uncertain. Clinical practice varied widely, with some clinicians advocating for earlier initiation at higher eGFR levels to potentially improve survival, reduce complications, and improve quality of life. Others argued that earlier dialysis exposed patients to the risks, costs, and burdens of dialysis without proven benefit. Observational studies had suggested possible advantages of starting dialysis earlier, but these were limited by confounding and selection bias. The IDEAL trial was designed to provide randomized evidence comparing early versus late initiation of dialysis in patients with stage 5 CKD, to determine whether earlier initiation improved survival or other clinical outcomes.

8.2 Study Design

Type: Randomized, controlled trial
Population: 828 adults age 18 or older with progressive chronic kidney disease and eGFR between 10.0–15.0 ml/1.73 m^2
Intervention: Initiation of dialysis when eGFR 10.0–14.0 ml/minute (early start) vs. eGFR 5.0–7.0 ml/minute (late start)
Primary Outcome: All-cause mortality
Secondary Outcomes:

- Cardiovascular events
- Infectious events
- Complications of dialysis

8.3 Results

Primary Outcome: No survival benefit was observed between the early and late start groups (HR for death in early start group 1.04; [95% CI: 0.83–1.30; p = 0.75]).
Secondary Outcomes: There was no significant difference observed between groups in any of the secondary outcomes.

8.4 Key Takeaways

- Early initiation of dialysis at higher eGFR did not improve survival compared with late initiation.
- There was no difference in all cause mortality, cardiovascular events, infections, or dialysis-related complications between groups.
- Quality of life outcomes were similar regardless of timing of dialysis initiation.
- Many patients assigned to early start still initiated dialysis later due to absence of symptoms, reflecting real-world clinical decision-making.
- The trial showed that starting dialysis based on symptoms and clinical indicators, not eGFR alone, is safe and appropriate.
- IDEAL influenced guidelines to move away from fixed eGFR thresholds and emphasize individualized, symptom-based initiation of dialysis.

8.5 Clinical Application

- Do not initiate dialysis solely on the basis of an eGFR threshold; use symptoms and clinical indicators to guide timing.
- Monitor patients with advanced CKD closely for signs of uremia, fluid overload, electrolyte disturbances, or malnutrition.
- Recognize that dialysis can be safely deferred until GFR falls below ~7 ml/min/1.73 m^2 if patients remain asymptomatic.
- Use shared decision-making to balance symptom control, quality of life, and patient readiness rather than relying on lab values alone.

8.6 When to Discuss on Rounds

Discuss this trial on rounds with the following scenarios:

- When debating the optimal timing of dialysis initiation in a patient with advanced CKD.
- When emphasizing that early initiation of dialysis does not improve mortality or cardiovascular outcomes.

8.7 Relevant Guidelines

The current **KDIGO** CKD guideline update recommends starting dialysis for symptoms or complications of kidney failure rather than at a fixed eGFR threshold. In stable, asymptomatic patients, dialysis can often be safely deferred until eGFR falls to ~5–10 ml/min/1.73 m^2 with close monitoring. Guidelines emphasize early planning for dialysis access and patient education when eGFR reaches ~15–20 ml/min/1.73 m^2, but actual initiation should be individualized.

9 PATHWAY-2 Trial Summary [9]

Full Title: Spironolactone Versus Placebo, Bisoprolol, and Doxazosin to Determine the Optimal Treatment For Drug-Resistant Hypertension: a Randomized, Double-Blind, Crossover Trial
Publication Year: 2015
Journal: The Lancet

9.1 Background

Resistant hypertension, defined as uncontrolled blood pressure despite the use of at least three antihypertensive agents (including a diuretic), is a common and high-risk clinical problem. Patients with resistant hypertension have increased risk of stroke, myocardial infarction, kidney disease progression, and mortality. Prior to PATHWAY-2, the optimal fourth-line therapy for resistant hypertension was uncertain. Beta-blockers, alpha-blockers, and mineralocorticoid receptor antagonists (MRAs) were all used in practice, but there was limited evidence from randomized controlled trials comparing these options. Observational and mechanistic studies had suggested that excess sodium retention and inappropriate aldosterone activity played a key role in resistant hypertension, raising the possibility that MRAs like spironolactone could be especially effective. The PATHWAY-2 trial was designed to directly test spironolactone against alternative add-on therapies in resistant hypertension using a rigorous randomized, double-blind, crossover design.

9.2 Study Design

Type: Randomized, double-blind, placebo-controlled, crossover trial
Population: 314 adults age 18–79 years with a systolic blood pressure of >140 mmHg despite treatment with maximally tolerated doses of ACE/ARB, CCB, and a thiazide diuretic
Intervention: All participants received each of the following as an add-on to their triple therapy (ACEi/ARB + CCB + Thiazide):

- Spironolactone (25–50 mg daily)
- Bisoprolol
- Doxazosin
- Placebo

Primary Outcome: Reduction in average home systolic blood pressure

9.3 Results

Primary Outcome:

- Spironolactone was superior to placebo, the mean of the other two active treatments (doxazosin and bisoprolol), as well as doxazosin and bisoprolol individually, in reducing systolic blood pressure ($p < 0.0001$).

9.4 Key Takeaways

- Almost 60% of patients achieved blood pressure control on spironolactone, making it the most effective fourth-line agent.
- The blood pressure response to spironolactone was greatest in patients with low plasma renin, supporting sodium retention as the main mechanism of resistant hypertension.
- Spironolactone showed a clear dose-response effect, with greater BP reductions at higher doses (50 mg vs 25 mg).
- Adverse events, including hyperkalemia, renal impairment, and gynecomastia, were uncommon and similar to other treatments, though electrolytes and renal function should be monitored.
- The study established spironolactone as the preferred fourth-line therapy for resistant hypertension, reshaping guideline recommendations worldwide.

9.5 Clinical Application

- Use spironolactone as the preferred fourth-line agent for resistant hypertension after ACEi/ARB, calcium channel blocker, and thiazide diuretic.
- Monitor potassium and renal function closely, especially in patients with diabetes or borderline kidney function.
- Consider bisoprolol or doxazosin only when spironolactone is not tolerated or contraindicated.
- Recognize that resistant hypertension is often due to sodium and aldosterone-driven mechanisms, making mineralocorticoid receptor antagonism the most effective strategy.

9.6 When to Discuss on Rounds

Discuss this trial on rounds with the following scenarios:

- When managing a patient with persistent hypertension despite being on the maximally tolerated triple therapy.
- When discussing aldosterone and sodium retention as common underlying mechanisms of resistant hypertension.
- When monitoring a patient started on spironolactone and emphasizing the need for potassium and renal function checks.
- When considering alternatives for patients who cannot tolerate spironolactone, such as doxazosin or bisoprolol.

9.7 *Relevant Guidelines*

The **NICE, AHA/ACC, and ESC/ESH** hypertension guidelines were all strongly influenced by the PATHWAY-2 trial. Each incorporated spironolactone as the preferred fourth-line therapy for resistant hypertension.

10 CREDENCE Trial Summary [10]

Full Title: Canagliflozin and Renal Outcomes in Type 2 Diabetes and Nephropathy
Publication Year: 2019
Journal: New England Journal of Medicine

10.1 *Background*

Before the CREDENCE trial, diabetic kidney disease (DKD) remained a leading cause of end-stage renal disease (ESRD) despite standard therapy with ACE inhibitors or ARBs. Sodium-glucose cotransporter-2 (SGLT2) inhibitors, initially developed for glycemic control, showed unexpected renal-protective benefits in cardiovascular trials. The CREDENCE trial was specifically designed to evaluate the renal effects and safety of canagliflozin, an SGLT2 inhibitor, in patients with type 2 diabetes and established nephropathy.

10.2 *Study Design*

Type: Randomized, double-blind, placebo-controlled trial
Population: 4,401 patients with type 2 diabetes, albuminuric CKD (eGFR 30–90 mL/min/1.73 m^2, urinary albumin-to-creatinine ratio > 300 mg/g), on standard therapy including ACE/ARBs
Intervention: Canagliflozin (100 mg daily) vs. placebo
Primary Outcome: Composite of ESRD, doubling of serum creatinine, or renal or cardiovascular death
Secondary Outcomes:

- Composite of cardiovascular death or hospitalization for heart failure
- Composite of cardiovascular death, MI, or stroke
- Hospitalization for heart failure
- Individual components of the composite primary and secondary outcomes

10.3 Results

Primary Outcome: Significant 30% reduction in primary composite renal outcome with canagliflozin compared to placebo (HR 0.70; [95% CI: 0.59–0.82; p = 0.00001).

Secondary Outcomes:

- Composite of cardiovascular death or hospitalization for heart failure: Significantly less in the Canagliflozin group vs placebo (HR 0.69; [95% CI: 0.57–0.83; p < 0.001]).
- Composite of cardiovascular death, MI, or stroke: Significant reduction in Canagliflozin vs placebo (HR 0.80; [95% CI: 0.67–0.95; p = 0.01]).
- Hospitalization for heart failure: Significant reduction in hospitalizations for heart failure was observed (HR 0.61; [95% CI: 0.47–0.80; p < 0.001]).
- Individual outcomes:
  - Doubling in serum creatinine: Decreased in the Canagliflozin group (HR 0.60; [95% CI: 0.48–0.76; p < 0.001]).
  - ESRD: Significant reduction was observed in the Canagliflozin group (HR 0.68; [95% CI: 0.54–0.86; p = 0.002]).
  - Cardiovascular death: Lower incidence in the Canagliflozin group vs placebo (HR 0.78; [95% CI: 0.61–1.00; p = 0.05]).

10.4 Key Takeaways

- Canagliflozin provided significant renal protection, reducing the progression to ESRD, doubling of creatinine, and renal death in patients with diabetic kidney disease.
- It demonstrates significant cardiovascular benefits, particularly reducing heart failure hospitalizations.
- Benefits were observed despite only modest reductions in HbA1c, blood pressure, and weight, suggesting mechanisms beyond glycemic control.
- Early dip in eGFR was followed by slower long-term decline in kidney function in the canagliflozin group.
- Safety profile was reassuring, with no excess risk of amputation or fracture compared to placebo, though diabetic ketoacidosis occurred slightly more often.
- The trial was stopped early for efficacy, strengthening the significance of the findings but possibly inflating effect sizes.
- CREDENCE established SGLT2 inhibitors as foundational therapy for kidney protection in type 2 diabetes with CKD, on top of RAAS blockade.

10.5 Clinical Application

- Initiate SGLTT2 inhibitors (canagliflozin and similar drugs) in patients with diabetic kidney disease alongside standard ACE inhibitor/ARB therapy.
- Use SGLT2 inhibitors to reduce risk of kidney failure, cardiovascular death, myocardial infarction, stroke, and hospitalization for heart failure.
- Routinely monitor renal function, electrolytes, and potential side effects, emphasizing safety profiles of SGLT2 inhibitors.
- Expect an initial dip in eGFR followed by long-term renal preservation.

10.6 When to Discuss on Rounds

Discuss this trial on rounds with the following scenarios:

- When managing diabetic patients with declining renal function despite standard RAAS blockade.
- When discussing SGLT2 inhibitors as standard of care for reducing risk of kidney failure and cardiovascular events.
- When discussing the dual renal and cardiovascular protective effects of SGLT2 inhibitors in diabetic nephropathy.

10.7 Relevant Guidelines

The **KDIGO** and **ADA** guidelines strongly recommend adding SGLT2 inhibitors to standard care for patients with Type 2 diabetes and CKD, significantly informed by the outcomes of the CREDENCE trial.

References

1. Brenner BM, Cooper ME, de Zeeuw D, et al. Effects of losartan on renal and cardiovascular outcomes in patients with type 2 diabetes and nephropathy. N Engl J Med. 2001;345(12):861–9. https://doi.org/10.1056/NEJMoa011161.
2. Torres VE, Chapman AB, Devuyst O, et al. Tolvaptan in patients with autosomal dominant polycystic kidney disease. N Engl J Med. 2012;367(25):2407–18. https://doi.org/10.1056/NEJMoa1205511.
3. Baigent C, Landray MJ, Reith C, et al. The effects of lowering LDL cholesterol with simvastatin plus ezetimibe in patients with chronic kidney disease (Study of Heart and Renal Protection): a randomized placebo-controlled trial. Lancet. 2011;377(9784):2181–92. https://doi.org/10.1016/S0140-6736(11)60739-3.
4. Fellström BC, Jardine AG, Schmieder RE, et al. Rosuvastatin and cardiovascular events in patients undergoing hemodialysis [published correction appears in N Engl J Med. 2010

Apr 15;362(15):1450]. N Engl J Med. 2009;360(14):1395–407. https://doi.org/10.1056/NEJMoa0810177.

5. Singh AK, Szczech L, Tang KL, et al. Correction of anemia with epoetin alfa in chronic kidney disease. N Engl J Med. 2006;355(20):2085–98. https://doi.org/10.1056/NEJMoa065485.
6. EVOLVE Trial Investigators, Chertow GM, Block GA, et al. Effect of cinacalcet on cardiovascular disease in patients undergoing dialysis. N Engl J Med. 2012;367(26):2482–94. https://doi.org/10.1056/NEJMoa1205624.
7. Macdougall IC, White C, Anker SD, et al. Intravenous Iron in Patients Undergoing Maintenance Hemodialysis [published correction appears in N Engl J Med. 2019 Jan 31;380(5):502. Doi: 10.1056/NEJMx180044]. N Engl J Med. 2019;380(5):447–58. https://doi.org/10.1056/NEJMoa1810742.
8. Cooper BA, Branley P, Bulfone L, et al. A randomized, controlled trial of early versus late initiation of dialysis. N Engl J Med. 2010;363(7):609–19. https://doi.org/10.1056/NEJMoa1000552.
9. Williams B, MacDonald TM, Morant S, et al. Spironolactone versus placebo, bisoprolol, and doxazosin to determine the optimal treatment for drug-resistant hypertension (PATHWAY-2): a randomised, double-blind, crossover trial. Lancet. 2015;386(10008):2059–68. https://doi.org/10.1016/S0140-6736(15)00257-3.
10. Perkovic V, Jardine MJ, Neal B, et al. Canagliflozin and renal outcomes in type 2 diabetes and nephropathy. N Engl J Med. 2019;380(24):2295–306. https://doi.org/10.1056/NEJMoa1811744.

Chapter 7
Hematology/Oncology

1 ECOG 1484 Trial Summary [1]

Full Title: CHOP Chemotherapy with or without Radiation Therapy for Intermediate-Grade or Aggressive Non-Hodgkin's Lymphoma
Publication Year: 2004
Journal: Journal of Clinical Oncology

1.1 Background

Before ECOG 1484, optimal management of localized aggressive non-Hodgkin lymphoma (such as diffuse large B-cell lymphoma, DLBCL) was controversial. Chemotherapy alone, radiation alone, or combined modality therapy had been used, but evidence was limited. ECOG 1484 aimed to determine whether adding involved-field radiation therapy (RT) after chemotherapy with CHOP (cyclophosphamide, doxorubicin, vincristine, prednisone) could improve outcomes compared to chemotherapy alone.

1.2 Study Design

Type: Randomized, controlled trial
Population: 172 patients with intermediate-grade NHL who achieved complete remission after initial CHOP chemotherapy
Intervention: CHOP chemotherapy alone vs. CHOP chemotherapy followed by involved-field radiotherapy (30 Gy)
Primary Outcome: Disease-free survival

A. Love, *The Essential Evidence*, https://doi.org/10.1007/978-3-032-12399-2_7

Secondary Outcomes:

- Overall survival
- Complete response rates
- Relapse patterns
- Toxicity and treatment-related adverse events

1.3 Results

Primary Outcome: 6-year disease-free survival was significantly improved with addition of radiotherapy compared to chemotherapy alone (73% vs. 56%; $p = 0.05$).

Secondary Outcomes:

- Overall survival: No significant difference in survival was observed between groups.
- Relapse rate: There were far fewer relapses at initial disease sites with radiotherapy, however results were not significant.
- Toxicity: Radiotherapy was well tolerated with manageable toxicity profile; no substantial increase in severe long-term adverse events.

1.4 Key Takeaways

- Consolidative involved-field radiotherapy after complete remission with CHOP chemotherapy significantly improved disease-free survival in patients with intermediate-grade NHL.
- Although overall survival benefit was not statistically significant, a trend towards improved long-term outcomes supports consolidative radiotherapy, especially for selected patients at high relapse risk.
- Most relapses in the observation arm occurred at prior disease sites, while RT reduced local relapse risk.
- The trial showed that systemic relapse remained the dominant mode of failure despite improved local control with RT.

1.5 Clinical Application

- Consider consolidative radiotherapy after achieving complete remission with chemotherapy (CHOP regimen) in intermediate-grade NHL, particularly in patients at higher risk of relapse.

- Individualize treatment decisions based on patient risk factors, disease characteristics, and potential radiotherapy toxicity.

1.6 When to Discuss on Rounds

Discuss this trial on rounds with the following scenarios:

- When evaluating treatment options for patients with intermediate-grade NHL who achieved remission after chemotherapy.
- When discussing management strategies to prolong disease-free survival and prevent relapses in aggressive NHL.
- When teaching trainees about multimodal therapy approaches for lymphoma.

1.7 Relevant Guidelines

National Comprehensive Cancer Network (NCCN) guidelines for diffuse large B-cell lymphoma note that consolidative involved-site radiotherapy can be considered in patients with limited-stage disease, especially those with bulky disease or extranodal involvement, reflecting evidence from ECOG 1484 and similar studies. However, with the advent of rituximab-based chemoimmunotherapy (R-CHOP), the role of RT has become more selective, often reserved for patients with bulky presentations or residual PET-avid sites after systemic therapy. KDIGO and ASCO do not issue specific guidance on lymphoma RT, but NCCN remains the most widely referenced standard.

2 CLOT Trial Summary [2]

Full Title: Low-Molecular-Weight Heparin versus a Coumarin for the Prevention of Recurrent Venous Thromboembolism in Patients with Cancer
Publication Year: 2003
Journal: New England Journal of Medicine

2.1 Background

Prior to the CLOT trial, cancer patients with venous thromboembolism (VTE) were traditionally managed with heparin followed by oral warfarin therapy. However, recurrence rates of VTE and bleeding complications were high in cancer patients receiving warfarin. The CLOT trial aimed to evaluate whether extended treatment with a low-molecular-weight heparin (dalteparin) would be more effective and safer than warfarin in reducing recurrent VTE in cancer patients.

2.2 *Study Design*

Type: Randomized, controlled, open-label trial
Population: 676 patients with active cancer and acute symptomatic VTE
Intervention: Dalteparin 200 IU/kg once daily for five to seven days vs. warfarin for six months
Primary Outcome: Symptomatic, objectively confirmed recurrent VTE
Secondary Outcomes:

- Major and minor bleeding
- Overall survival
- Safety and tolerability

2.3 *Results*

Primary Outcome: Significant reduction in recurrent VTE with dalteparin compared to warfarin (9% vs. 16%; HR 0.48; [95% CI: 0.30–0.77; p = 0.002]).
Secondary Outcomes:

- Maor and minor bleeding: Similar rates of major bleeding between dalteparin and warfarin groups (6% vs. 4%, p = 0.27).
- Overall survival: No significant difference in overall survival between groups.
- Safety and tolerability: Dalteparin was well-tolerated despite prolonged injections.

2.4 *Key Takeaways*

- Dalteparin (LMWH) significantly reduced recurrence of venous thromboembolism in cancer patients compared to oral warfarin.
- Mortality rates were similar between groups, with most deaths due to progressive cancer.
- Major bleeding rates did not differ significantly between dalteparin and oral anticoagulation.
- Dalteparin was effective and safe despite requiring long-term subcutaneous injections, with acceptable patient adherence.

- The trial provided definitive evidence that LMWH is superior to warfarin for secondary prophylaxis of cancer-associated VTE.

2.5 *Clinical Application*

- Initiate LMWH therapy instead of warfarin in patients with active cancer who develop acute VTE.
- Consider patients preference and comfort, balancing efficacy benefits of LMWH against inconvenience of daily injections.
- Counsel patients on the need for daily injections and provide support for self-administration to improve adherence.
- Monitor for bleeding complications, though the risk is not significantly higher than with warfarin.
- Reassess anticoagulation strategy as cancer status changes (progression, remission, or transition to palliative care).
- Weigh cost and convenience of LMWH against its demonstrated superiority in preventing recurrent VTE.

2.6 *When to Discuss on Rounds*

Discuss this trial on rounds with the following scenarios:

- When managing VTE in cancer patients and selecting optimal anticoagulation therapy.
- When highlighting that bleeding risk with LMWH is comparable to warfarin, despite its greater efficacy in reducing recurrence.
- When evaluating recurrent thrombosis risks and anticoagulant safety profiles in cancer-associated VTE.

2.7 *Relevant Guidelines*

The **American Society of Clinical Oncology (ASCO)**, **NCCN**, and the **International Society on Thrombosis and Haemostasis (ISTH)** guidelines for cancer-associated thrombosis incorporated findings from the CLOT trial, recommending low-molecular-weight heparin (LMWH) over vitamin K antagonists as first-line therapy for at least the first 3–6 months of treatment. More recently, guidelines from **American Society of Hematology (ASH)**, ASCO, and NCCN have expanded to include direct oral anticoagulants (DOACs, such as apixaban or rivaroxaban) as acceptable alternatives in carefully selected patients, but LMWH remains preferred in those with high bleeding risk, gastrointestinal malignancies, or concerns about drug interactions. The CLOT trial was pivotal in establishing LMWH as the initial standard of care for secondary prevention of VTE in cancer.

3 RE-LY Trial Summary [3]

Full Title: Dabigatran versus Warfarin in Patients with Atrial Fibrillation: Randomized Evaluation of Long-Term Anticoagulation Therapy
Publication Year: 2009
Journal: New England Journal of Medicine

3.1 Background

Before the RE-LY trial, warfarin was the standard anticoagulant used for stroke prevention in patients with atrial fibrillation (AF). Warfarin required regular monitoring and dose adjustments, increasing patient inconvenience and risk of bleeding. Dabigatran, a novel oral direct thrombin inhibitor, offered fixed dosing without routine monitoring. The RE-LY trial aimed to compare efficacy and safety of dabigatran with warfarin for stroke prevention in AF.

3.2 Study Design

Type: Randomized, open-label, controlled trial
Population: 18,113 patients with non-valvular atrial fibrillation and additional stroke risk factors
Intervention: Dabigatran (110 mg or 150 mg twice daily) vs. dose-adjusted warfarin (target INR 2.0–3.0)
Primary Outcome: Stroke or systemic embolism
Primary Safety Outcome: Major hemorrhage
Secondary Outcomes:

- Stroke
- Systemic embolism
- Death

3.3 Results

Primary Outcome:

- Dabigatran 150 mg was superior in reducing stroke or systemic embolism compared to warfarin (RR 0.66; [95% CI: 0.53–0.82; $p < 0.001$]).
- Dabigatran 110 mg was non-inferior to warfarin ($p < 0.001$), but was not superior (RR 0.91; [95% CI: 0.74–1.11; $p = 0.34$]).

Secondary Outcomes:

- Stroke: Hemorrhagic stroke occurred in 0.38% of patients per year in the warfarin group compared to 0.12% of patients per year in the 110 dabigatran group (RR 0.31; [95% CI: 0.17–0.56; $p < 0.001$]) and 0.10% of patients per year in the 150 mg dabigatran group (RR 0.26; [95% CI: 0.14–0.49; $p < 0.001$]).
- No significant difference was observed between groups in rates of systemic embolism or death

3.4 Key Takeaways

- Both 110 mg and 150 mg doses of dabigatran were noninferior to warfarin for prevention of stroke or systemic embolism in atrial fibrillation.
- Dabigatran 150 mg twice daily was superior to warfarin, reducing stroke and systemic embolism by 34%.
- Both dabigatran doses reduced hemorrhagic stroke by more than two-thirds compared with warfarin.
- Dabigatran 150 mg was associated with higher rates of major gastrointestinal bleeding compared with warfarin.
- Overall mortality was similar across groups, with a trend toward lower all-cause mortality with dabigatran.
- RE-LY established dabigatran as the first direct oral anticoagulant (DOAC) alternative to warfarin for atrial fibrillation, reshaping clinical practice.

3.5 Clinical Application

- Use dabigatran (and other direct oral anticoagulants) as first-line therapy in stroke prevention for patients with non-valvular atrial fibrillation, especially when warfarin monitoring is challenging.
- Consider patient-specific factors, including renal function, bleeding risk, and medication adherence, when choosing anticoagulants.

3.6 *When to Discuss on Rounds*

Discuss this trial on rounds with the following scenarios:

- When selecting anticoagulation strategies for patients with new-onset atrial fibrillation.
- When evaluating the choice between warfarin and direct oral anticoagulants based on individual patients profiles.
- When reviewing DOAC selection, discuss that dabigatran was the first approved, but factor Xa inhibitors are now more commonly used due to ease of dosing and lower GI bleeding risk.

3.7 *Relevant Guidelines*

The **AHA, ACC,** and **ESC** guidelines recommend direct oral anticoagulants (including dabigatran) as a first-line therapy for stroke prevention in atrial fibrillation, heavily influenced by results from the RE-LY trial. While apixaban and other factor Xa inhibitors are now more commonly favored due to broader safety and tolerability, dabigatran remains a guideline-endorsed option, especially when careful renal function–based dosing and GI bleeding risk monitoring are applied.

4 AMPLIFY Trial Summary [4]

Full Titles: Oral Apixaban for the Treatment of Acute Venous Thromboembolism
Publication Year: 2013
Journal: New England Journal of Medicine

4.1 *Background*

While warfarin had long been the standard oral anticoagulant for venous thromboembolism (VTE), it required bridging with parenteral anticoagulants and regular INR monitoring. Direct oral anticoagulants (DOACs) like apixaban emerged as simpler alternatives. The AMPLIFY trial evaluated apixaban as a single oral agent for the treatment of acute DVT and PE, comparing it with conventional therapy (enoxaparin plus warfarin).

4.2 Study Design

Type: Randomized, double-blind, non-inferiority trial
Population: 5,395 patients with acute symptomatic proximal DVT or PE
Intervention: Apixaban 10 mg twice daily for 7 days, then 5 mg twice daily for 6 months vs. standard therapy with enoxaparin followed by warfarin (INR 2.0–3.0) for 6 months
Primary Outcome: Recurrent symptomatic VTE or VTE-related death
Secondary Outcomes:

- Major bleeding
- Clinically relevant non-major bleeding
- All-cause mortality

4.3 Results

Primary Outcome: Apixaban was non-inferior to standard therapy for prevention of recurrent VTE or VTE-related death (2.3% vs. 2.7%; HR 0.83; [95% CI: 0.60–1.18; $p < 0.001$ for non-inferiority]).
Secondary Outcomes:

- Major bleeding: Was significantly lower with apixaban (0.6% vs. 1.8%; HR 0.31; [95% CI: 0.17–0.55; $p < 0.001$ for superiority]).
- Clinically relevant non-major bleeding: Significantly reduced with apixaban (3.8% vs. 8.0%; HR 0.48; [95% CI: 0.38—0.60]).
- There was no significant difference in all-cause mortality observed between groups.

4.4 Key Takeaways

- Apixaban is as effective as conventional anticoagulation for acute VTE but significantly safer in terms of bleeding risk.
- Even compared with well-controlled warfarin (INR therapeutic >68%), apixaban maintained efficacy and reduced bleeding.
- No significant difference in all-cause mortality between apixaban and conventional therapy.
- Safety profile was favorable, with no excess in liver toxicity or other unexpected adverse effects.

4.5 Clinical Application

- Consider apixaban as a first-line therapy for most patients with acute DVT or PE.
- Apixaban is especially useful in outpatient or low-risk PE settings due to oral-only regimen and lower bleeding risk.
- Monitor renal function and weight carefully, as additional data are needed in patients with creatinine clearance <50 mL/min or low body weight.
- Recognize apixaban as part of the broader shift toward DOACs as standard of care for VTE treatment, replacing warfarin in most scenarios.

4.6 When to Discuss on Rounds

Discuss this trial on rounds with the following scenarios:

- When admitting a patient with acute DVT or PE and deciding between starting heparin/warfarin versus a DOAC.
- When explaining why DOACs are preferred over warfarin in most VTE cases, highlight that apixaban was equally effective without the need for bridging or INR monitoring.
- When managing patients in outpatient settings or those with barriers to INR monitoring.

4.7 Relevant Guidelines

The **CHEST** VTE guideline and **ASH** guidelines recommend DOACs over warfarin for initial and long-term treatment of most patients with acute DVT/PE, with apixaban specifically endorsed as a first-line option based on AMPLIFY's noninferior efficacy and markedly lower major bleeding. The **ESC** PE guidelines likewise favors DOACs over VKAs in non–high-risk PE, and prefer apixaban for its no-bridge, fixed-dose regimen and safety profile; exceptions (e.g., severe renal failure, antiphospholipid syndrome, pregnancy) still favor non-DOAC strategies.

5 4T Score Validation Trial Summary [5]

Full Title: Evaluation of Pretest Clinical Score (4Ts) for the Diagnosis of Heparin-Induced Thrombocytopenia in Two Clinical Settings
Publication Year: 2006
Journal: Journal of Thrombosis and Haemostasis

5.1 Background

Heparin-induced thrombocytopenia (HIT) is a potentially life-threatening, immune-mediated condition. Prior to this trial, there was no validated clinical scoring tool to assess pretest probability of HIT. Many patients were over tested and overtreated, leading to unnecessary use of alternative anticoagulants. This study evaluated the diagnostic accuracy of the newly developed 4 T score across two tertiary centers.

5.2 Study Design

Type: Prospective cohort validation study
Population: 307 patients with suspected HIT from two academic hospitals (Hamilton, Canada and Greifswald, Germany)
Intervention:

- Application of the 4 T clinical scoring system (Thrombocytopenia, Timing, Thrombosis, and other causes)
- Blinded scoring by investigators prior to lab testing
- Comparison against gold standard functional assays (serotonin release assay or heparin-induced platelet activation assay)

Primary Outcome: Diagnostic performance (sensitivity, specificity, PPV, NPV) of the 4 T score for laboratory-confirmed HIT

5.3 Results

Low 4t Score (0–3):
- Negative Predictive Value (NPV): 100%
- Sensitivity: 98%
- No patients with a low score had positive confirmatory HIT tests.

Intermediate (4–5) or High (6–8) Scores:
- Required further laboratory testing due to insufficient specificity
- Positive Predictive Value (PPV): ~14% for intermediate, ~64% for high
- Higher scores correlated with increasing probability of HIT

5.4 Key Takeaways

- The 4 T score is a highly sensitive tool for ruling out HIT when the score is low.
- A low 4 T score effectively excludes HIT without further testing, preventing unnecessary treatment.

- Intermediate and high scores require confirmatory laboratory testing with functional assays.
- This study provided the evidence that made the 4 T score the standard clinical prediction rule for HIT.

5.5 Clinical Application

- Use the 4 T sore to stratify pretest probability before ordering HIT labs.
- Avoid testing and treatment in patients with low 4 T scores to reduce overdiagnosis and overtreatment.
- Order confirmatory testing in intermediate/high-risk patients and consider non-heparin anticoagulation pending results.

5.6 When to Discuss on Rounds

Discuss this trial on rounds with the following scenarios:

- When evaluating thrombocytopenia in hospitalized patients exposed to heparin.
- When teaching about reducing unnecessary HIT testing and improving diagnostic stewardship.
- When deciding whether to stop heparin and start alternative anticoagulation for suspected HIT.

5.7 Relevant Guidelines

Guidelines from **ASH, ACCP/CHEST,** and **British Society for Haematology (BSH)/ ISTH** all endorse the 4Ts score to guide evaluation of suspected HIT. Testing is not recommended in low-probability patients. For intermediate or high 4Ts, stop heparin, start a non-heparin anticoagulant, and order a PF4/heparin immunoassay, followed by a functional assay if positive. Warfarin should be avoided until platelets recover.

6 IRIS Trial Summary [6]

Full Title: Imatinib Compared with Interferon and Low-Dose Cytarabine for Newly Diagnosed Chronic-Phase Chronic Myeloid Leukemia
Publication Year: 2003 (5-year follow-up published 2006)
Journal: New England Journal of Medicine

6.1 Background

Chronic myeloid leukemia (CML) is characterized by the BCR-ABl fusion gene (Philadelphia chromosome), which produces a constitutively active tyrosine kinase. Before the IRIS trial, the standard treatment for chronic-phase CML was interferon-alpha plus cytarabine, which had modest response rates and significant toxicity. Imatinib, a tyrosine kinase inhibitor targeting BCR-ABL, had shown promise in early studies. The IRIS trial was designed to compare imatinib to interferon-alpha plus cytarabine in newly diagnosed CML.

6.2 Study Design

Type: International, randomized, open-label, phase III trial
Population: 1,106 patients with newly diagnosed chronic-phase CML
Intervention: Imatinib 400 mg daily vs. interferon-alpha + low-dose cytarabine
Primary Outcome: Disease progression
Secondary Outcomes:

- Rate of complete hematologic response
- Rate of major cytogenic response
- Safety and tolerability

6.3 Results

Primary Outcome: Imatinib group had significantly higher rate of freedom from progression at 18 months (96.7% vs. 91.5%; $p < 0.001$).
Secondary Outcomes:

- Rate of complete hematologic response: Higher rate in the imatinib group than in the combination-therapy group (95.3% vs. 55.5%; $p < 0.001$).
- Rate of major cytogenic response: Was also higher in the imatinib group (85.2% vs. 22.1%; $p < 0.001$).

- Safety and tolerability: Imatinib was generally safe and well tolerated, with most adverse events being mild to moderate (edema, nausea, cramps, rash), and severe toxicities were rare, especially compared to the higher rates of intolerance and grade 3–4 toxicities seen with combination therapy.

6.4 Key Takeaways

- Imatinib dramatically improved cytogenic and molecular response rates, reduced disease progression, and was better tolerated than prior standard therapy.
- This trial revolutionized the treatment of CML and established targeted therapy as the new standard of care.

6.5 Clinical Application

- Initiate imatinib (or second-generation TKIs) as the first-line therapy in patients with chronic-phase CML.
- Expect rapid hematologic and cytogenetic responses, even in higher-risk patients.
- Prefer imatinib over interferon-based regimens due to superior efficacy and better tolerability.
- Consider bone marrow transplantation only in selected high-risk patients or those with inadequate response to imatinib.
- Monitor for mild adverse effects such as edema, rash, nausea, and muscle cramps, which are generally manageable.

6.6 When to Discuss on Rounds

Discuss this trial on rounds with the following scenarios:

- When initiating treatment for a newly diagnosed CML patient.
- When reviewing the dramatic differences in cytogenetic response rates between imatinib and interferon-based therapy.
- When discussing the shift away from early bone marrow transplantation toward tyrosine kinase inhibitor–based therapy.
- When highlighting imatinib's role in delaying progression to accelerated or blast phase CML.

6.7 Relevant Guidelines

The **NCCN** and **European LeukemiaNet (ELN)** guidelines designate tyrosine kinase inhibitors, with imatinib or newer agents (dasatinib, nilotinib, bosutinib), as first-line therapy for chronic-phase CML. This recommendation is directly informed by the landmark IRIS trial, which demonstrated superior hematologic and cytogenetic responses, improved progression-free survival, and better tolerability compared to interferon plus cytarabine. Bone marrow transplantation is now reserved for patients with advanced disease or resistance to TKIs.

7 ECOG E2100 Trial Summary [7]

Full Title: Paclitaxel plus Bevacizumab versus Paclitaxel Alone for Metastatic Breast Cancer
Publication Year: 2007
Journal: New England Journal of Medicine

7.1 Background

In metastatic breast cancer, treatment is often palliative, aiming to prolong survival and improve quality of life. Bevacizumb, a monoclonal antibody targeting VEGF, had shown potential in improving tumor response in earlier studies. The ECOG E2100 trial investigated whether adding bevacizumab to standard paclitaxel would improve outcomes in patients with HER2-negative metastatic breast cancer.

7.2 Study Design

Type: Randomized, open-label, phase III trial
Population: 722 women with HER2-negative, previously untreated metastatic breast cancer
Intervention: Paclitaxel alone (90 mg/m^2 weekly x 3 every 4 weeks) vs. paclitaxel + bevacizumab (10 mg/kg every 2 weeks)
Primary Outcome: Progression-free survival (PFS)
Secondary Outcomes:

- Overall survival (OS)
- Objective response rate (ORR)
- Quality of life
- Safety and adverse events

7.3 Results

Primary Outcome: Median progression-free survival (PFS) was significantly longer in the paclitaxel + bevacizumab group compared to paclitaxel alone (11.8 months vs. 5.9 months; HR 0.60, $p < 0.001$)

Secondary Outcomes:

- Overall survival: No significant difference was observed between the groups 26.7 vs. 25.2 months ($p = 0.16$).
- Objective response rate (ORR): Was higher in the combination group (36.9%) vs. paclitaxel alone (21.2%); ($p < 0.001$).
- Quality of life: No significant difference between groups.
- Safety and adverse events: The bevacizumab group had higher rates of hypertension (14.8% vs. 0.0%, $p < 0.001$), proteinuria (3.6% vs. 0.0%, $p < 0.001$), headache (2.2% vs. 0.0%, $p = 0.008$), and cerebrovascular ischemia (1.9% vs. 0.0%, $p = 0.02$). Treatment discontinuation due to toxicity was relatively uncommon.

7.4 Key Takeaways

- Adding bevacizumab to paclitaxel significantly improved progression-free survival and tumor response rates in HER2-negative metastatic breast cancer.
- One-year survival was higher with combination therapy, but median overall survival was not significantly different
- Toxicities were generally manageable, though grade 3–4 neuropathy, infections, fatigue, hypertension, cerebrovascular ischemia, and headaches were more common with bevacizumab.
- The trial sparked significant debate and later led to the FDA to revoke bevacizumab's breast cancer indication due to safety concerns and lack of survival benefit.

7.5 Clinical Application

- The ECOG E2100 trial established proof-of-concept that adding anti-VEGF therapy to chemotherapy could improve progression-free survival and response rates in metastatic breast cancer, even though overall survival was not improved.
- Bevacizumab is no longer FDA-approved for breast cancer, but the trial remains an important landmark in oncology because it demonstrated the role of angiogenesis inhibition in solid tumors.
- Bevacizumab continues to be used in other malignancies (e.g., colorectal cancer, non–small cell lung cancer, renal cell carcinoma, glioblastoma), where the balance of efficacy and safety has been more favorable.

7.6 *When to Discuss on Rounds*

Discuss this trial on rounds with the following scenarios:

- When reviewing the history of anti-angiogenic therapy in breast cancer, bring up ECOG E2100 as the landmark trial that initially showed improved progression-free survival with bevacizumab plus paclitaxel.
- When discussing why the FDA sometimes revokes approvals, cite ECOG E2100 as an example where improved PFS and response rate did not translate into improved overall survival, raising concerns about meaningful benefit.
- When comparing bevacizumab's role across cancers, discuss why it lost its breast cancer indication but remains approved in colorectal, lung, renal, and brain cancers.

7.7 *Relevant Guidelines*

The FDA revoked bevacizumab's breast cancer indication in 2011 after subsequent data failed to confirm an overall survival benefit, despite the improved progression-free survival seen in ECOG E2100. Current **NCCN** and **ASCO** guidelines for metastatic breast cancer do not recommend bevacizumab as part of standard therapy. Instead, ECOG E2100 is referenced historically as an example of how regulatory approvals can be withdrawn when benefits in PFS do not translate into overall survival or quality-of-life improvements. Bevacizumab remains guideline-endorsed for other malignancies, including colorectal cancer, non–small cell lung cancer, renal cell carcinoma, ovarian cancer, and glioblastoma, but not for breast cancer.

8 KEYNOTE-024 Trial Summary [8]

Full Title: Pembrolizumab versus Chemotherapy for PD-L1-Positive Non-Small-Cell Lung Cancer
Publication Year: 2016
Journal: New England Journal of Medicine

8.1 *Background*

Before KEYNOTE-024, platinum-based chemotherapy was the standard first-line treatment for metastatic non-small-cell lung cancer (NSCLC). Immunotherapy targeting PD-1/PD-L1 had shown promise in pretreated patients. This trial aimed to assess whether pembrolizumab, an anti-PD-1 antibody, could outperform chemotherapy as first-line treatment in patients with high PD-L1 expression (≥50%) and no EGFR or ALK mutations.

8.2 Study Design

Type: Randomized, open-label, phase III trial
Population: 305 patients with untreated stage IV NSCLC and PD-L1 expression ≥50%, without EGFR or ALK mutations
Intervention: Pembrolizumab 200 mg IV every 3 weeks for up to 35 cycles vs. investigator's choice of platinum-based chemotherapy (4–6 cycles) ± pemetrexed maintenance
Primary Outcome: Progression-free survival (PFS)
Secondary Outcomes:

- Overall survival
- Objective response rate
- Safety and adverse events

8.3 Results

Primary Outcome: Median progression free survival was significantly longer with pembrolizumab compared to chemotherapy (10.3 months vs. 6.0 months; HR for disease progression 0.50; [95% CI: 0.37–0.68; p < 0.001]).
Secondary Outcomes:

- Overall survival: At 6 months, overall survival (OS) was significantly higher in the pembrolizumab group (80.2%) vs. chemotherapy (72.4%); (HR for death 0.60; [95% CI: 0.41–.89; p = 0.005]).
- Objective response rate: Was higher with pembrolizumab (44.8%) vs. chemotherapy (27.8%).
- Adverse events occurred in 26.6% of the pembrolizumab vs. 53.3% in the chemotherapy group. Common immune-related adverse events with pembrolizumab included pneumonitis, colitis, and endocrinopathies.

8.4 Key Takeaways

- Pembrolizumab significantly improved progression-free and overall survival compare to chemotherapy in advanced NSCLC with high PD-L1 expression.
- It was associated with fewer high-grade adverse events and a better safety profile.

- Immune-mediated adverse events (e.g., pneumonitis, colitis, skin reactions) were more common with pembrolizumab, but most were manageable and non-fatal.
- Benefit of pembrolizumab was consistent across subgroups, including squamous histology and patients with brain metastases.
- Trial was stopped early due to clear survival benefit, and chemotherapy patients were allowed crossover to pembrolizumab.
- This trial established pembrolizumab as first-line therapy in PD-L1-high NSCLC.

8.5 Clinical Application

- Use pembrolizumab as first-line treatment in patients with stage IV NSCLC and PD-L1 $\geq$ 50% without EGFR/ALK mutations.
- Consider early testing for PD-L1 status in patients with newly diagnosed metastatic NSCLC.
- Monitor for immune-related adverse effects and educate patients accordingly.

8.6 When to Discuss on Rounds

Discuss this trial on rounds with the following scenarios:

- When initiating first-line therapy for metastatic NSCLC.
- When discussing treatment options in a patient without EGFR or ALK driver mutations, note that pembrolizumab provides superior overall survival and fewer toxicities than platinum doublets.
- When reviewing response durability, emphasize that pembrolizumab showed longer progression-free survival and longer-lasting responses compared with chemotherapy.
- When comparing toxicity profiles between immunotherapy and chemotherapy.

8.7 Relevant Guidelines

The KEYNOTE-024 trial directly informed major international lung cancer guidelines. **NCCN**, **ASCO**, and **ESMO** all endorse pembrolizumab monotherapy as the preferred first-line treatment for patients with advanced or metastatic NSCLC who have PD-L1 expression $\geq$50% and no actionable driver mutations such as EGFR or ALK.

9 TOPPS Trial Summary [9]

Full Title: A No-Prophylaxis Platelet-Transfusion Strategy for Hematologic Cancers
Publication Year: 2013
Journal: New England Journal of Medicine

9.1 *Background*

Patients with hematologic malignancies undergoing chemotherapy often develop severe thrombocytopenia. Platelet transfusions are commonly given prophylactically to prevent bleeding, but their necessity in all patients was unclear. The TOPPS trial assessed whether omitting prophylactic platelet transfusions increased bleeding risk in patients with thrombocytopenia due to intensive chemotherapy.

9.2 *Study Design*

Type: Multicenter, randomized, controlled, open-label trial
Population: 600 adult patients with hematologic malignancies undergoing intensive chemotherapy or stem cell transplant
Intervention: Prophylactic platelet transfusions given when platelet count $<10\text{x}10^9$/L, regardless of bleeding vs. platelets given only in response to clinically significant bleeding (WHO grade ≥ 2)
Primary Outcome: Proportion of patients with WHO grade 2–4 bleeding
Secondary Outcomes:

- Number of bleeding days
- Time from randomization to first bleeding event
- Bleeding event of WHO grade 3 or 4
- Number of platelet and red-cell transfusions
- Number of days with a platelet count less than 20×10^9 per liter
- Time until recovery from thrombocytopenia
- Time in hospital
- Serious adverse events

9.3 *Results*

Primary Outcome:
- WHO grade 2–4 bleeding occurred in 50% of patients in the therapeutic group vs. 43% in the prophylactic group ($p = 0.06$ for noninferiority).

- Although not statistically significant, the therapeutic-only group had a trend toward increased bleeding, especially in patients receiving chemotherapy (as opposed to stem cell transplant).

Secondary Outcomes:

- Number of bleeding days: Was higher in the no-prophylaxis group than in the prophylaxis group (RR 1.52; [95% CI: 1.14–2.03; p = 0.004]).
- Time to first bleeding event: Was significantly shorter in the no-prophylaxis group (p = 0.02).
- WHO grade 3 or 4 bleeding: Higher in the no-prophylaxis group, but was not significant.
- Number of days with low platelets: Was observed to be greater in the no-prophylaxis group than those in the prophylaxis group (p < 0.001).
- No significant difference was observed between groups in time to recovery from thrombocytopenia and time spent in the hospital.
- Serious adverse events were similar between groups (p = 0.63).

9.4 *Key Takeaways*

- Prophylactic platelet transfusions reduced bleeding risk compared to a no-prophylaxis strategy
- Therapeutic-only transfusion strategy may be reasonable in select settings but may increase bleeding risk, especially in patients receiving chemotherapy (vs. stem cell transplant).
- Reinforced current practice of prophylactic transfusion in patients with hematologic malignancies receiving intensive chemotherapy.

9.5 *Clinical Application*

- Continue prophylactic platelet transfusion for patients with hematologic malignancy receiving induction chemotherapy.
- In select low-risk or post-transplant settings, therapeutic-only transfusion may be considered under close monitoring.
- Educate care teams about individualized bleeding risk when designing transfusion plans.

9.6 *When to Discuss on Rounds*

Discuss this trial on rounds with the following scenarios:

- When deciding on platelet transfusion threshold for neutropenic or thrombocytopenic patients.

- When discussing risks of bleeding vs. transfusion overuse in oncology or transplant settings.
- When reviewing institutional transfusion guidelines and cost-conscious care.

9.7 Relevant Guidelines

The findings of the TOPPS trial directly informed the **American Association of Blood Banks (AABB)** 2015 clinical practice guidelines and are referenced in **NCCN** guidelines for hematologic malignancies and stem cell transplantation. These guidelines recommend prophylactic platelet transfusion at a threshold of $<10 \times 10^9/L$ for hospitalized patients with therapy-induced hypoproliferative thrombocytopenia, reflecting the evidence that prophylaxis reduces bleeding risk compared with a therapeutic-only strategy.

10 ALCYONE Trial Summary [10]

Full Title: Daratumumab plus Bortezomib, Melphalan, and Prednisone for Untreated Myeloma
Publication Year: 2017
Journal: New England Journal of Medicine

10.1 Background

Before the ALCYONE trial, frontline therapy for transplant-ineligible newly diagnosed multiple myeloma typically involved a combination of bortezomib, melphalan, and prednisone (VMP). Daratumumab, an anti-CD38 monoclonal antibody, had shown promise in relapsed myeloma. ALCYONE evaluated whether adding daratumumab to standard VMP would improve outcomes in newly diagnosed, transplant-ineligible patients.

10.2 Study Design

Type: Phase III, randomized, open-label trial
Population: 706 patients with newly diagnosed multiple myeloma who were ineligible for autologous stem cell transplant
Intervention: Experimental arm (Daratumumab + bortezomib + melphalan + prednisone [D-VMP]) vs. control arm (Bortezomib + melphalan + prednisone [VMP])

Primary Outcome: Progression-free survival
Secondary Outcomes:

- Overall response rate
- Complete response or better
- Negative status for minimal residual disease
- Overall survival
- Safety and adverse events

10.3 Results

Primary Outcome: 18-month progression-free survival rate was 71.6% in the experimental group and 50.2% in the control group (HR for disease progression 0.50; [95% CI: 0.38–0.65; $p < 0.001$]).
Secondary Outcomes:

- Overall response rate: 90.9% in the experimental group vs 73.9% in the control group ($p < 0.001$)
- Complete response or better: 42.6% in the experimental group vs. 24.4% in the control group ($p < 0.001$).
- Negative status for minimal residual disease: 22.3% of patients in the experimental group were negative for minimal residual disease compared to 6.2% in the control group ($p < 0.001$).
- There were higher rates of infections and infusion-related reactions in the daratumumab group, but these were generally manageable. Other adverse events included neutropenia, thrombocytopenia, and anemia.

10.4 Key Takeaways

- Adding daratumumab to bortezomib, melphalan, and prednisone (VMP) significantly improved progression-free survival, reducing the risk of progression or death by 50% compared with VMP alone.
- Benefits were consistent across subgroups, including the elderly (≥75 years), those with ISS stage III disease, and patients with renal impairment.
- Patients with high-risk cytogenetics derived benefit, though to a lesser extent than those with standard risk.
- The addition of daratumumab did not increase chemotherapy-related toxicities; however, there were higher rates of infection, particularly pneumonia, and infusion-related reactions, which were mostly grade 1–2 and manageable.
- Compared with prior frontline myeloma trials (e.g., VISTA, FIRST), daratumumab-based therapy demonstrated a greater magnitude of benefit, establishing it as a new frontline option for transplant-ineligible newly diagnosed multiple myeloma.

10.5 Clinical Application

- Use D-VMP as first-line therapy in patients with newly diagnosed multiple myeloma who are not candidates for transplant.
- Plan infusion logistics: weekly dosing initially, then every 3 weeks (cycles 3–6) and every 4 weeks thereafter; ensure clinic capacity for long first infusions.
- Premedicate (steroid, antihistamine, antipyretic) and monitor for infusion-related reactions, most often during the first dose; consider split/extended first infusion.
- Monitor for infusion reactions and infection risk associated with daratumumab.
- Incorporate MRD assessment into treatment response evaluation when available.

10.6 When to Discuss on Rounds

Discuss this trial on rounds with the following scenarios:

- When starting therapy in an older or transplant-ineligible patient with multiple myeloma.
- When comparing depth of response and MRD between different frontline myeloma regimens.
- When counseling about toxicity, note increased infections (especially pneumonia) but no rise in treatment discontinuation or mortality.
- When considering patient subgroups, remember benefit was seen across age, renal impairment, and ISS stage, though attenuated in high-risk cytogenetics.

10.7 Relevant Guidelines

The **NCCN** guidelines for multiple myeloma and the **European Hematology Association-European Society for Medical Oncology** clinical practice guidelines both recommend daratumumab plus bortezomib, melphalan, and prednisone (D-VMP) as a frontline standard of care for transplant-ineligible, newly diagnosed multiple myeloma patients. These guidelines cite the ALCYONE trial as pivotal evidence showing improved progression-free survival, higher rates of deep response, and acceptable safety compared with VMP alone.

References

1. Horning SJ, Weller E, Kim K, et al. Chemotherapy with or without radiotherapy in limited-stage diffuse aggressive non-Hodgkin's lymphoma: Eastern Cooperative Oncology Group study 1484. J Clin Oncol. 2004;22(15):3032–8. https://doi.org/10.1200/JCO.2004.06.088.
2. Lee AY, Levine MN, Baker RI, et al. Low-molecular-weight heparin versus a coumarin for the prevention of recurrent venous thromboembolism in patients with cancer. N Engl J Med. 2003;349(2):146–53. https://doi.org/10.1056/NEJMoa025313.
3. Connolly SJ, Ezekowitz MD, Yusuf S, et al. Dabigatran versus warfarin in patients with atrial fibrillation [published correction appears in N Engl J Med. 2010 Nov 4;363(19):1877]. N Engl J Med. 2009;361(12):1139–51. https://doi.org/10.1056/NEJMoa0905561.
4. Agnelli G, Buller HR, Cohen A, et al. Oral apixaban for the treatment of acute venous thromboembolism. N Engl J Med. 2013;369(9):799–808. https://doi.org/10.1056/NEJMoa1302507.
5. Lo GK, Juhl D, Warkentin TE, Sigouin CS, Eichler P, Greinacher A. Evaluation of pretest clinical score (4 T's) for the diagnosis of heparin-induced thrombocytopenia in two clinical settings. J Thromb Haemost. 2006;4(4):759–65. https://doi.org/10.1111/j.1538-7836.2006.01787.x.
6. O'Brien SG, Guilhot F, Larson RA, et al. Imatinib compared with interferon and low-dose cytarabine for newly diagnosed chronic-phase chronic myeloid leukemia. N Engl J Med. 2003;348(11):994–1004. https://doi.org/10.1056/NEJMoa022457.
7. Miller K, Wang M, Gralow J, et al. Paclitaxel plus bevacizumab versus paclitaxel alone for metastatic breast cancer. N Engl J Med. 2007;357(26):2666–76. https://doi.org/10.1056/NEJMoa072113.
8. Reck M, Rodríguez-Abreu D, Robinson AG, et al. Pembrolizumab versus chemotherapy for PD-L1-positive non-small-cell lung cancer. N Engl J Med. 2016;375(19):1823–33. https://doi.org/10.1056/NEJMoa1606774.
9. Stanworth SJ, Estcourt LJ, Powter G, et al. A no-prophylaxis platelet-transfusion strategy for hematologic cancers. Lancet. 2013;382(9892):314–22. https://doi.org/10.1016/S0140-6736(13)60195-4.
10. Mateos MV, Dimopoulos MA, Cavo M, et al. Daratumumab plus bortezomib, melphalan, and prednisone for untreated myeloma. N Engl J Med. 2018;378(6):518–28. https://doi.org/10.1056/NewEnglandJournalofMedicineoa1714678.

Chapter 8
Rheumatology

1 TEMPO Trial Summary [1]

Full Title: Therapeutic Effect of the Combination of Etanercept and Methotrexate Compared With Each Treatment Alone in Patients with Rheumatoid Arthritis: Double-Blind Randomized Controlled Trial
Publication Year: 2004
Journal: The Lancet

1.1 Background

Before the TEMPO trial, methotrexate was the cornerstone of rheumatoid arthritis (RA) therapy, but many patients continued to experience progressive joint damage and symptoms despite treatment. Etanercept, a TNF-alpha inhibitor, had shown efficacy as monotherapy in RA, but the benefits of combining etanercept and methotrexate was unclear. The TEMP trial evaluated whether combination therapy provided superior clinical and radiographic outcomes compared to each agent alone.

1.2 Study Design

Type: Randomized, double-blind, controlled trial
Population: 686 patients with active RA despite prior disease-modifying antirheumatic drug (DMARD) use
Intervention: Etanercept monotherapy (25 mg twice weekly) vs. methotrexate monotherapy (up to 20 mg weekly) vs. combination etanercept + methotrexate

A. Love, *The Essential Evidence*, https://doi.org/10.1007/978-3-032-12399-2_8

Primary Outcome:

- Numeric index of American College of Rheumatology (ACR-N) response at 24 weeks
- Radiographic change in baseline to week 52 in total joint damage assessed with modified Sharp score.

1.3 Results

Primary Outcomes:

- ACR-N AUC
  - Greatest in the combination group compared to etanercept and methotrexate alone ($p < 0.0001$).
  - Mean difference in ACR-N AUC was greater in combination group compared to methotrexate alone ($p < 0.0001$).
  - ACR-N AUC greater in etanercept compared to methotrexate ($p = 0.0034$).
- Radiographic changes:
  - Combination therapy was greater than methotrexate or etanercept alone in prevent joint damage with a mean total Sharp score of −0.54 vs. 2.80 ($p < 0.0001$) and 0.52 ($p = 0.0006$) respectively.
  - Mean total sharp score between combination therapy and methotrexate alone was −3.34 ($p < 0.0001$).
  - Mean total sharp score between etanercept and methotrexate was -27 ($p = 0.0469$).

1.4 Key Takeaways

- Combination etanercept+methotrexate produced greater overall clinical response (ACR-N AUC) than either methotrexate or etanercept alone at 24 weeks.
- Disease activity fell fastest and deepest with combination therapy, yielding the lowest Disease Activity Score (DAS) at 52 weeks.
- Radiographic progression (total Sharp score, erosions, joint-space narrowing) was least with combination therapy and less with etanercept than methotrexate; combination showed mean negative progression (suggesting possible repair).
- Fewer withdrawals for lack of efficacy occurred with combination therapy than with either monotherapy.
- Prior methotrexate exposure did not modify the superior efficacy of combination therapy across primary endpoints.

- Etanercept (alone or with methotrexate) was generally well tolerated; infection and serious infection rates were similar across arms, and no opportunistic infections or TB occurred.
- Overall adverse-event profile favored combination therapy over methotrexate for hepatic enzyme elevations and study discontinuations, with injection-site reactions more common when etanercept was used.

1.5 *Clinical Application*

- Use etanercept plus methotrexate in patients with established RA who have active disease despite prior methotrexate, as combination therapy provides superior control.
- Expect higher rates of remission and improved function with combination therapy compared with either drug alone.
- Consider combination therapy early in patients with aggressive disease, since it slows or halts radiographic progression and may allow for joint repair.
- Reserve etanercept monotherapy for patients intolerant of methotrexate, recognizing it is less effective than the combination.
- Reassure patients that combination therapy did not show higher infection or malignancy rates compared to monotherapy in this trial.

1.6 *When to Discuss on Rounds*

Discuss this trial on rounds with the following scenarios:

- When selecting optimal therapy for RA patients not responding adequately to methotrexate monotherapy.
- When comparing monotherapy versus combination biologic and DMARD approaches in established RA.
- When reviewing strategies to prevent joint damage and disease progression in RA.

1.7 *Relevant Guidelines*

The **American College of Rheumatology (ACR)** and **European League Against Rheumatism (EULAR)** guidelines strongly recommend combination therapy (biologic plus methotrexate) as standard care in moderate-to-severe RA not responding to DMARD monotherapy, based largely on results from the TEMP trial.

2 TICORA Trial Summary [2]

Full Title: Effect of a Treatment Strategy of Tight Control For Rheumatoid Arthritis: a Single-Blind Randomized Controlled Trial
Publication Year: 2004
Journal: The Lancet

2.1 Background

Before the TICORA trial, treatment for rheumatoid arthritis (RA) often involved infrequent monitoring and slow adjustment of medications. Clinical remission was rarely achieved, and progression of joint damage was common. TICORA aimed to assess whether "tight control"-intensive treatment guided by regular disease activity assessment-could improve outcomes compared to routine care in early RA patients.

2.2 Study Design

Type: Randomized, controlled, open-label trial
Population: 111 patients with early RA(<5 years duration)
Intervention: Monthly clinical assessments using Disease Activity Score (DAS) with aggressive escalation of therapy to achieve low disease activity (DAS < 2.4) (tight control group) vs. every 3 months visits with therapy adjusted at clinical discretion (routine care group)
Primary Outcomes:

- Mean fall in DAS
- Proportion of patients with a good response

Secondary Outcomes:

- Proportion of patients in remission (EULAR)
- ACR response rates

2.3 Results

Primary Outcome:

- Mean fall in DAS: Was significantly greater in tight control group at 18 months (−3.5 vs. -1.9; [95% CI: 1.1–2.1; $p < 0.0001$]).
- Patients with a good response: Patients in the tight control group were more likely to have a good response ($p < 0.0001$) or be in remission ($p < 0.0001$).

Secondary Outcomes:

- EULAR remission: Greater patients in remission in the intensive group compared to the routine care group (65% vs. 16%; OR 9.7; [95% CI: 3.9–23.9; $p < 0.0001$]).
- ACR response: Greater in in intensive group vs. routine care group ($p < 0.0001$).

2.4 *Key Takeaways*

- Tight control of RA using frequent disease activity monitoring and aggressive therapy escalation significantly improved clinical outcomes, reduces joint damage, and enhances quality of life.
- Patients in the intensive group showed greater improvements in disease activity, pain, function, and quality of life than those in routine management.
- Benefits were achieved using conventional DMARDs with structured escalation and frequent monitoring, without biologics.
- Intensive management was cost-neutral compared with routine care, with higher outpatient costs offset by lower inpatient costs
- This trial strongly influenced RA management guidelines, shifting clinical practice towards the treat-to-target paradigm.

2.5 *Clinical Application*

- Employ a treat-to-target strategy with regular DAS or clinical assessments (every 1–2 months) in RA patients, especially in early disease.
- Aim for rapid remission or low disease activity by frequently escalating therapy based on disease activity scores.
- Utilize intra-articular steroids proactively as part of intensive management to quickly suppress flares
- Monitor closely to balance therapeutic efficacy against potential medication-related adverse events.

2.6 *When to Discuss on Rounds*

Discuss this trial on rounds with the following scenarios:

- When emphasizing the importance of treat-to-target strategies in early rheumatoid arthritis.
- When comparing outcomes of intensive management versus routine care in chronic inflammatory diseases.

- When discussing the role of frequent monitoring and structured treatment escalation in achieving remission.
- When reviewing the benefits of combination DMARD therapy and proactive steroid use in tight control regimens

2.7 Relevant Guidelines

The **ACR** and **EULAR** guidelines strongly endorse a tight control (treat-to-target) strategy in RA management, citing the results from the TICORA trial.

3 GO-FORWARD Trial Summary [3]

Full Title: Golimumab, a New Human Anti-TNF-a Monoclonal Antibody, Administered Subcutaneously Every Four Weeks in Patients with Active Rheumatoid Arthritis Despite Methotrexate Therapy.
Publication Year: 2009
Journal: Annals of Rheumatic Disease

3.1 Background

Many patients with rheumatoid arthritis (RA) fail to achieve adequate disease control despite methotrexate (MTX) monotherapy. Golimumab, a fully human monoclonal antibody against tumor necrosis factor-alpha (TNF-a), was developed as a subcutaneous biologic treatment option. The GO-FORWARD trial evaluated the efficacy and safety of golimumab alone or in combination with methotrexate in patients with active RA despite ongoing methotrexate therapy.

3.2 Study Design

Type: Randomized, double-blind, placebo-controlled trial
Population: 444 adult patients with active RA inadequately responding to methotrexate
Intervention: Patients randomized into four groups:

1. Golimumab 100 mg + MTX
2. Golimumab 50 mg + MTX

3. Golimumab 100 mg monotherapy
4. Placebo + MTX

Primary Outcome: American College of Rheumatology 20 (ACR20) response at week 14

Secondary Outcomes:

- ACR50 and ACR70 responses
- Disease Activity Score (DAS28) remission rates
- Improvements in physical function (Health Assessment Questionnaire; HAQ)
- Safety and adverse events

3.3 Results

Primary Outcome:

- ACR20 Response at Week 14:
  - Golimumab 100 mg + MTX: 56% ($p < 0.001$ vs. placebo + MTX)
  - Golimumab 50 mg + MTX: 55% ($p < 0.001$ vs. placebo + MTX)
  - Golimumab 100 mg monotherapy: 44% ($p = 0.059$ vs. placebo + MTX)
  - Placebo + MTX: 33%

Secondary Outcomes:

- ACR50 Response at Week 14:
  - Golimumab 100 mg + MTX: 33% ($p < 0.001$)
  - Golimumab 50 mg + MTX: 35% ($p < 0.001$)
  - Golimumab 100 mg monotherapy: 18% ($p = 0.56$)
  - Placebo + MTX: 10%
- ACR70 Response at Week 14:
  - Golimumab 100 mg + MTX: 13% ($p = 0.021$)
  - Golimumab 50 mg + MTX: 20% ($p = 0.002$)
  - Golimumab 100 mg monotherapy: 7% ($p = 0.43$)
  - Placebo + MTX: 4%
- DAS28 Remission:
  - Higher in combination therapy groups compared to placebo + MTX.
- Physical Function (HAQ) Improvement:
  - Significantly greater improvement with golimumab + MTX compared to placebo + MTX ($p < 0.001$).

- Safety:
  - Adverse events were similar across groups; infections were slightly higher in golimumab groups but generally mild and manageable.

3.4 Key Takeaways

- Golimumab in combination with methotrexate significantly improves clinical outcomes (ACR20, ACR50, ACR70) and physical function in patients inadequately controlled on MTX monotherapy.
- Golimumab monotherapy was less effective compared to combination therapy.
- Golimumab provided an additional safe and effective biologic option for patients with persistent active RA despite MTX.

3.5 Clinical Application

- Consider golimumab combined with methotrexate in patients with active RA inadequately controlled by methotrexate alone.
- Recognize golimumab as a well-tolerated, subcutaneously administered biologic therapy option for RA.
- Evaluate clinical response regularly, considering escalation of therapy in patients not achieving adequate control with methotrexate.

3.6 When to Discuss on Rounds

Discuss this trial on rounds with the following scenarios:

- When evaluating biologic therapy options for RA patients inadequately responding to methotrexate alone.
- When discussing the relative efficacy and safety profiles of TNF inhibitors in RA.
- When teaching trainees about personalized biologic therapy choices in rheumatoid arthritis management.

3.7 Relevant Guidelines

The **ACR** and **EULAR** guidelines endorse the use of TNF inhibitors, including golimumab, in combination with methotrexate for patients with inadequate response to DMARD monotherapy, based on findings from the GO-FORWARD trial.

4 RAVE Trial Summary [4]

Full Title: Rituximab versus Cyclophosphamide for ANCA-Associated Vasculitis
Publication Year: 2010
Journal: New England Journal of Medicine

4.1 *Background*

Before the RAVE trial, cyclophosphamide plus corticosteroids was the standard induction therapy for ANCA-associated vasculitis (AAV), including granulomatosis with polyangiitis (GPA, formerly Wegener's) and microscopic polyangiitis (MPA). Cyclophosphamide is effective but associated with significant toxicity. Rituximab, a monoclonal antibody targeting CD20+ B-cells, emerged as a potential alternative treatment. The RAVE trial compared rituximab to cyclophosphamide for remission induction in patients with severe ANCA-associated vasculitis.

4.2 *Study Design*

Type: Randomized, double-blind, noninferiority trial
Population: 197 patients with severe GPA or MPA
Intervention: Rituximab (375 mg/m^2 weekly x 4) + corticosteroids vs. oral cyclophosphamide (2 mg/kg/day) + corticosteroids, followed by azathioprine after remission
Primary Outcome: Remission of disease without the use of prednisone at six months
Secondary Outcomes:

- Rates of disease flares
- Disease remission while receiving less than 10 mg per day of prednisone
- Rates of adverse events

4.3 *Results*

Primary Outcome:

- Complete remission achieved in 64% of rituximab patients vs. 53% cyclophosphamide patients at 6 months (noninferiority confirmed; $p < 0.001$ for noninferiority).

Secondary Outcomes:

- Rates of disease flares: No significant difference was observed between groups.
- Remission while on less than 10 mg prednisone: 70 patients treated with rituximab remained in remission while receiving less than 10 mg prednisone daily compared to 61 patients in the control group, though this was no significant ($p = 0.10$).
- Adverse events: No significant difference was observed in the numbers of adverse events between groups.

4.4 Key Takeaways

- Rituximab was noninferior to cyclophosphamide for induction therapy of severe ANCA-associated vasculitis.
- In relapsing disease at baseline, rituximab was significantly more effective suggesting superiority in this subgroup.
- Outcomes were similar between rituximab and cyclophosphamide in patients with major renal involvement or alveolar hemorrhage.
- Adverse event rates were comparable between groups, though cyclophosphamide caused more leukopenia; no major new safety concerns with rituximab were identified.
- Both regimens showed similar effects on damage accrual and quality of life at 6 months.
- The trial was limited to ANCA-positive patients with severe disease, excluding those with advanced renal failure or requiring ventilatory support.
- Long-term data are needed to clarify rituximab's role in maintenance therapy and retreatment, especially after B-cell reconstitution.

4.5 Clinical Application

- Use rituximab as first-line induction therapy for patients with GPA or MPA, especially those who have relapsed disease or have contraindications to cyclophosphamide.
- Rituximab is particularly valuable for patients with relapsing disease, where it showed superior efficacy over cyclophosphamide.
- Rituximab may be favored in younger patients or those where cyclophosphamide avoidance is important due to risks of infertility or malignancy.
- Monitor closely for infusion reactions and infections during rituximab therapy.
- Monitoring ANCA levels may provide insight into treatment effect, but clinical response should guide management since ANCA negativity did not always correlate with remission.
- Tailor treatment choices based on patient-specific factors, including previous treatment exposure, disease severity, and side-effect profile considerations.

4.6 When to Discuss on Rounds

Discuss this trial on rounds with the following scenarios:

- When selecting induction therapies for newly diagnosed or relapsing ANCA-associated vasculitis patients.
- When reviewing risks of cyclophosphamide such as infertility or malignancy and considering alternatives.
- When discussing personalized therapeutic choices for vasculitis patients based on disease phenotype and patient comorbidities.

4.7 Relevant Guidelines

The **ACR, EULAR,** and **KDIGO** guidelines recommend Rituximab as an induction therapy for severe ANCA-associated vasculitis, directly influenced by findings from the RAVE trial.

5 RITUXVAS Trial Summary [5]

Full Title: Rituximab versus Cyclophosphamide in ANCA-Associated Renal Vasculitis
Publication Year: 2010
Journal: New England Journal of Medicine

5.1 Background

Before the RITUXVAS trial, cyclophosphamide plus glucocorticoids was the standard induction therapy for patients with severe ANCA-associated vasculitis (AAV) involving significant renal disease. However, cyclophosphamide therapy is associated with serious toxicity, including infection, malignancy, and infertility. Rituximab, a monoclonal antibody targeting CD20+ B-cells, presented a promising alternative. The RITUXVAS trial evaluated rituximab combined with a shorter cyclophosphamide regimen compared to the standard cyclophosphamide regimen for remission induction in patients with severe renal involvement due to ANCA-associated vasculitis.

5.2 *Study Design*

Type: Randomized, controlled, open-label, non-inferiority trial

Population: 44 patients newly diagnosed with ANCA-associated vasculitis (GPA or MPA) with significant renal involvement.

Intervention: Rituximab (375 mg/m^2 weekly x 4 doses) plus two intravenous cyclophosphamide pulses, followed by azathioprine maintenance vs. intravenous cyclophosphamide pulses (15 mg/kg every 2 weeks for 3 doses, then every 3 weeks for additional 3–6 months), followed by azathioprine maintenance

- Both groups received glucocorticoids tapered over 5 months

Primary Outcome: Sustained remission at 12 months (absence of active disease without need for additional immunosuppressants)

Secondary Outcomes:

- Rates of adverse events (particularly infections)
- Renal function outcomes (change in estimated glomerular filtration rate [eGFR])
- Mortality
- Disease relapse rates

5.3 *Results*

Primary Outcome:

- Sustained remission at 12 months:
  - Rituximab group: 76% (16 of 21 patients)
  - Control (cyclophosphamide) group: 82% (18 of 22 patients)
  - Non-inferiority achieved (p = 0.68)

Secondary Outcomes:

- Adverse Events:
  - Similar rates of serious infections between groups (rituximab: 18 episodes; cyclophosphamide: 20 episodes)
  - Infusion-related reactions more common in rituximab group
  - Leukopenia more common in cyclophosphamide group
- Renal outcomes:
  - Median change in eGFR similar between groups (+11 mL/min in rituximab vs. +9 mL/min in cyclophosphamide group; no significant difference)

- Mortality:
  - No significant difference between groups (rituximab group: 4 deaths; cyclophosphamide group: 3 deaths)
- Disease relapse rates:
  - Low and comparable between both groups at 12 months

5.4 *Key Takeaways*

- Rituximab combined with a reduced cyclophosphamide regimen is non-inferior to standard cyclophosphamide therapy in inducing sustained remission in ANCA-associated vasculitis with significant renal involvement.
- Rituximab regimen is associated with fewer hematologic toxicities and comparable infectious risks.
- This trial strongly supports rituximab as an effective alternative induction therapy to reduce cumulative cyclophosphamide exposure and toxicity in renal vasculitis.

5.5 *Clinical Application*

- Use rituximab-based regimens as effective alternatives to prolonged cyclophosphamide induction therapy in patients with severe ANCA-associated renal vasculitis.
- Consider patient-specific factors, such as toxicity risk, fertility preservation, and infection risk, when choosing between rituximab and cyclophosphamide-based induction regimens.
- Closely monitor renal function and adverse events, particularly infections and infusion reactions, during treatment.

5.6 *When to Discuss on Rounds*

Discuss this trial on rounds with the following scenarios:

- When selecting induction therapy for patients presenting with severe ANCA-associated vasculitis and significant renal involvement.
- When teaching trainees about managing immunosuppressive toxicity and therapeutic strategies to minimize long-term risks.
- When discussing individualized therapeutic strategies balancing disease control and treatment-related risks in vasculitis.

5.7 Relevant Guidelines

The **ACR, EULAR,** and **KDIGO** guidelines recommend rituximab-based induction regimens for severe ANCA-associated vasculitis involving renal disease, informed significantly by the RUTXVAS trial findings.

6 BLISS-52 and BLISS-76 Trial Summaries [6, 7]

Full Title:

- BLISS-52: Efficacy and Safety of Belimumab in Patients with Active Systemic Lupus Erythematous
- BLISS-76: Belimumab, a BLyS-specific Inhibitor, Reduced Disease Activity and Severe Flares in Systemic Lupus Erythematosus

Publication Year: 2011
Journal:

- BLISS-52: The Lancet
- BLISS-76: Arthritis & Rheumatism

6.1 Background

Systemic lupus erythematosus (SLE) is a chronic autoimmune disease historically treated with non-specific immunosuppressants, corticosteroids, and antimalarial agents, often leading to significant side effects and incomplete disease control. Belimumab, a monoclonal antibody targeting B-lymphocyte stimulator (BLyS), was developed as the first targeted biologic therapy specifically approved for SLE. The BLISS-52 and BLISS-76 trials evaluated the efficacy and safety of belimumab added to standard-of-care therapy in patients with active SLE.

6.2 Study Design

Type: Randomized, double-blind, placebo-controlled, phase III trials
Population:

- BLISS-52: 865 patients from Asia-Pacific, Latin America, Eastern Europe
- BLISS-76: 819 patients from North America, Europe

Intervention: Intravenous belimumab (1 mg/kg or 10 mg/kg) vs. placebo given at weeks 0, 2, 4, and then every 4 weeks plus standard SLE care

Primary Outcome: SLE Responder Index (SRI-4) response at 52 (≥4-point reduction in SELENA-SLEDAI, no worsening in BILAG, no worsening in Physician's Global Assessment)

Secondary Outcome:

- Reduction in severe disease flares
- Steroid dose reduction
- Safety and adverse events

6.3 *Results*

Primary Outcome:

- BLISS-52 Trial SRI-4 response at 52 weeks:
  - Belimumab 10 mg/kg: 58% ($p < 0.0001$)
  - Belimumab 1 mg/kg: 51% ($p = 0.013$)
  - Placebo: 44%
- BLISS-76 Trial SRI-4 response at 52 weeks:
  - Belimumab 10 mg/kg: 43% ($p = 0.021$)
  - Belimumab 1 mg/kg: 40% (p = 0.0.89, non-significant)
  - Placebo: 34%

Secondary Outcomes:

- Severe Flares:
  - Significantly reduced severe flare rates with belimumab (10 mg/kg) vs. placebo in both trials.
- Steroid Reduction:
  - Greater proportion of patients achieved meaningful corticosteroid dose reduction with belimumab 10 mg/kg compared to placebo.
- Safety:
  - Rates of serious adverse events were comparable across groups.
  - Slightly higher rates of infusion reactions, mild infections, and hypersensitivity observed with belimumab but generally manageable.

6.4 Key Takeaways

- Belimumab significantly improved SLE disease control (as measured by the SRI-4 response) and reduces severe flares when added to standard therapy.
- Enabled significant steroid-sparing effects in SLE patients, thus reducing corticosteroid-related adverse effects.
- Represents the first targeted biologic therapy specifically approved for systemic lupus erythematosus, changing the landscape of lupus management.

6.5 Clinical Application

- Consider belimumab therapy in patients with persistently active SLE despite standard-of-care therapy, especially in patients with serological evidence of active disease (elevated anti-dsDNA, low complement).
- Regularly monitor disease activity and consider gradual corticosteroid tapering once disease activity improves with belimumab therapy.
- Educated patients about infusion reactions and infection risk associated with belimumab.

6.6 When to Discuss on Rounds

Discuss this trial on rounds with the following scenarios:

- When initiating or escalating therapy for patients with moderate-to-severe active lupus despite standard therapy.
- When teaching trainees about the role and rationale for biologic therapies in SLE management.
- When reviewing strategies to minimize corticosteroid-related morbidity in chronic autoimmune conditions.

6.7 Relevant Guidelines

The **ACR** and **EULAR** guidelines endorse belimumab in patients with active systemic lupus erythematosus inadequately controlled by conventional therapy, directly referencing BLISS trials findings.

7 NOR-SWITCH Trial [8]

Full Title: Switching from Originator Infliximab to Biosimilar CT-P13 Compared with Continued Treatment with Originator Infliximab (NOR-SWITCH): A 52-Week Randomized, Double-Blind, Non-Inferiority Trial
Publication Year: 2017
Journal: The Lancet

7.1 Background

Biologic medications, including infliximab, have significantly improved outcomes in autoimmune diseases, but their high cost limits access. Biosimilars are less costly alternatives that are structurally similar to originator biologics. Prior to the NOR-SWITCH trial, there was uncertainty regarding the efficacy, safety, and immunogenicity of switching stable patients from originator infliximab to its biosimilar CTP13 . The NOR-SWITCH trial evaluated the safety and efficacy of switching from originator infliximab to biosimilar CT-P13 across multiple autoimmune diseases.

7.2 Study Design

Type: Randomized, double-blind, non-inferiority trial
Population: 482 stable patients on originator infliximab with inflammatory diseases: rheumatoid arthritis, spondylarthritis, psoriatic arthritis, Crohn's disease, ulcerative colitis, or chronic plaque psoriasis
Intervention: Patients switched from originator infliximab to biosimilar CT-P13 vs. continued originator infliximab
Primary Outcome: Disease worsening at 52 weeks, defined by composite disease-specific endpoints
Secondary Outcomes:

- Time to disease worsening
- Study drug discontinuation
- Overall remission status based on the main composite measures
- Changes in erythrocyte sedimentation rate (ESR) and C-reactive protein (CRP)

7.3 Results

Primary Outcome:

- Disease worsening occurred in 26% of the switch group vs. 30% of the control group, demonstrating non-inferiority of switching to CT-P13 (95% CI -12.7 to 3.9; within pre-specified non-inferiority margin of 15%).

Secondary Outcomes:

- Time to disease worsening: No significant difference was observed between the groups. Disease worsening occurred at similar rates and times.
- Drug discontinuation: Rates of discontinuation were comparable between groups, with no excess risk observed in patients switched to the biosimilar.
- Overall remission: Remission rates at 52 weeks were maintained in both groups, with no significant difference between biosimilar and infliximab.
- ESR/CRP: Both inflammatory markers remained stable and showed no clinically relevant difference between groups during follow-up.

7.4 Key Takeaways

- Switching from infliximab originator to the biosimilar CT-P13 was not inferior to continued originator therapy for disease worsening, within the prespecified 15% non-inferiority margin.
- Secondary endpoints including ESR, CRP, patient- and physician-reported disease activity, and disease-specific composite scores showed no clinically meaningful differences between groups.
- Adverse events and serious adverse events occurred at comparable rates, with no new safety signals; infusion reactions were slightly more frequent in the originator group.
- Immunogenicity and drug trough levels were similar between arms, with no excess development of anti-drug antibodies in the biosimilar group.
- Subgroup analyses by disease type (RA, spondyloarthritis, psoriatic arthritis, IBD, psoriasis) suggested consistency, though the trial was not powered to prove non-inferiority within each disease individually.
- Results support that a single switch from infliximab originator to CT-P13 is safe and effective, but generalizability to multiple switches or other biologics remains uncertain.

7.5 *Clinical Application*

- Safely transition patients from originator biologics to biosimilars without compromising disease control, especially in stable patients.
- Encourage use of biosimilars as cost-effective alternatives to increase patient access to biologic therapy.
- Educate patients and providers regarding the safety and efficacy of biosimilar drugs.

7.6 *When to Discuss on Rounds*

Discuss this trial on rounds with the following scenarios:

- When considering switching biologic therapy to biosimilars in stable patients with autoimmune diseases.
- When explaining that efficacy and safety are generally preserved when switching from a biologic originator to a biosimilar.
- When evaluating strategies for cost-effective management of chronic inflammatory diseases.

7.7 *Relevant Guidelines*

The **ACR**, the **EULAR**, and the **American Gastroenterological Association (AGA)** endorse the use of biosimilars as safe and effective alternatives to originator biologics in patients with rheumatologic and gastrointestinal diseases. These guidelines support clinician-led switching in stable patients, emphasizing shared decision-making and continued disease activity monitoring.

8 PEXIVAS Trial Summary [9]

Full Title: Plasma Exchange and Glucocorticoids in Severe ANCA-Associated Vasculitis
Publication Year: 2020
Journal: New England Journal of Medicine

8.1 Background

Before the PEXIVAS trial, plasma exchange (PLEX) was often used in severe ANCA-associated vasculitis (AAV), particularly for patients with rapidly progressive glomerulonephritis or diffuse alveolar hemorrhage, based on small randomized studies and observational data suggesting potential benefit in reducing progression to end-stage kidney disease. However, evidence for a survival advantage or durable renal protection was inconsistent and limited by trial size. At the same time, standard high-dose glucocorticoid regimens were known to increase infection risk and long-term toxicity, but uncertainty remained over whether reduced-dose regimens could maintain efficacy. The PEXIVAS trial was conducted to provide definitive answers regarding the role of plasma exchange and the optimal steroid dosing strategy in severe AAV.

8.2 Study Design

Type: Multicenter, international, randomized controlled trial
Population: 352 patients with severe ANCA-associated vasculitis (defined as an estimated glomerular filtration rate of <50 ml per minute per 1.73 m^2 of body-surface area or diffuse pulmonary hemorrhage)
Interventions:

- Plasma exchange within 14 days after randomization vs. no plasma exchange
- Standard- dose glucocorticoid regimen vs. reduced-dose regimen of glucocorticoids

Primary Outcomes: Composite of all-cause mortality or end-stage kidney disease
Secondary Outcomes:

- All-cause mortality
- End-stage kidney disease
- Sustained remission
- Serious adverse events
- Serious infections within 1 year
- Health-related quality of life

8.3 Results

Primary Outcome:

- The primary outcome occurred in 28.4% of patients in the plasma-exchange group compared to 31.0% of patients in the control group, which was not statistically significant (HR 0.86; [95% CI: 0.65–1.13; p = 0.27]).
- Death from any cause or end-stage kidney disease occurred in 27.9% of patients in the reduced-dose group compared to 25.5% in the standard-dose group, which met criterion for noninferiority.

Secondary Outcomes:

- All-cause mortality: No significant difference between plasma exchange and no plasma exchange; mortality was similar across glucocorticoid regimens as well.
- End-stage kidney disease: Plasma exchange did not significantly reduce the risk of progression to ESKD compared with no plasma exchange.
- Sustained remission: Rates of sustained remission were similar across plasma exchange and control groups, and between standard-dose and reduced-dose glucocorticoid regimens.
- Serious adverse events: Overall rates were comparable between plasma exchange and control groups; however, the reduced-dose glucocorticoid regimen was associated with fewer serious adverse events compared to the standard-dose group.
- Serious infections within 1 year: Significantly fewer occurred in the reduced-dose glucocorticoid group compared to the standard-dose group; plasma exchange had no impact.
- Health-related quality of life: No significant differences were observed between groups for quality-of-life outcomes.

8.4 Key Takeaways

- Plasma exchange did not reduce the incidence of death or end-stage kidney disease (ESKD) compared with no plasma exchange.
- The reduced-dose glucocorticoid regimen was noninferior to the standard-dose regimen for preventing death or ESKD.
- Patients on the reduced-dose regimen experienced significantly fewer serious infections in the first year compared with those on standard-dose steroids.
- Rates of sustained remission, serious adverse events, and health-related quality of life outcomes were similar between groups.
- The trial's findings challenge prior smaller studies that suggested benefit of plasma exchange, including in patients with pulmonary hemorrhage.
- Results support that lower-dose glucocorticoids can be used safely, reducing infection risk while maintaining efficacy in severe ANCA-associated vasculitis.

8.5 Clinical Application

- Plasma exchange should not be routinely used for severe ANCA-associated vasculitis, as it does not improve survival or reduce risk of ESKD.
- Consider reserving plasma exchange only for select cases (e.g., catastrophic pulmonary hemorrhage) where benefit is still uncertain.

- A reduced-dose glucocorticoid regimen can be safely used as initial therapy, lowering infection risk without compromising efficacy.
- When starting induction therapy, clinicians can confidently taper steroids earlier while maintaining disease control.

8.6 When to Discuss on Rounds

Discuss this trial on rounds with the following scenarios:

- When discussing management of patients with ANCA-associated vasculitis.
- When deciding whether to add plasma exchange to induction therapy.
- When choosing between high-dose versus reduced-dose glucocorticoid regimens.
- When reviewing evidence for preventing progression to end-stage kidney disease in vasculitis.

8.7 Relevant Guidelines

The **ACR/Vasculitis Foundation** guidelines and the **EULAR** guidelines incorporate the findings of the PEXIVAS trial. Both recommend against the routine use of plasma exchange in ANCA-associated vasculitis, even in patients with severe renal involvement, though they allow consideration in select cases such as life-threatening pulmonary hemorrhage. Additionally, these guidelines support reduced-dose glucocorticoid regimens for remission induction, citing PEXIVAS as evidence that lower steroid exposure is noninferior for survival and kidney outcomes while reducing infection risk.

9 AGREE Trial Summary [10]

Full Title: Clinical Efficacy and Safety of Abatacept in Methotrexate-Naive Patients With Early Rheumatoid Arthritis and Poor Prognostic Factors
Publication Year: 2009
Journal: Annals of the Rheumatic Diseases

9.1 Background

Early treatment of rheumatoid arthritis (RA) is essential to prevent joint damage and functional impairment. Abatacept, a selective T-cell co-stimulation modulator, had demonstrated efficacy in patients inadequately responsive to methotrexate (MTX). Prior to the AGREE trial, the role of abatacept as initial therapy in MTX-naive patients with early RA was unclear. The AGREE trial evaluated whether combination therapy with abatacept plus MTX could achieve superior clinical remission rates and prevent joint damage compared to MTX alone in early RA.

9.2 Study Design

Type: Randomized, double-blind, placebo-controlled trial
Population: 500 patients with early erosive RA (symptom duration ≤2 years), methotrexate-naive
Intervention: Abatacept plus MTX: IV abatacept (~10 mg/kg) plus MTX weekly vs. MTX weekly plus placebo infusions
Primary Outcomes:

- Remission rates (DAS28-CRP <2.6) at one year
- Joint damage progression (modified Sharp total score) at one year

Secondary Outcomes:

- ACR50/70/90 responses
- Joint-space narrowing
- Physical function
- Health Assessment Questionnaire Disability Index (HAQ-DI) improvement

9.3 Results

Primary Outcomes:

- Remission rates: Significantly higher remission rates (DAS28-CRP <2.6) at 1 year with abatacept plus MTX compared to MTX monotherapy (41.4% vs. 23.3%; $p < 0.001$).
- Joint damage: Significantly less radiographic evidence of joint damage progression in the abatacept group plus MTX compared to MTX monotherapy ($p = 0.04$).

Secondary Outcomes:

- ACR response rates:
  - ACR50: Significantly higher with abatacept plus MTX (57.4% vs. 42.3%; $p < 0.001$).
  - ACR70: Higher with abatacept plus MTX (42.6% vs. 27.3%; $p < 0.001$).
  - ACR90: Higher with abatacept plus MTX (16.4% vs. 6.7%; $p = 0.001$).
- Joint-space narrowing: Progression was significantly reduced with combination therapy compared with methotrexate only, indicating better protection against structural damage.
- Physical function: Improved more with abatacept plus methotrexate, with patients reporting less disability and better daily functioning ($p = 0.005$).
- HAQ-DI improvement: Greater improvement with abatacept plus MTX compared to MTX alone ($p = 0.024$).

9.4 Key Takeaways

- Abatacept combined with methotrexate significantly increased clinical remission rates, reduced joint damage progression, and improved functional outcomes compared to methotrexate alone in early RA patients.
- Safety outcomes, including adverse events and serious infections, were comparable between groups, with no new safety signals.

9.5 Clinical Application

- Consider abatacept plus MTX as initial therapy in patients with early erosive RA to achieve rapid and sustained remission and minimize long-term joint damage.
- Monitor closely for infections and adverse events, though overall tolerability of abatacept is favorable.
- Educate patients about the importance of early aggressive treatment in RA management to prevent irreversible joint damage.

9.6 When to Discuss on Rounds

Discuss this trial on rounds with the following scenarios:

- When discussing treatment options for early RA patients with high-risk features such as seropositivity and erosions.
- When explaining why biologics may be started earlier in aggressive RA rather than waiting for methotrexate failure.
- When considering quality-of-life outcomes in addition to disease activity in RA management.

9.7 *Relevant Guidelines*

The **ACR** and **EULAR** guidelines support early aggressive therapy with combination biologic DMARDs (such as abatacept plus MTX) in early RA patients to achieve rapid remission, informed by findings from the AGREE trial.

10 CARES Trial Summary [11]

Full Title: Cardiovascular Safety of Febuxostat or Allopurinol in Patients with Gout
Publication Year: 2018
Journal: New England Journal of Medicine

10.1 *Background*

Gout is associated with increased cardiovascular risk, and urate-lowering therapy is often lifelong. Febuxostat, a xanthine oxidase inhibitor, was developed as an alternative to allopurinol, especially for patients with intolerance or renal dysfunction. However, concerns were raised about its cardiovascular safety, prompting the CARES trial to compare outcomes between febuxostat and allopurinol in high-risk patients.

10.2 *Study Design*

Type: Multicenter, double-blind, noninferiority trial
Population: 6190 patients with a diagnosis of gout
Intervention: Fuboxostat 40 mg once daily if serum urate level was less than 6.0 mg/dl after 2 weeks of therapy or 80 mg daily if serum urate >6.0 mg/dl vs. renally dosed allopurinol starting at 300 mg once daily and increased in 100 mg increments until serum urate was <6.0 mg/dl
Primary Outcome: Composite of cardiovascular death, nonfatal myocardial infarction, nonfatal stroke, or unstable angina with urgent revascularization
Secondary Outcomes:

- Composite of cardiovascular death, nonfatal myocardial infarction, or nonfatal stroke
- Individual components of the composite primary outcome

10.3 Results

Primary Outcome: The primary composite outcome occurred in 10.8% of patients in the febuxostat group compared to 10.4% in the allopurinol group (HR 1.03; [95% CI: 1.23; p = 0.002]).

Secondary Outcomes:

- There was no statistically significant difference observed in the secondary composite outcome, nonfatal MI, nonfatal stroke, or need for revascularization.
- Cardiovascular death: Occurred more often in the febuxostat group vs. the allopurinol group (HR 1.34; [95% CI: 1.03–1.73; p = 0.03]).
- All-cause mortality: Deaths from any cause occurred more frequently in the febuxostat group vs. allopurinol (HR 1.22; [95% CI: 1.01–1.47; p = 0.04]).

10.4 Key Takeaways

- Febuxostat and allopurinol had similar rates of major adverse cardiovascular events (MACE), meeting criteria for non-inferiority.
- Rates of nonfatal events (MI, stroke, revascularization, HF hospitalization, arrhythmia) were similar between groups.
- Gout control (urate lowering and flare rates) was comparable between febuxostat and allopurinol.
- The mechanism of excess cardiovascular deaths with febuxostat remains unclear, as preclinical data showed no direct cardiotoxicity.
- Trial limitations included high discontinuation and loss to follow-up rates, but the mortality imbalance persisted across analyses.

10.5 Clinical Application

- Use allopurinol as first-line urate-lowering therapy for most patients with gout, especially those with cardiovascular disease.
- Reserve **febuxostat** only for patients who cannot tolerate or have contraindications to allopurinol.
- Monitor closely for **cardiovascular events** in patients already on febuxostat, especially those with prior MI, stroke, or heart failure.

10.6 When to Discuss on Rounds

Discuss this trial on rounds with the following scenarios:

- When presenting a patient with gout and cardiovascular disease who needs urate-lowering therapy, mention the CARES trial to highlight the mortality concerns with febuxostat compared to allopurinol.
- When discussing why allopurinol is considered the preferred first-line urate-lowering therapy in guidelines.
- When comparing different xanthine oxidase inhibitors, explain that urate control is similar between febuxostat and allopurinol, but cardiovascular outcomes differ.

10.7 Relevant Guidelines

The **ACR** gout guidelines recommend allopurinol as the preferred first-line urate-lowering therapy, including in patients with chronic kidney disease, largely influenced by safety concerns raised in the CARES trial. Febuxostat is reserved for patients who cannot tolerate or do not respond adequately to allopurinol. Similarly, the **EULAR** guidelines emphasize caution with febuxostat use in patients with established cardiovascular disease, citing the increased cardiovascular and all-cause mortality observed in CARES.

References

1. Klareskog L, van der Heijde D, de Jager JP, et al. TEMPO Study Investigators. Therapeutic effect of the combination of etanercept and methotrexate compared with each treatment alone in patients with rheumatoid arthritis. N Engl J Med. 2004;350(25):2531–42. https://doi.org/10.1056/NEJMoa031424.
2. Grigor C, Capell H, Stirling A, et al. Effect of a treatment strategy of tight control for rheumatoid arthritis (the TICORA study): a single-blind randomized controlled trial. Lancet. 2004;364(9430):263–9. https://doi.org/10.1016/S0140-6736(04)16676-2.
3. Keystone EC, Genovese MC, Klareskog L, et al. Golimumab, a human antibody to tumour necrosis factor {alpha} given by monthly subcutaneous injections, in active rheumatoid arthritis despite methotrexate therapy: the GO-FORWARD Study [published correction appears in Ann Rheum Dis. 2011;70(1):238]. Ann Rheum Dis. 2009;68(6):789–96. https://doi.org/10.1136/ard.2008.099010.
4. Stone JH, Merkel PA, Spiera R, et al. Rituximab versus cyclophosphamide for ANCA-associated vasculitis. N Engl J Med. 2010;363(3):221–32. https://doi.org/10.1056/NEJMoa0909905.
5. Jones RB, Tervaert JW, Hauser T, et al. Rituximab versus cyclophosphamide in ANCA-associated renal vasculitis. N Engl J Med 2010;363(3):211–220. doi:https://doi.org/10.1056/NEJMoa0909169.
6. Navarra SV, Guzmán RM, Gallacher AE, et al. Efficacy and safety of belimumab in patients with active systemic lupus erythematosus: a randomised, placebo-controlled, phase 3 trial. Lancet. 2011;377(9767):721–31. https://doi.org/10.1016/S0140-6736(10)61354-2.

7. Furie R, Petri M, Zamani O, et al. A phase III, randomized, placebo-controlled study of belimumab, a monoclonal antibody that inhibits B lymphocyte stimulator, in patients with systemic lupus erythematosus. Arthritis Rheum. 2011;63(12):3918–30. https://doi.org/10.1002/art.30613.
8. Jørgensen KK, Olsen IC, Goll GL, et al. Switching from originator infliximab to biosimilar CT-P13 compared with maintained treatment with originator infliximab (NOR-SWITCH): a 52-week, randomised, double-blind, non-inferiority trial [published correction appears in Lancet. 2017 Jun 10;389(10086):2286. Doi: 10.1016/S0140-6736(17)31423-X]. Lancet. 2017;389(10086):2304–16. https://doi.org/10.1016/S0140-6736(17)30068-5.
9. Walsh M, Merkel PA, Peh CA, et al. Plasma exchange and glucocorticoids in severe ANCA-associated vasculitis. N Engl J Med. 2020;382(7):622–31. https://doi.org/10.1056/NEJMoa1803537.
10. Westhovens R, Robles M, Ximenes AC, et al. Clinical efficacy and safety of abatacept in methotrexate-naive patients with early rheumatoid arthritis and poor prognostic factors. Ann Rheum Dis. 2009;68(12):1870–7. https://doi.org/10.1136/ard.2008.101121.
11. White WB, Saag KG, Becker MA, et al. Cardiovascular safety of Febuxostat or allopurinol in patients with gout. N Engl J Med. 2018;378(13):1200–10. https://doi.org/10.1056/NEJMoa1710895.

Chapter 9
Gastroenterology

1 STOPAH Trial Summary [1]

Full Title: Prednisolone or Pentoxifylline for Alcoholic Hepatitis
Publication Year: 2015
Journal: New England Journal of Medicine

1.1 Background

Alcoholic hepatitis is associated with significant morbidity and mortality. Before the STOPAH trial, guidelines recommended corticosteroids or pentoxifylline for severe alcoholic hepatitis, though evidence supporting their benefit was inconsistent and uncertain. The STOPAH trial was designed to evaluate the effectiveness of prednisolone and pentoxifylline, either alone or combined, compared to placebo in reducing short-term mortality among patients with severe alcoholic hepatitis.

1.2 Study Design

Type: Multicenter, randomized, double-blind, placebo-controlled trial (factorial 2x2 design)
Population: 1103 patients with severe alcoholic hepatitis (Maddrey's discriminant function ≥32)
Intervention: Patients were randomized into four groups:

A. Love, *The Essential Evidence*, https://doi.org/10.1007/978-3-032-12399-2_9

1. Prednisolone (40 mg daily for 28 days) plus pentoxifylline placebo
2. Pentoxifylline (400 mg three times daily for 28 days) plus prednisolone placebo
3. Combination therapy (prednisolone plus pentoxifylline)
4. Double placebo

Primary Outcome: 28-day mortality
Secondary Outcomes:

- Death or liver transplantation at 90 days
- Death or liver transplantation at 1 year

1.3 Results

Primary Outcome:

- Prednisolone-placebo: 14% of patients died at 28 days (OR 0.72; [95% CI: 0.52–1.02; p = 0.06]).
- Pentoxifylline-placebo: 19% of patients died at 28 days (OR 1.07; [95% CI: 0.77–1.49; p = 0.69]).
- No benefit seen with combination therapy compared to placebo (p = 0.41).

Secondary Outcomes: Prednisolone and pentoxifylline were found to have no influence on mortality or the need for liver transplantation at 90 days and 1 year.

1.4 Key Takeaways

- Prednisolone showed a borderline reduction in short-term mortality (28-day) but no longer-term survival benefit.
- Pentoxifylline provided no survival advantage.
- Infections were more frequent in patients receiving prednisolone, but this did not translate into higher infection-related mortality.
- The study led clinicians to reconsider routine use of these therapies, emphasizing individualized risk-benefit assessment, particularly considering infection risks.

1.5 Clinical Application

- Consider prednisolone in select patients with severe alcoholic hepatitis and low infection risk, acknowledging limited evidence of long-term benefit.
- Do not routinely use pentoxifylline, as it shows no benefit.

- Monitor closely for infections when prescribing corticosteroids, given the increased risk observed with prednisolone.
- Counsel patients and families that prognosis remains poor despite therapy, emphasizing the critical role of alcohol cessation for long-term survival.
- Prioritize supportive care and alcohol cessation efforts as primary management strategies.

1.6 When to Discuss on Rounds

Discuss this trial on rounds with the following scenarios:

- When evaluating treatment options for hospitalized patients with severe alcoholic hepatitis.
- When explaining why pentoxifylline is no longer recommended for alcoholic hepatitis.
- When discussing the limitations of prednisolone, including short-term but not long-term benefit.
- When discussing guidelines and evidence-based management of alcoholic liver disease.
- When counseling about prognosis and emphasizing alcohol cessation as the most important determinant of long-term survival.

1.7 Relevant Guidelines

The **American Association for the Study of Liver Diseases (AASLD)** and **European Association for the Study of the Liver (EASL)** guidelines acknowledge the STOPAH trial results, recommending selective corticosteroid use in severe alcoholic hepatitis while strongly emphasizing supportive care and alcohol abstinence.

2 Early TIPS Trial [2]

Full Title: Early Use of TIPS in Patients with Cirrhosis and Variceal Bleeding
Publication Year: 2010
Journal: New England Journal of Medicine

2.1 Background

Acute variceal bleeding in patients with cirrhosis carries significant mortality risk. Standard treatment involves endoscopic band ligation, vasoactive drugs, and antibiotics. Transjugular intrahepatic portosystemic shunt (TIPS) was traditionally reserved as rescue therapy after standard treatments failed. The Early TIPS trial evaluated whether early TIPS placement within 72 hours of initial bleeding would improve survival and prevent rebleeding in high-risk cirrhotic patients compared to standard therapy.

2.2 Study Design

Type: Randomized, controlled trial
Population: 63 patients with cirrhosis and variceal bleeding at high risk of treatment failure (Child-Pugh class B with active bleeding at endoscopy or Child-Pugh class C)
Intervention: TIPS placed within 72 hours of initial bleeding plus standard medical therapy vs. endoscopic band ligation plus vasoactive drugs (octreotide), antibiotics, and TIPS only as rescue therapy
Primary Outcome: Rebleeding or failure to control acute bleeding at 1 year
Secondary Outcomes:

- Survival at 6 weeks and at 1 year
- Failure to control acute bleeding
- Early rebleeding
- Rate of rebleeding between 6 weeks and 1 year
- Number of days in the intensive care unit

2.3 Results

Primary Outcome:

- Significantly lower rebleeding rates with early TIPS vs. standard therapy (1 patient vs. 14 patients; $p < 0.001$).

Secondary Outcomes:

- Survival:
  - 6 weeks: Survival was higher in the early TIPS group at 97% compared to 67% in the pharmacotherapy group (ARR 30%; [95% CI: 12–48])
  - 1 year: Higher survival at 1 year in the early TIPS group than in the pharmacotherapy group 86% vs. 61% (ARR 25%; [95% CI: 2–48])

- Early rebleeding: Occurred in 7 patients in the pharmacotherapy group and 0 in the early TIPS group.
- Rebleeding >6 wk-1 yr.: Occurred in 3 patients in the pharmacotherapy group and 0 in the early TIPS group.
- Days in ICU: Significantly greater amount of days were spent in the ICU in the pharmacotherapy group (8.6 ± 9 vs. 3.6 ± 4, p = 0.01).

2.4 Key Takeaways

- Early TIPS placement with e-PTFE–covered stents in high-risk patients (Child–Pugh class C or class B with active bleeding) significantly reduced failure to control bleeding and rebleeding compared to pharmacotherapy plus endoscopic band ligation.
- Survival was markedly improved with early TIPS, with higher 6-week and 1-year survival rates compared to standard therapy.
- Rescue TIPS after treatment failure was associated with poor outcomes and high mortality, underscoring the benefit of early intervention rather than delayed use.
- Early TIPS did not increase the risk of hepatic encephalopathy compared with standard care.
- These findings challenge the prior paradigm of reserving TIPS only as a rescue therapy, supporting its proactive use in carefully selected high-risk patients.

2.5 Clinical Application

- Use early TIPS in patients with acute variceal bleeding who are high risk, particularly Child–Pugh class C or class B with active bleeding.
- Reserve TIPS as rescue therapy only in lower-risk patients, as outcomes with delayed rescue TIPS are significantly worse.
- Reassure that early TIPS does not significantly increase hepatic encephalopathy risk compared to standard therapy.
- Recognize that early TIPS improves both rebleeding control and overall survival, shifting practice beyond its prior role as salvage therapy.

2.6 When to Discuss on Rounds

Discuss this trial on rounds with the following scenarios:

- When managing acute variceal bleeding in cirrhotic patients, especially those at high risk.

- When reviewing acute gastrointestinal bleeding management protocols in patients with decompensated cirrhosis.
- When highlighting that rescue TIPS after treatment failure carries high mortality, making early intervention more effective.

2.7 Relevant Guidelines

The **AASLD** and **EASL** guidelines now strongly recommend early TIPS placement for patients at high risk of treatment failure in acute variceal bleeding, based on findings from this landmark trial.

3 SONIC Trial Summary [3]

Full Title: Infliximab, Azathioprine, or Combination Therapy for Crohn's Disease
Publication Year: 2010
Journal: New England Journal of Medicine

3.1 Background

Traditionally, moderate-to-severe Crohn's disease (CD) was managed with a step-up approach, starting with immunomodulators like azathioprine and escalating to biologics like infliximab upon failure. The SONIC trial was designed to assess whether combination therapy from the outset could achieve superior clinical remission and mucosal healing compared to monotherapy with either in treatment-naive patients.

3.2 Study Design

Type: Randomized, double-blind, controlled trial
Population: 508 adults with moderate-to-severe CD, treatment-naive to biologics and immunomodulators
Intervention: Infliximab plus azathioprine vs. infliximab monotherapy vs. azathioprine monotherapy
Primary Outcome: Corticosteroid-free clinical remission at 26 weeks
Secondary Outcomes:

- Mucosal healing at 26 weeks
- Rate of any remission
- IBDQ score (quality of life)
- Change in CRP level form baseline to week 26

3.3 Results

Primary Outcome: Combination therapy resulted in significantly higher steroid-free remission (56.8%) compared with infliximab alone (44.4%, $p = 0.02$) and azathioprine alone (30.0%, $p < 0.001$).

Secondary Outcomes:

- Mucosal healing:
  - Baseline mucosal ulcerations were found in 65.7% of patients in the combination therapy group, 58.6% of patients in the infliximab group, and 67.6% of patients in the azathioprine group.
  - At week 26 mucosal healing had occurred in 43.9% of patients in the combination therapy group, 30.1% in the infliximab group, and 16.5% in the azathioprine group (infliximab vs. azathioprine $p = 0.02$, combination therapy vs. azathioprine $p < 0.001$, and combination therapy vs. infliximab $p = 0.06$).
- Rate of any remission: At week 26, corticosteroid-free remission rates were 56.8% (combo), 44.4% (infliximab), and 30.0% (azathioprine).
- IBDQ score: Mean improvement was greatest in the combination group, intermediate in infliximab, and lowest in azathioprine ($P < 0.001$ for combo vs. azathioprine, $P = 0.02$ for combo vs. infliximab).
- Change in CRP: Larger reductions seen in the combination group and infliximab group, both significantly greater than azathioprine alone.

3.4 Key Takeaways

- Early initiation of combination therapy with infliximab and azathioprine significantly improves remission and mucosal healing compared to monotherapy.
- Infliximab monotherapy was more effective than azathioprine alone but less effective than combination therapy.
- Combination therapy reduced the development of anti-infliximab antibodies and maintained higher drug trough levels, supporting improved durability of response.
- Safety profiles were broadly similar across groups, though combination therapy carries known risks of rare but serious adverse events, including infections and malignancy.

- Overall, SONIC established infliximab–azathioprine combination therapy as the most effective induction approach for biologic- and immunomodulator-naïve Crohn's disease patients.

3.5 Clinical Application

- Initiate combination therapy early in moderate-to-severe CD patients who have not yet received biologics or immunomodulators.
- Prefer combination therapy over azathioprine monotherapy, which is less effective for induction of remission.
- Consider infliximab monotherapy when azathioprine is contraindicated or not tolerated, recognizing it is less effective than combination therapy.
- Monitor CRP and endoscopic findings, as patients with objective inflammation benefit most from infliximab-based therapy.
- Be cautious with long-term combination therapy, balancing superior efficacy against risks of infection and rare malignancies.

3.6 When to Discuss on Rounds

Discuss this trial on rounds with the following scenarios:

- When initiating therapy in newly diagnosed Crohn's patients.
- When discussing the advantages of combination therapy vs. monotherapy.
- When reviewing goals of therapy, especially mucosal healing and remission rates.
- When discussing how combination therapy reduces anti-drug antibody formation and maintains higher infliximab trough levels.
- When weighing efficacy benefits against safety concerns of dual immunosuppression.

3.7 Relevant Guidelines

The **American Gastroenterological Association (AGA)** and the **European Crohn's and Colitis Organization (ECCO)** recommend early combination therapy for induction in moderate-to-severe Crohn's disease, based primarily on the SONIC trial.

4 OCTAVE Trials (OCTAVE Induction 1 & 2) Summary [4]

Full Title: Tofacitinib as Induction Therapy for Ulcerative Colitis
Publication Year: 2017
Journal: New England Journal of Medicine

4.1 Background

Patients with moderate-to-severe ulcerative colitis (UC) often fail or lose response to anti-TNF therapy, prompting a need for alternative therapeutic targets. Tofacitinib, an oral JAK inhibitor, offers a novel mechanism of action. The OCTAVE Induction trials evaluated the efficacy and safety of tofacitinib as induction therapy for UC.

4.2 Study Design

Type: Two parallel randomized, double-blind, placebo-controlled, phase III trials
Population: 1139 adults with moderate-to-severe UC (Mayo score 6–12, endoscopic subscore ≥2), many previously exposed to biologics
Intervention: Tofacitinib 10 mg twice daily vs. placebo for 8 weeks
Primary Outcome: Clinical remission at week 8 (total Mayo score ≤ 2, no subscore >1)
Secondary Outcomes: Mucosal healing at 8 weeks

4.3 Results

Primary Outcome:

OCTAVE Induction 1: Tofacitinib 18.5% vs. placebo 8.2% ($p = 0.007$)
OCTAVE Induction 2: Tofacitinib 16.6% vs. placebo 3.6% ($p < 0.001$)

Secondary Outcome:

Mucosal healing: Significantly greater in tofacitinib groups (OCTAVE 1: 31.3%, OCTAVE 2: 28.4%) compared to placebo (OCTAVE 1: 15.6%, OCTAVE 2: 11.6%; $p < 0.001$)

4.4 Key Takeaways

Tofacitinib 10 mg BID was significantly more effective than placebo for induction of remission at 8 weeks in moderate-to-severe ulcerative colitis.

Mucosal healing rates were higher with tofacitinib compared with placebo during induction and maintenance phases.

Clinical benefit was consistent in patients regardless of prior anti-TNF exposure or failure, supporting efficacy in both biologic-naïve and experienced populations.

Improvements were observed early, with symptom relief and partial Mayo score reduction as early as 2 weeks.

Patient-reported outcomes (IBDQ scores, quality of life) improved significantly with tofacitinib in both induction and maintenance trials.

Safety profile included increased rates of infections (notably herpes zoster), mild lipid elevations, and rare serious adverse events such as GI perforation and non-melanoma skin cancer.

Serious infection rates were low overall but numerically higher during induction; herpes zoster risk was more pronounced with the 10 mg dose.

OCTAVE trials established tofacitinib as an effective oral non-biologic option for patients with moderate-to-severe ulcerative colitis who fail or cannot tolerate conventional or biologic therapies.

4.5 Clinical Application

- Use tofacitinib as induction therapy for moderate-to-severe UC, particularly after failure of biologic therapies.
- Consider tofacitinib for patients preferring an oral agent over infusion or injection therapies.
- Use tofacitinib 5 mg BID for maintenance in responders; reserve 10 mg BID for patients with inadequate response, balancing efficacy with infection risk.
- Proactively monitor patients for infections and lipid abnormalities associated with JAK inhibitors.
- Avoid in patients with high malignancy risk (e.g., prior skin cancers) unless benefits outweigh risks.

4.6 When to Discuss on Rounds

Discuss this trial on rounds with the following scenarios:

- When managing moderate-to-severe UC patients who are refractory to or intolerant of biologics.

- When teaching trainees about novel oral therapies and risks associated with JAK inhibitors.
- When counseling patients about options following biologic therapy failure.

4.7 Relevant Guidelines

The **AGA** and the **ACG** recommend tofacitinib as an induction and maintenance therapy option for patients with moderate-to-severe UC who failed conventional or biologic therapies, directly referencing OCTAVE trial data.

5 HALT-C Trial Summary [5]

Full Title: Prolonged Therapy of Advanced Chronic Hepatitis C with Low-Dose Peginterferon
Publication Year: 2008
Journal: New England Journal of Medicine

5.1 Background

Chronic hepatitis C Infection leads to progressive liver fibrosis and cirrhosis, especially in patients unresponsive to initial antiviral therapy. Prior to the direct-acting antiviral (DAA) era, prolonged interferon therapy was hypothesized to halt fibrosis progression. The HALT-C trial assessed whether prolonged low-dose peginterferon alfa-2a could prevent clinical progression in chronic hepatitis C patients who previously failed standard antiviral treatment.

5.2 Study Design

Type: Multicenter, randomized, controlled trial
Population: 1050 chronic hepatitis C patients with advanced fibrosis or compensated cirrhosis who failed previous antiviral treatment
Intervention: Peginterferon alfa-2a (90 μg weekly) maintenance therapy vs. no treatment (observation)
Primary Outcome: Clinical progression (defined as death, hepatocellular carcinoma, hepatic decompensation, or increased Child-Pugh score)
Secondary Outcomes:

- Change in quality of life
- Serious adverse events
- Increase in fibrosis from baseline
- Development of presumed hepatocellular carcinoma (HCC)

5.3 *Results*

Primary Outcome: No significant difference was observed in the primary outcome between maintenance therapy (34.1%) and the control group (33.8%) (HR 1.01; [95% CI: 0.81–1.27; p = 0.90]).

Secondary Outcomes:

- Change in quality of life: No significant differences were observed between maintenance peginterferon and placebo; patients in both groups reported declines over time, largely reflecting disease progression rather than treatment effect.
- Serious adverse events: Occurred more frequently in the peginterferon group (38%) compared with placebo (34%), though the difference was not statistically significant.
- Increase in fibrosis from baseline: Progression of fibrosis on serial biopsies was similar between the two groups, with no clear benefit of maintenance peginterferon in slowing histologic progression.
- Development of HCC: Rates of HCC were not significantly different between groups, occurring in about 7% of the peginterferon group and 6% of the placebo group during follow-up.

5.4 *Key Takeaways*

- Long-term low-dose peginterferon therapy provides no clinical or histologic benefit in chronic hepatitis C patients who failed standard antiviral therapy.
- The trial significantly influenced hepatitis C management prior to the introduction of DAAs, shifting focus away from interferon-based maintenance therapy.
- The trial highlights the importance of achieving sustained virologic response with effective antiviral therapy rather than relying on suppressive interferon strategies.
- This trial represents a historical pivot point that highlights how limited and toxic older therapies were, underscoring the transformative impact of modern direct-acting antivirals.

5.5 Clinical Application

- Maintenance peginterferon should not be prescribed for patients with chronic hepatitis C who did not achieve a sustained virologic response.
- Clinical management of these patients should focus on cirrhosis care and hepatocellular carcinoma surveillance rather than interferon maintenance.
- The trial underscored the need for effective antiviral therapy that achieves viral eradication instead of long-term suppression.
- Patients with advanced fibrosis should be prioritized for curative direct-acting antiviral regimens, which are now the standard of care and achieve sustained virologic response in the vast majority of patients.

5.6 When to Discuss on Rounds

Discuss this trial on rounds with the following scenarios:

- When evaluating the historical context and effectiveness of interferon-based therapy for hepatitis C.
- When explaining rationale for transition from interferon-based to DAA-based treatments.

5.7 Relevant Guidelines

The **AASLD** and **EASL** guidelines recommend against interferon maintenance therapy for hepatitis C, based on evidence from HALT-C. Instead, both societies endorse direct-acting antivirals as the standard of care for all patients with chronic HCV infection, given their high rates of sustained virologic response and ability to halt disease progression. HALT-C remains historically important because it established that interferon maintenance provided no long-term benefit, paving the way for guidelines to shift focus toward curative therapies rather than disease suppression.

6 POISE Trial Summary [6]

Full Title: A Placebo-Controlled Trial of Obeticholic Acid in Primary Biliary Cholangitis
Publication Year: 2016
Journal: New England Journal of Medicine

6.1 Background

Primary biliary cholangitis (PBC) is a chronic autoimmune liver disease treated first-line with ursodeoxycholic acid (UDCA). However, many patients have an inadequate response. Obeticholic acid (OCA), a farnesoid X receptor agonist, was developed as a second-line therapy. The POISE trial evaluated the efficacy and safety of OCA in patients with PBC who were inadequately responding to UDCA.

6.2 Study Design

Type: Randomized, placebo-controlled, double-blind phase III trial
Population: 217 patients with PBC inadequately responsive or intolerant to UDCA
Intervention: OCA 5–10 mg daily (dose titration) or placebo
Primary Outcome: Reduction in alkaline phosphatase (ALP) levels below 1.67x upper limit of normal, ≥15% decrease from baseline, and normal bilirubin at 12 months
Secondary Outcomes:

- Change in liver biochemistry (bilirubin, AST, ALT)
- Safety, adverse events, and pruritis severity

6.3 Results

Primary Outcome: Significantly higher response in OCA group (47%) compared to placebo group (10%; $p < 0.001$).
Secondary Outcomes:

- Change in liver biochemistry:
  - Obeticholic acid significantly reduced alkaline phosphatase compared to placebo at 12 months, with mean reductions of −113 U/L (5–10 mg) and − 130 U/L (10 mg) versus −14 U/L in placebo ($P < 0.001$ for both).
  - Total bilirubin decreased slightly in both obeticholic acid groups (−0.02 and − 0.05 mg/dL) but increased in placebo (+0.12 mg/dL) ($P < 0.001$ for both comparisons).
  - Other liver enzymes (GGT, ALT, AST, conjugated bilirubin) improved significantly in the obeticholic acid groups versus placebo ($P < 0.001$).
  - No significant improvements were seen in albumin, INR, prothrombin time, or noninvasive fibrosis scores (transient elastography, ELF score).

Adverse events:

- Pruritus worsened significantly in the 10 mg group early in treatment, leading to more discontinuations compared with the 5–10 mg titration group.
- Bone health showed modest benefit, with smaller decreases in femoral bone mineral density in both obeticholic acid groups compared with placebo ($P < 0.05$).

6.4 Key Takeaways

- OCA significantly improves biochemical markers in PBC patients inadequately responsive to UDCA.
- Additional improvements were seen in GGT, ALT, AST, and inflammatory markers (hs-CRP, TNF-α, immunoglobulins).
- No significant benefit was observed in noninvasive fibrosis measures over 12 months.
- Pruritus was the most common side effect, especially at the 10 mg dose, sometimes requiring discontinuation.
- The trial established obeticholic acid as an effective add-on therapy to ursodiol in patients with inadequate biochemical response.

6.5 Clinical Application

- Consider OCA for patients with inadequate biochemical response to UDCA in PBC.
- It can be used as monotherapy if patients are intolerant of ursodiol.
- Patients should be monitored for changes in alkaline phosphatase, bilirubin, and lipid profiles.
- Educate patients about pruritis risk and manage symptomatically or via dose titration.

6.6 When to Discuss on Rounds

Discuss this trial on rounds with the following scenarios:

- When a patient with PBC on ursodiol has persistently elevated alkaline phosphatase despite adherence.
- When discussing next-line therapy options for PBC beyond ursodiol.
- When considering how to monitor for treatment response in PBC using alkaline phosphatase and bilirubin.

6.7 Relevant Guidelines

The **AASLD** and **EASL** guidelines both recognize obeticholic acid as a second-line therapy for primary biliary cholangitis in patients who have an inadequate biochemical response to ursodiol or who are intolerant to it.

7 TARGET Trial Summary [7]

Full Title: Rifaximin Treatment in Hepatic Encephalopathy
Publication Year: 2010
Journal: New England Journal of Medicine

7.1 Background

Hepatic encephalopathy (HE) frequently occurs in patients with advanced cirrhosis, significantly affecting their quality of life and prognosis. Lactulose has historically been the standard treatment, though recurrence remains high. The TARGET trial evaluated rifaximin. A nonabsorbable antibiotic, to determine its effectiveness in preventing recurrent episodes of hepatic encephalopathy.

7.2 Study Design

Type: Randomized, double-blind, placebo-controlled trial
Population: 299 patients with cirrhosis and a history of recurrent HE already receiving lactulose
Intervention: Rifaximin (550 mg twice daily) vs. placebo
Primary Outcome: Time to first breakthrough episode of HE
Secondary Outcome: Hospitalizations due to HE

7.3 Results

Primary Outcome: Rifaximin significantly reduced the risk of recurrent HE episodes compared to placebo (22.1% rifaximin vs. 45.9% placebo; HR 0.42; [95% CI: 0.28–0.64; $p < 0.001$]).

Secondary Outcome: Significantly fewer hospitalizations occurred in the rifaximin group compared to placebo (13.6% vs. 22.6%; HR 0.50; [95% CI: 0.29–0.87; p = 0.01])

7.4 Key Takeaways

- Rifaximin effectively reduced recurrent hepatic encephalopathy episodes and associated hospitalizations in patients already on lactulose.
- Benefits of rifaximin were consistent across subgroups and were observed early, within 28 days of initiation.
- Adverse events were similar between rifaximin and placebo groups, supporting a favorable safety profile.
- No significant increase in Clostridium difficile infections or other major infectious complications was noted, although vigilance is required.
- The trial established rifaximin as an effective long-term therapy for secondary prevention of recurrent hepatic encephalopathy, beyond its role in acute treatment.

7.5 Clinical Application

- Initiate rifaximin alongside lactulose in cirrhotic patients with recurrent hepatic encephalopathy to reduce recurrence and hospitalizations.
- Rifaximin may be used to reduce hospitalizations related to hepatic encephalopathy.
- Educate patients on adherence and safety profiles, emphasizing excellent tolerability.
- Rifaximin is generally safe for long-term use, making it an appropriate chronic therapy option in advanced liver disease.

7.6 When to Discuss on Rounds

Discuss this trial on rounds with the following scenarios:

- When evaluating treatment plans for patients with recurrent hepatic encephalopathy despite lactulose therapy.
- When discussing management strategies to reduce hospitalizations in cirrhosis patients.
- When reviewing evidence-based options for long-term management of hepatic encephalopathy.

7.7 *Relevant Guidelines*

The **AASLD** and **EASL** guidelines recommend rifaximin in combination with lactulose as standard-of-care for recurrent hepatic encephalopathy, based on TARGET trial results.

8 ANSWER Trial Summary [8]

Full Title: Long-Term Albumin Administration in Decompensated Cirrhosis: an Open-Label Randomised Trial
Publication Year: 2018
Journal: The Lancet

8.1 *Background*

Patients with decompensated cirrhosis often experience recurrent ascites and frequent hospitalizations, leading to poor survival and a high healthcare burden. Albumin is commonly administered acutely for complications such as large-volume paracentesis and spontaneous bacterial peritonitis, but its long-term use was not well studied. The ANSWER trial evaluated whether long-term albumin administration, in addition to standard medical treatment, would improve outcomes in patients with decompensated cirrhosis and ascites.

8.2 *Study Design*

Type: Multicenter, open-label, randomized controlled trial
Population: 440 patients with cirrhosis and grade 2 or 3 ascites (requiring ≥1 paracentesis in the prior 12 weeks)
Intervention: Standard medical treatment (SMT) alone vs. SMT + long-term albumin administration (40 g albumin twice weekly for 2 weeks, then 40 g weekly thereafter)
Primary Outcome: 18-month survival
Secondary Outcomes:

- Number of therapeutic paracenteses
- Cumulative diuretic dosage
- Hyponatremia
- Incidence of cirrhosis-related complications
- Number and duration of hospital admissions

- Treatment cost-effectiveness

8.3 *Results*

Primary Outcome: 18-month survival was significantly higher survival in the albumin + SMT group vs. SMT alone (77% vs. 66%; HR 0.62; [95% CI: 0.40–0.95; $p = 0.028$]).

Secondary Outcomes:

- Therapeutic paracentesis: Patients receiving long-term albumin required significantly fewer paracenteses compared with standard medical treatment (SMT) alone ($p < 0.0001$).
- Cumulative diuretic dosage: Albumin-treated patients required lower cumulative doses of diuretics ($p < 0.001$).
- Hyponatremia: The incidence of hyponatremia was reduced in the albumin group compared with SMT (9% vs. 19%; $p = 0.002$).
- Cirrhosis-related complications: Patients on albumin had lower rates of complications such as spontaneous bacterial peritonitis, renal dysfunction, and hepatic encephalopathy.
- Hospital admissions: Both the number of hospital admissions and total days hospitalized were reduced in the albumin group ($p < 0.001$).

8.4 *Key Takeaways*

- Long-term albumin therapy significantly improved survival in patients with decompensated cirrhosis and ascites.
- The risk of cirrhosis-related complications, including SBP, renal dysfunction, and hepatic encephalopathy, was reduced with albumin.
- The trial challenged the traditional view that albumin's role in cirrhosis is limited to acute settings (e.g., large-volume paracentesis, SBP, HRS).
- The trial provided a new treatment paradigm for advanced cirrhosis, influencing how hepatologists view chronic albumin infusion.

8.5 *Clinical Application*

- Albumin infusion is standard of care in acute settings such as after large-volume paracentesis, in spontaneous bacterial peritonitis, and in hepatorenal syndrome.
- Long-term albumin infusion for recurrent ascites is not routinely practiced, despite benefits shown in the ANSWER trial, because of cost, logistics, and limited guideline endorsement.

- In practice, most hepatologists will prioritize diuretics, paracentesis, and transplant evaluation, reserving long-term albumin infusion for select, refractory cases at specialized centers.
- Clinicians should know about this trial to understand the evolving landscape, even if it has not yet shifted day-to-day practice.

8.6 When to Discuss on Rounds

Discuss this trial on rounds with the following scenarios:

- When a patient with decompensated cirrhosis is admitted for recurrent tense ascites and you're discussing management beyond diuretics and paracentesis.
- When albumin is being ordered after large-volume paracentesis, SBP, or hepatorenal syndrome, bring up that albumin has also been studied as a chronic, disease-modifying therapy in cirrhosis.

8.7 Relevant Guidelines

Major hepatology guidelines, including those from the **AASLD** and the **EASL**, continue to recommend albumin primarily for specific, short-term indications: prevention of paracentesis-induced circulatory dysfunction, treatment of spontaneous bacterial peritonitis, and management of hepatorenal syndrome. While the ANSWER trial demonstrated survival and quality-of-life benefits with long-term albumin infusions in patients with decompensated cirrhosis and recurrent ascites, this strategy has not yet been widely incorporated into routine guideline-based care. The AASLD highlights cost and logistical barriers, and EASL acknowledges the findings but emphasizes the need for confirmatory trials before broad adoption. Thus, guidelines currently position long-term albumin as investigational rather than standard practice.

9 PIVENS Trial Summary [9]

Full Title: Pioglitazone, Vitamin E, or Placebo for Nonalcoholic Steatohepatitis
Publication Year: 2010
Journal: New England Journal of Medicine

9.1 Background

Nonalcoholic steatohepatitis (NASH) is a progressive liver disease characterized by hepatic inflammation and fibrosis, associated with insulin resistance and oxidative stress. Prior to the PIVENS trial, there were no widely accepted pharmacological treatments for NASH. Pioglitazone, an insulin-sensitizing agent, and vitamin E, a potent antioxidant, emerged as potential treatments. This trial aimed to determine the efficacy of pioglitazone or vitamin E compared to placebo for histological improvement with biopsy-confirmed NASH who did not have diabetes.

9.2 Study Design

Type: Randomized, double-blind, placebo-controlled trial
Population: 247 nondiabetic adults with biopsy-proven NASH
Intervention: Pioglitazone 30 mg daily vs. Vitamin E 800 IU daily vs. placebo, administered for 96 weeks
Primary Outcome: Histologic improvement in NASH
Secondary Outcomes:

- Changes in the overall activity score for NAFLD
- Individual component scores for:
  - Steatosis
  - Lobular inflammation
  - Hepatocellular ballooning
  - Fibrosis
- Changes in serum aminotransferase levels

9.3 Results

Primary Outcome:

- Vitamin E showed significant histologic improvement compared with placebo (43% vs. 19%, $p = 0.001$).
- Pioglitazone showed a trend toward improvement but did not achieve the predefined significance level (34% vs. 19%, $p = 0.04$; predefined threshold was $p < 0.025$).

Secondary Outcomes:

- Activity score for NAFLD: Significant decrease was observed in the activity score for NAFLD in both the vitamin E and Pioglitazone group as compared to placebo ($p < 0.001$).
- Steatosis: Improved in 54% of patients in the vitamin E group and 69% of patients in the pioglitazone group compared to only 31% in the placebo group ($p = 0.005$ for vitamin E) ($p < 0.001$ for pioglitazone).
- Lobular inflammation: Both vitamin E and pioglitazone significant improved inflammation compared to placebo ($p = 0.02$ vitamin E) ($p = 0.004$ pioglitazone).
- Hepatocellular ballooning: Significantly improved in both groups compared to placebo ($p < 0.001$ vitamin E) ($p = 0.002$ pioglitazone).
- Fibrosis: There was no significant difference observed between groups and placebo with improvement of fibrosis.
- Aminotransferase levels: In both groups there was a significant decrease in mean aspartate aminotransferase and alanine aminotransferase levels.

9.4 Key Takeaways

- Vitamin E significantly improved histologic features of NASH and met the pre-specified primary endpoint
- Pioglitazone did not meet the primary endpoint but showed significant benefits in steatosis, lobular inflammation, ballooning, insulin resistance, liver enzymes, and resolution of NASH in many patients.
- Neither therapy led to significant improvement in fibrosis scores, highlighting the ongoing challenge of reversing advanced liver injury.
- Pioglitazone was associated with weight gain despite metabolic benefits, which limits long-term tolerability.
- Vitamin E was generally well tolerated but carries concerns about uncertain long-term risks (e.g., diabetes risk, possible cancer risk from other studies).
- The trial established vitamin E as a therapeutic option in non-diabetic patients with biopsy-proven NASH, influencing guideline recommendations.

9.5 Clinical Application

- Vitamin E can be considered for non-diabetic adults with biopsy-proven NASH.
- Pioglitazone may be considered in select patients with NASH, particularly when metabolic syndrome or insulin resistance is present, but its use is limited by weight gain and potential long-term adverse effects.
- Neither agent improved fibrosis, so they should not be expected to reverse advanced liver disease.

- Both treatments likely require chronic use to maintain benefit, as discontinuation is associated with relapse.
- Clinical decision-making should balance potential benefits against risks, especially given uncertainties about long-term safety.
- First-line management of NASH remains lifestyle modification and weight loss, with pharmacologic therapy reserved for carefully selected patients.

9.6 When to Discuss on Rounds

Discuss this trial on rounds with the following scenarios:

- When determining pharmacologic options for nondiabetic patients with biopsy-confirmed NASH.
- When counseling patients regarding the side effects of pioglitazone, such as edema and weight gain.
- When highlighting that neither vitamin E nor pioglitazone improves fibrosis in NASH.
- When emphasizing that lifestyle modification and weight loss remain the cornerstone of therapy.

9.7 Relevant Guidelines

The **AASLD** and **EASL** guidelines cite PIVENS when outlining pharmacologic therapy for biopsy-proven NASH in non-diabetic adults recommending vitamin E (α-tocopherol) 800 IU daily to improve steatohepatitis based on its histologic benefit. It is not recommended for patients with diabetes, cirrhosis, or simple steatosis, and potential long-term risks (e.g., hemorrhagic stroke, prostate cancer signal) should be discussed.

10 COLONPREV Trial Summary [10]

Full Title: Colonoscopy versus Fecal Immunochemical Testing in Colorectal-Cancer Screening
Publication Year: 2012
Journal: New England Journal of Medicine

10.1 Background

Colorectal cancer (CRC) screening reduces incidence and mortality, but optimal screening strategies remain debated. Colonoscopy allows direct visualization and polyp removal, while fecal immunochemical testing (FIT) is non-invasive, cost-effective, and increases patient adherence. Prior to COLONPREV, no large randomized trials had directly compared colonoscopy and FIT regarding CRC detection rates, advanced adenoma detection, or adherence to screening recommendations.

10.2 Study Design

Type: Multicenter, randomized controlled trial
Population: 53,302 asymptomatic adults (aged 50–69) at average risk for CRC
Intervention: One-time screening colonoscopy vs. Biennial FIT (every two years)
Primary Outcome: Rate of death from colorectal cancer at 10 years (long-term follow-up ongoing)
Secondary Outcomes:

- CRC detection rates at initial screening
- Advanced adenoma detection rates
- Screening participation and adherence rates

10.3 Results

Primary Outcome:

- Long-term mortality data ongoing; initial results focused primarily on CRC and advanced adenoma detection rates at initial screening rounds.

Secondary Outcomes:

- CRC detection at baseline: Similar detection rates between groups (0.1% colonoscopy group vs. 0.1% FIT group; OR 0.99; [95% CI: 0.61–1.64; $p = 0.99$]).
- Advanced adenoma detection: Higher detection rate in colonoscopy group (1.9%) compared to FIT group (0.9%) (OR 2.30; [95% CI: 1.97–2.69; $p < 0.001$]).
- Participation/adherence:
  - Higher initial adherence rate in FIT group (34.2%) compared with colonoscopy group (24.6%) ($p < 0.001$).
  - Cumulative adherence after multiple FIT rounds approached adherence rates for colonoscopy.

10.4 Key Takeaways

- Participation was higher with FIT than colonoscopy, highlighting real-world differences in patient acceptance of screening strategies.
- Detection of colorectal cancer was similar between FIT and colonoscopy in the first screening round, with no difference in tumor stage.
- Colonoscopy was superior for detecting advanced and nonadvanced adenomas, especially in the proximal colon, which could translate into better long-term cancer prevention.
- FIT detected fewer adenomas, but this may reduce unnecessary colonoscopies for low-risk lesions, lowering complications and costs.
- Complication rates were significantly higher with colonoscopy, reflecting procedure-related risks.
- The ultimate comparison—impact on colorectal cancer mortality—awaits the planned 10-year follow-up.

10.5 Clinical Application

- Colonoscopy remains the gold standard screening test because of its higher detection of advanced and nonadvanced adenomas, particularly in the proximal colon.
- FIT is a reasonable alternative for patients who decline colonoscopy, given its higher participation rates and similar initial detection of colorectal cancer.
- FIT may help reduce unnecessary colonoscopies by detecting fewer low-risk adenomas, which can lower complication rates and resource use.
- In clinical practice, screening choice should be individualized, balancing patient preferences, risk tolerance, and resource availability.
- The trial reinforces the importance of offering both colonoscopy and FIT as acceptable screening strategies to maximize population-level participation.

10.6 When to Discuss on Rounds

Discuss this trial on rounds with the following scenarios:

- When counseling average-risk patients about colorectal cancer screening options.
- When discussing patient compliance and screening adherence as important determinants of screening effectiveness.
- When teaching trainees about the pros and cons of different CRC screening modalities.

- When weighing the balance between procedure-related risks (like bleeding or perforation) and diagnostic yield.
- When emphasizing that mortality benefit data are pending long-term follow-up, so both strategies remain valid options.

10.7 Relevant Guidelines

The **American Cancer Society (ACS)** and **USPSTF** guidelines recommend either colonoscopy every 10 years or FIT annually/biennially as effective CRC screening strategies, referencing COLONPREV among other studies as evidence supporting these recommendations.

References

1. Thursz MR, Richardson P, Allison M, et al. STOPAH Trial. Prednisolone or pentoxifylline for alcoholic hepatitis. N Engl J Med. 2015;372(17):1619–28. https://doi.org/10.1056/NEJMoa1412278.
2. García-Pagán JC, Caca K, Bureau C, et al. Early use of TIPS in patients with cirrhosis and variceal bleeding. N Engl J Med. 2010;362(25):2370–9. https://doi.org/10.1056/NEJMoa0910102.
3. Colombel JF, Sandborn WJ, Reinisch W, et al. Infliximab, azathioprine, or combination therapy for Crohn's disease. N Engl J Med. 2010;362(15):1383–95. https://doi.org/10.1056/NEJMoa0904492.
4. Sandborn WJ, Su C, Sands BE, et al. Tofacitinib as induction and maintenance therapy for ulcerative colitis. N Engl J Med. 2017;376(18):1723–36. https://doi.org/10.1056/NEJMoa1606910.
5. Di Bisceglie AM, Shiffman ML, Everson GT, et al. Prolonged therapy of advanced chronic hepatitis C with low-dose peginterferon. N Engl J Med. 2008;359(23):2429–41. https://doi.org/10.1056/NEJMoa0707615.
6. Nevens F, Andreone P, Mazzella G, et al. A placebo-controlled trial of Obeticholic acid in primary biliary cholangitis. N Engl J Med. 2016;375(7):631–43. https://doi.org/10.1056/NEJMoa1509840.
7. Bass NM, Mullen KD, Sanyal A, et al. Rifaximin treatment in hepatic encephalopathy. N Engl J Med. 2010;362(12):1071–81. https://doi.org/10.1056/NEJMoa0907893.
8. Caraceni P, Riggio O, Angeli P, et al. Long-term albumin administration in decompensated cirrhosis (ANSWER): an open-label randomized trial [published correction appears in Lancet. 2018;392(10145):386. Doi: 10.1016/S0140-6736(18)31709-4]. Lancet. 2018;391(10138):2417–29. https://doi.org/10.1016/S0140-6736(18)30840-7.
9. Sanyal AJ, Chalasani N, Kowdley KV, et al. Pioglitazone, vitamin E, or placebo for nonalcoholic steatohepatitis. N Engl J Med. 2010;362(18):1675–85. https://doi.org/10.1056/NEJMoa0907929.
10. Quintero E, Castells A, Bujanda L, et al. Colonoscopy versus fecal immunochemical testing in colorectal-cancer screening [published correction appears in N Engl J Med. 2016 May 12;374(19):1898. Doi: 10.1056/NEJMx150040.]. N Engl J Med. 2012;366(8):697–706. https://doi.org/10.1056/NEJMoa1108895.

Chapter 10
Infectious Diseases

1 ACTT-1 Trial Summary [1]

Full Title: Remdesivir for the Treatment of Covid-19 - Final Report
Publication Year: 2020
Journal: New England Journal of Medicine

1.1 Background

Early in the COVID-19 pandemic, effective antiviral therapies were urgently needed. Remdesivir, a nucleoside analog originally developed for Ebola, emerged as a potential antiviral against SARS-CoV-2. The Adaptive COVID-19 Treatment Trial (ACTT-1) aimed to evaluate the efficacy and safety of intravenous remdesivir compared to placebo in hospitalized COVID-19 patients.

1.2 Study Design

Type: Randomized, double-blind, placebo-controlled trial
Population: 1062 hospitalized patients with laboratory-confirmed COVID-19 and evidence of lower respiratory tract infection
Intervention: Remdesivir (200 mg loading dose, then 100 mg daily for up to 10 days) vs. placebo
Primary Outcome: Time to clinical recovery (discharge or hospitalization for infection-control purposes only)
Secondary Outcomes:

A. Love, *The Essential Evidence*, https://doi.org/10.1007/978-3-032-12399-2_10

- Clinical status at day 15
- Assessed on ordinal scale:

  1. Not hospitalized, no limitations on activities
  2. Not hospitalized, but with activity limitations or requiring home oxygen
  3. Hospitalized, not requiring oxygen and no longer needing ongoing medical care
  4. Hospitalized, not requiring oxygen but still needing medical care
  5. Hospitalized, requiring supplemental oxygen
  6. Hospitalized, requiring noninvasive ventilation or high-flow oxygen devices
  7. Hospitalized, requiring invasive mechanical ventilation or ECMO
  8. Death

- 15 day mortality
- 29 day mortality
- Time to improvement of one category and of two categories from the baseline ordinal score
- Number of days with supplemental O2 with noninvasive ventilation or high-flow O2, and with invasive ventilation or ECMO up to day 29

1.3 Results

Primary Outcome: Median recovery time was significantly shorter with remdesivir at 10 days compared to 15 days with placebo (RR 1.29; [95% CI: 1.12–1.49; $p < 0.001$).

Secondary Outcomes:

- Clinical status at day 15: Odds of improvement at day 15 were higher in the remdesivir group (OR 1.5; [95% CI: 1.2–1.9]).
- 15-day mortality: Mortality was 6.7% in the remdesivir group compared to 11.9% in the placebo group (HR 0.55; [95% CI: 0.36–0.83]).
- 29-day mortality: Mortality was 11.4% in remdesivir group vs. 15.2% in the placebo group (HR 0.73; [95% CI: 0.52–1.03]).
- Time to improvement: There was a shorter time to improvement in the remdesivir group at a median on 7 days vs. 9 days in the placebo group in one category (RR 1.23; [95% CI: 1.08–1.41]) and two categories 11 vs. 14 days (RR 1.29; [95% CI: 1.12–1.48]).
- Oxygen requirement: In 913 patients receiving oxygen in enrollment, those in the remdesivir group received oxygen for fewer days than patients in the placebo group (median 13 days vs. 21 days). There was also lower incidence of those newly requiring O2 in the remdesivir group vs. placebo (36% vs. 44%).

1.4 Key Takeaways

- Remdesivir shortened recovery time in hospitalized COVID-19 patients compared to placebo.
- The greatest benefit occurred in patients requiring low-flow oxygen at baseline.
- Patients already on mechanical ventilation or ECMO did not show clear benefit.
- Mortality was numerically lower with remdesivir but did not reach statistical significance overall.
- Starting remdesivir earlier in the course of illness led to greater benefit.
- Treatment reduced the risk of progression to higher levels of respiratory support.
- Serious adverse events, particularly respiratory failure, were less frequent in the remdesivir group.
- This trial established remdesivir as the first antiviral with proven clinical benefit in COVID-19.

1.5 Clinical Application

- Initiate remdesivir therapy promptly in hospitalized COVID-19 patients requiring oxygen but not yet critically ill.
- Initiate remdesivir as early as possible in the disease course to maximize benefit.
- Recognize that remdesivir alone does not significantly reduce mortality and should be combined with other evidence-based therapies (e.g., dexamethasone in hypoxic patients).
- Monitor renal and hepatic function during treatment, as with other antivirals.
- Counsel patients and families that remdesivir may shorten recovery and reduce progression of illness but is not a cure.

1.6 When to Discuss on Rounds

Discuss this trial on rounds with the following scenarios:

- When managing hospitalized COVD-19 patients requiring supplemental oxygen.
- When discussing antiviral therapy options and guidelines for COVID-19.
- When explaining that remdesivir should be used alongside other therapies like dexamethasone, since antivirals alone are insufficient.
- When teaching about how this trial led to remdesivir's FDA Emergency Use Authorization during the pandemic.

1.7 Relevant Guidelines

The **National Institutes of Health**, **WHO**, and **Infectious Diseases Society of America** guidelines strongly recommend remdesivir for hospitalized COVID-19 patients requiring supplemental oxygen, directly citing ACTT-1 findings. Collectively, the guidelines position remdesivir as part of combination therapy—typically alongside corticosteroids—in moderate to severe disease, while not recommending routine use in patients with mild illness or in those already receiving mechanical ventilation.

2 MERINO Trial Summary [2]

Full Title: Effect of Piperacillin-Tazobactam vs Meropenem on 30-Day Mortality for Patients With E. coli or Klebsiella pneumoniae Bloodstream Infection and Ceftriaxone Resistance: A Randomized Clinical Trial
Publication Year: 2018
Journal: Journal of the American Medical Association

2.1 Background

Extended-spectrum beta-lactamase (ESBL)-producing Enterobacterales infections have been traditionally treated with carbapenems. Rising carbapenem resistance, however, has prompted exploration of carbapenem-sparing treatments like piperacillin-tazobactam. The MERINO trial aimed to determine if piperacillin-tazobactam could be used safely as an alternative to meropenem in bloodstream infections caused by ESBL-producing organisms.

2.2 Study Design

Type: International, multicenter, randomized non-inferiority trial
Population: 391 patients with bloodstream infection caused by ceftriaxone-resistant E. coli or Klebsiella pneumoniae
Intervention: Piperacillin-tazobactam (4.5 g IV Q6H) vs. Meropenem (1 g IV Q8H) for a minimum of 4 days, then tailored therapy, total treatment 7–14 days
Primary Outcome: All-cause mortality at 30 days
Secondary Outcomes:

- Clinical and microbiologic success at day 4 after randomization
- Microbiologic resolution of infection
- Relapsed bloodstream infection

2.3 Results

Primary Outcome: Significantly higher mortality with piperacillin-tazobactam compared to meropenem (12.3% vs 3.7%; risk difference 8.6%; [95% CI: – ∞ – 14.5%; p = 0.90 for noninferiority]), failing non-inferiority criteria.

Secondary Outcomes:

- Clinical resolution: Lower clinical success rate with piperacillin-tazobactam compared to meropenem.
- Clinical and microbiological resolution at day 4: Occurred in 68.4% of patients in the piperacillin-tazobactam group compared with 74.6% of patients in the meropenem group (risk difference −6.2%; [95% CI: −15.5-3.1%; p = 0.19]).
- There was no significant difference observed between groups in microbiologic resolution of infection and relapse of bloodstream infection.

2.4 Key Takeaways

- The MERINO trial tested whether piperacillin–tazobactam could be a safe alternative to meropenem for bloodstream infections caused by ceftriaxone-resistant *E. coli* or *K. pneumoniae*.
- The study was stopped early due to excess mortality in the piperacillin–tazobactam arm, with 30-day mortality 12.3% vs 3.7% for meropenem.
- Noninferiority of piperacillin–tazobactam compared to meropenem was not demonstrated; instead, results suggested inferiority.
- Mortality differences persisted across subgroups, even in urinary tract sources, which are usually considered lower-risk.
- Secondary outcomes (clinical resolution, microbiological cure, relapse, *C. difficile*) were similar, but mortality drove the difference.
- The trial reinforced that meropenem (a carbapenem) should remain the preferred definitive therapy for ESBL-producing bacteremia.
- Results highlighted the danger of relying on piperacillin–tazobactam despite in vitro susceptibility, as clinical outcomes did not align with lab MIC data.
- Limitations included some crossover with empirical therapy, unblinded design, and regional dosing variations, but the mortality signal was consistent and robust.
- The study had major practice-changing implications, strongly influencing guidelines to recommend carbapenems as first-line treatment for serious ESBL bloodstream infections.

2.5 Clinical Application

- Prefer meropenem over piperacillin-tazobactam in severe bloodstream infections caused by ESBL-producing *E. coli* or *Klebsiella pneumoniae.*
- Do not rely on piperacillin–tazobactam for definitive therapy in ESBL bacteremia, even when lab testing shows susceptibility, because clinical outcomes show higher mortality.
- Piperacillin–tazobactam may still have a role in less severe, non-bacteremic infections (such as some urinary tract infections) caused by ESBL producers, though this is not directly addressed by MERINO.
- This trial underscores the importance of antibiotic stewardship—reserving carbapenems for severe ESBL infections while exploring newer BLBLI agents (e.g., ceftolozane-tazobactam, ceftazidime-avibactam) for future roles.

2.6 When to Discuss on Rounds

Discuss this trial on rounds with the following scenarios:

- When selecting antibiotic regimens for patients with known or suspected ESBL bacteremia.
- When teaching the difference between in vitro susceptibility testing and real-world clinical outcomes, highlighting why "susceptible" on paper doesn't always mean effective in patients.
- When emphasizing antibiotic stewardship and explaining why carbapenem use should be reserved for severe ESBL infections but cannot be replaced by piperacillin–tazobactam in bacteremia.

2.7 Relevant Guidelines

Infectious Diseases Society of America (IDSA) and international guidelines endorse carbapenems (e.g., meropenem) as first-line therapy for ESBL bloodstream infections, strongly referencing MERINO trial outcomes. These guidelines also advise against using piperacillin–tazobactam for definitive therapy of ESBL bacteremia, even if in vitro susceptibility is reported, because of higher observed mortality compared with meropenem.

3 POET Trial Summary [3]

- **Full Title:** Partial Oral versus Intravenous Antibiotic Treatment of Endocarditis
- **Publication Year:** 2018
- **Journal:** New England Journal of Medicine

3.1 Background

Traditionally, infective endocarditis (IE) is treated with prolonged intravenous (IV) antibiotics due to concerns about antibiotic penetration and bioavailability. However, prolonged IV therapy is associated with complications, including line infections and prolonged hospitalization. The POET trial evaluated whether stable patients with left-sided infective endocarditis could safely switch to oral antibiotics after an initial IV treatment period.

3.2 Study Design

- **Type:** Multicenter, randomized, open-label, non-inferiority trial
- **Population:** 400 adults with stable left-sided infective endocarditis (native or prosthetic valve)
- **Intervention:** Continued IV antibiotics vs. transition to oral antibiotics after at least 10 days of IV treatment
- **Primary Outcome:** Composite of all-cause mortality, unplanned cardiac surgery, embolic events, or relapse of bacteremia within 6 months

3.3 Results

- **Primary Outcome:** Oral antibiotics group met criteria for non-inferiority compared to IV antibiotics group (9% oral vs. 12.1% IV; difference −3.1%; [95% CI: −3.4 to 9.6; p = 0.40]).

3.4 Key Takeaways

- Switching to oral therapy after about 17 days of IV antibiotics was noninferior to completing the entire course IV, with similar rates of death, embolic events, unplanned cardiac surgery, or relapse of bacteremia.
- Oral therapy regimens used two antibiotics with high bioavailability (e.g., linezolid, fluoroquinolones, rifampin, dicloxacillin), carefully selected based on culture results and susceptibility testing.
- Patients in the oral group had a dramatically shorter hospital stay (median 3 days after randomization vs 19 days in the IV group), showing major potential for reducing hospitalization burden and costs.
- Outcomes were consistent across subgroups, including patients with prosthetic valves and those who underwent surgery.

- Safety outcomes and adverse effects were similar between IV and oral groups, with no signal of increased risk from oral therapy.
- The trial's results are only applicable to carefully selected patients: stable, good GI absorption, susceptible pathogens (streptococci, *E. faecalis*, *S. aureus* without MRSA, coagulase-negative staphylococci), and under close follow-up.
- This trial challenges the long-standing paradigm that all endocarditis must be treated with prolonged IV antibiotics, opening the door for outpatient and less invasive management in select cases.

3.5 Clinical Application

- Transition stable IE patients to oral antibiotics after initial IV therapy (~10) under appropriate clinical and microbiologic conditions.
- Consider this strategy in patients who are clinically stable, afebrile, and showing improvement on IV antibiotics.
- Reserve IV-only therapy for patients with unstable disease, resistant organisms, or impaired absorption where oral therapy is unreliable.

3.6 When to Discuss on Rounds

Discuss this trial on rounds with the following scenarios:

- When managing infective endocarditis patients after initial stabilization on IV antibiotics.
- When discussing criteria for transitioning endocarditis patients to oral antibiotics.
- When considering outpatient therapy for endocarditis but weighing the safety of oral versus IV regimens.
- When teaching about modern approaches to reducing hospitalization and IV-line complications.

3.7 Relevant Guidelines

The **ESC** and **AHA** guidelines now cautiously permits partial oral step-down for carefully selected, clinically stable patients with left-sided infective endocarditis after an initial period of effective IV therapy—essentially reflecting POET's criteria.

4 OVIVA Trial Summary [4]

Full Title: Oral versus Intravenous Antibiotics for Bone and Joint Infection
Publication Year: 2019
Journal: New England Journal of Medicine

4.1 Background

Historically, bone and joint infections (e.g., osteomyelitis, prosthetic joint infections) have been treated with prolonged intravenous antibiotics, necessitating lengthy hospital stays and IV-line maintenance. Oral antibiotic therapy could significantly reduce hospital stays and improve patient convenience, but effectiveness was uncertain. The OVIVA trial evaluated whether oral antibiotics are non-inferior to IV antibiotics for complex orthopedic infections.

4.2 Study Design

Type: Multicenter, randomized, open-label, non-inferiority trial
Population: 1054 adults with bone or joint infections requiring ≥6 weeks of antibiotic treatment
Intervention: Oral antibiotic regimen (tailored based on cultures/susceptibilities) vs. IV antibiotic regimen
Primary Outcome: Treatment failure at 1 year (defined as infection recurrence, unplanned surgical intervention, or adverse antibiotic-related events leading to discontinuation)
Secondary Outcomes:

- Probable or possible treatment failure
- Early discontinuation
- Intravenous catheter complications
- *C. diff*—associated diarrhea
- Serious adverse events

4.3 Results

Primary Outcome: Oral therapy was non-inferior to IV therapy regarding treatment failure at 1 year (oral: 13.2% vs IV: 14.6%; difference −1.4%, 95% CI: −5.6 to 2.9; non-inferiority met).

Secondary Outcomes:

- Probable or possible treatment failure: Occurred in 1.2% of patients in the IV group compared to 2.0% in the oral group.
- Early discontinuation: Occurred more commonly in the IV than oral group at 18.9% vs. 12.8% ($p = 0.006$).
- IV catheter complications: There were more complications with IV catheter in the IV group at 9.4% compared to 1.0% in the oral group ($p < 0.001$).
- There was no significant difference observed between groups with rates of *C. diff* infection or adverse events.

4.4 Key Takeaways

- Oral antibiotic therapy was noninferior to intravenous (IV) therapy for bone and joint infections when used during the first 6 weeks, with similar rates of treatment failure at 1 year.
- Switching to oral therapy was associated with fewer complications, particularly catheter-related events, and shorter hospital stays compared with prolonged IV therapy.
- The trial included a heterogeneous population (various organisms, surgical vs. nonsurgical cases, metalware infections), supporting the generalizability of results to routine clinical practice.
- Adherence to oral regimens was high, and treatment failure rates did not differ by pathogen, site of infection, or surgical approach, strengthening confidence in oral strategies when appropriate antibiotics are chosen.
- OVIVA challenged the long-standing belief that IV therapy is mandatory for prolonged courses in osteomyelitis and prosthetic joint infections, reshaping standard care by legitimizing oral step-down in stable patients.

4.5 Clinical Application

- Oral antibiotics can be used as an alternative to prolonged IV therapy in patients with bone and joint infections, provided that the organism is susceptible and oral agents with good bioavailability are available.
- Patients who are clinically stable after initial IV therapy can be safely transitioned to oral therapy without compromising outcomes.

- Using oral therapy helps reduce hospital length of stay, the need for prolonged IV access, and catheter-related complications.
- Oral regimens should be chosen carefully in consultation with infectious diseases specialists, ensuring adequate absorption, tissue penetration, and patient adherence.
- This approach is particularly useful in resource-limited settings or when outpatient parenteral antibiotic therapy (OPAT) is logistically difficult or risky.

4.6 When to Discuss on Rounds

Discuss this trial on rounds with the following scenarios:

- When managing a patient with osteomyelitis or prosthetic joint infection and considering whether prolonged IV antibiotics are necessary.
- When explaining to trainees that oral therapy can be noninferior to IV therapy for complex bone and joint infections if appropriate oral agents are available.

4.7 Relevant Guidelines

IDSA and the **European Society of Clinical Microbiology and Infectious Diseases** have incorporated the findings of the OVIVA trial into their recommendations. Both societies acknowledge that in appropriately selected patients with bone and joint infections, oral antibiotic therapy can be considered as an alternative to prolonged intravenous therapy once initial stabilization is achieved.

5 European Dexamethasone Study Summary [5]

Full Title: Dexamethasone in Adults with Bacterial Meningitis
Publication Year: 2002
Journal: New England Journal of Medicine

5.1 Background

Bacterial meningitis is associated with high mortality and severe neurological complications. Adjunctive corticosteroids had been proposed to reduce inflammation and improve clinical outcomes, but prior evidence was inconclusive. This pivotal

European multicenter study aimed to evaluate whether adjunctive dexamethasone, given early in the course of bacterial meningitis, could reduce mortality and neurologic sequelae.

5.2 *Study Design*

Type: Multicenter, randomized, double-blind, placebo-controlled trial
Population: 301 adults with suspected or confirmed bacterial meningitis
Intervention: IV dexamethasone (10 mg every 6 hours for 4 days) vs. placebo, initiated before or with the first dose of antibiotics
Primary Outcome: Score on the Glasgow Outcome Scale at eight weeks (A score of 5 indicating a favorable outcome, while a score of 1 to 4 indicating an unfavorable outcome)
Secondary Outcomes:

- Mortality rates
- Focal neurologic abnormalities
- Hearing loss
- Gastrointestinal bleeding
- Fungal infection
- Herpes zoster
- Hyperglycemia

5.3 *Results*

Primary Outcome: Dexamethasone significantly reduced the risk of unfavorable outcome compared to placebo (15% vs. 25%; RR 0.59; [95% CI: 0.37–0.84; p = 0.03]).
Secondary Outcomes:

- Mortality: Lower mortality in dexamethasone group (7% vs. 15%; RR 0.48; [95% CI: 0.24–0.96; p = 0.04]).
- There was no significant difference observed between groups in incidence of focal neurologic abnormalities, hearing loss, GI bleeding, fungal infection, herpes zoster infection, or hyperglycemia.

5.4 *Key Takeaways*

- Early adjunctive dexamethasone significantly reduced the risk of an unfavorable outcome at 8 weeks with the strongest benefit seen in pneumococcal meningitis.
- Mortality was lower in the dexamethasone group showing a clear survival advantage without increasing severe neurologic sequelae.

- Benefits included reduced rates of impaired consciousness, seizures, and cardiorespiratory failure during hospitalization.
- No meaningful benefit was seen in meningococcal meningitis, but subgroup sizes were small, and the trial still supports use across all bacterial meningitis.
- The regimen (10 mg IV every 6 hours for 4 days) was safe, with adverse events rare and not significantly different from placebo.
- The protective effect is contingent on timing — dexamethasone must be started before or with the first dose of antibiotics.
- The trial established corticosteroids as a cornerstone of treatment for adults with bacterial meningitis, especially for pneumococcal disease.

5.5 *Clinical Application*

- Use dexamethasone (10 mg IV every 6 hours for 4 days) in all adults with suspected bacterial meningitis, especially when pneumococcal disease is likely.
- Administer dexamethasone before or with the first dose of antibiotics to maximize benefit, as delayed use is not effective.
- Recognize that dexamethasone significantly reduces mortality and unfavorable outcomes, particularly in pneumococcal meningitis.
- Monitor for adverse effects such as hyperglycemia or GI complications, though these are rare.
- In patients receiving vancomycin for resistant pneumococcus, maintain vigilance as dexamethasone may theoretically reduce CSF penetration of vancomycin.
- Reinforce that dexamethasone does not improve rates of hearing loss but does not worsen neurologic sequelae either.

5.6 *When to Discuss on Rounds*

Discuss this trial on rounds with the following scenarios:

- When managing adult patients presenting with suspected bacterial meningitis.
- When teaching trainees about adjunctive therapies and timing of corticosteroid initiation in CNS infections.
- When emphasizing the importance of early steroid administration before or simultaneously with antibiotics.

5.7 *Relevant Guidelines*

IDSA and the **European Society of Clinical Microbiology and Infectious Diseases** recommend adjunctive dexamethasone in adults with suspected or confirmed bacterial meningitis, particularly when *Streptococcus pneumoniae* is likely.

6 NIX-TB Trial Summary [6]

Full Title: Treatment of Highly Drug-Resistant Pulmonary Tuberculosis
Publication Year: 2020
Journal: New England Journal of Medicine

6.1 *Background*

Multidrug-resistant tuberculosis (MDR-TB) and extensively drug-resistant tuberculosis (XDR-TB) pose major public health challenges with high mortality rates. Conventional therapies involve long durations, injectable drugs, and considerable toxicity. The NIX-TB trial evaluated an all-oral, shorter regimen combining bedaquiline, pretomanid, and linezolid (BPaL) for patients with difficult-to-treat MDR/XRD pulmonary tuberculosis.

6.2 *Study Design*

Type: Open-label, single-group, phase 3 clinical trial
Population: 109 patients with extensively drug-resistant or treatment-intolerant MDR-TB
Intervention: 6-month regimen of Bedaquiline + Pretomanid + Linezolid
Primary Outcome: Incidence of an unfavorable outcome (treatment failure or relapse during follow-up)
Secondary Outcome: Adverse events

6.3 *Results*

Primary Outcome: 10% of patients had an unfavorable outcome at 6 months after the end of treatment (95% CI: 83 to 95).

- 7 deaths
- 1 withdrawal of consent during treatment
- 2 relapses during follow-up
- 1 loss to follow-up

Secondary Outcomes: Peripheral neuropathy and myelosuppression were common due to linezolid, necessitating dose reduction in a substantial proportion.

6.4 Key Takeaways

- The trial tested a novel, all-oral regimen of bedaquiline, pretomanid, and linezolid (BPaL) given for 26 weeks in patients with XDR-TB and complicated MDR-TB, populations with historically very poor outcomes (<20% cure rates).
- 90% of patients achieved a favorable outcome at 6 months post-treatment, including 89% with XDR-TB and 92% with MDR-TB.
- Linezolid toxicity was frequent (81% neuropathy, 48% myelosuppression, ~40% anemia), but these side effects were generally manageable with dose adjustments or interruptions; very few patients required permanent discontinuation.
- The trial was single-group and conducted in South Africa, limiting generalizability, but outcomes were so dramatically improved compared with historical controls that the findings are viewed as transformative.
- Importantly, the regimen shortened therapy to 6 months (vs. 18–24 months historically), reducing treatment burden, risk of loss to follow-up, and economic hardship for patients.
- The results influenced WHO recommendations, which now endorse BPaL as an option for XDR-TB and certain MDR-TB cases.

6.5 Clinical Application

- Consider bedaquiline-pretomanid-linezolid regimen as first-line therapy in patients with extensively drug-resistant or treatment-resistant MDR pulmonary tuberculosis.
- Closely monitor linezolid-related toxicities (neuropathy, cytopenias) and adjust dosing accordingly.
- Programs implementing this regimen must be prepared for active pharmacovigilance and have resources for managing side effects.

6.6 *When to Discuss on Rounds*

Discuss this trial on rounds with the following scenarios:

- When evaluating treatment options for patients with MDR or XDR tuberculosis.
- When counseling patients regarding potential regimen toxicities and monitoring.
- When teaching trainees about modern treatment regimens for resistant tuberculosis.

6.7 *Relevant Guidelines*

The **WHO** endorses the BPaL regimen (bedaquiline, pretomanid, and linezolid) as a treatment option for patients with extensively drug-resistant tuberculosis (XDR-TB), treatment-intolerant MDR-TB, or nonresponsive MDR-TB. The **Centers for Disease Control and Prevention** and the **IDSA** have similarly recognized the BPaL regimen as a major advance in the management of highly resistant TB, though they emphasize its use within specialized programs with strong capacity for adverse event monitoring.

7 Fidaxomicin vs. Vancomycin for *C. difficile* Trial Summary [7]

Full Title: Fidaxomicin versus Vancomycin for *Clostridium difficile* Infection
Publication Year: 2011
Journal: New England Journal of Medicine

7.1 *Background*

Clostridium difficile infection (CDI) is a significant cause of healthcare-associated morbidity and mortality. Standard therapy with oral vancomycin was effective but associated with high recurrence rates. Fidaxomicin, a narrow-spectrum macrolide antibiotic, was developed to specifically target C. difficile with potentially fewer recurrences. This trial aimed to compare fidaxomicin and oral vancomycin for treatment of CDI.

7.2 *Study Design*

Type: Multicenter, randomized, double-blind, non-inferiority trial
Population: 629 patients with acute CDI

Intervention: Fidaxomicin 200 mg orally twice daily vs. Vancomycin 125 mg orally four times daily, each for 10 days

Primary Outcome: Clinical cure rate (resolution of diarrhea and no need for additional CDI treatment)

Secondary Outcomes:

- CDI recurrence rates within 4 weeks after therapy
- Resolution of diarrhea with no recurrence

7.3 Results

Primary Outcome: Fidaxomicin was non-inferior to vancomycin in achieving clinical cure (88.2% vs. 85.8%, respectively; p = 0.36).

Secondary Outcomes:

- Recurrence rates: Fidaxomicin significantly reduced CDI recurrence compared to vancomycin (15.4% vs. 25.3%; [95% CI: −16.6 to −2.9; p = 0.005]).
- Resolution of diarrhea: Fidaxomicin resulted in significantly higher rates of resolution of diarrhea without recurrence compared to vancomycin (74.6% vs. 64.1%; [95% CI: 3.1–17.7; p = 0.006]).
- Adverse events: Similar safety and adverse event rates between the two treatment groups.

7.4 Key Takeaways

- The trial demonstrated that fidaxomicin was noninferior to vancomycin for initial clinical cure of *C. difficile* infection.
- Fidaxomicin significantly reduced recurrence rates compared with vancomycin, particularly for non–NAP1/BI/027 strains.
- Fidaxomicin led to a higher proportion of patients achieving global cure (sustained resolution without recurrence) compared with vancomycin.
- Safety and tolerability were similar between the two agents, with no major differences in adverse event profiles.
- Microbiologic findings suggest fidaxomicin's bactericidal activity, narrow spectrum, and preservation of normal gut flora may explain its advantage in preventing recurrence.
- The study highlighted fidaxomicin's potential role not just in treating acute *C. difficile* infection but also in reducing relapse and transmission, an important public health consideration.

7.5 Clinical Application

- Fidaxomicin can be considered as a first-line therapy for *C. difficile* infection, especially in patients at high risk for recurrence.
- Vancomycin remains a reasonable alternative when cost or access to fidaxomicin is a barrier, as both are effective for initial clinical cure.
- Fidaxomicin's preservation of the normal gut flora makes it a good choice for patients with multiple comorbidities or prior recurrent infections.
- Clinicians should still weigh cost-effectiveness, as fidaxomicin is significantly more expensive than vancomycin, despite lower recurrence and rehospitalization rates.

7.6 When to Discuss on Rounds

Discuss this trial on rounds with the following scenarios:

- When initiating antibiotic therapy for new-onset CDI, especially in patients at risk or recurrence.
- When comparing fidaxomicin and vancomycin in terms of efficacy, recurrence rates, and cost.
- When teaching about how newer agents like fidaxomicin may change standard practice compared with traditional vancomycin or metronidazole therapy.

7.7 Relevant Guidelines

The **IDSA** and the **Society for Healthcare Epidemiology of America** recommend fidaxomicin as the preferred first-line therapy for both the initial episode and recurrences of *C. difficile* infection, given its lower rates of recurrence compared with vancomycin. The **ACG** and the **European Society of Clinical Microbiology and Infectious Diseases** provide similar guidance, emphasizing fidaxomicin as the optimal therapy when available, while acknowledging that vancomycin remains a reasonable alternative, particularly where cost or access is an issue.

8 PROACT Trial Summary [8]

Full Title: Procalcitonin-Guided Use of Antibiotics for Lower Respiratory Tract Infection
Publication Year: 2018
Journal: New England Journal of Medicine

8.1 Background

Procalcitonin is a biomarker that rises in bacterial infections and has been studied as a tool to guide antibiotic prescribing decisions. Previous European trials suggested procalcitonin-guided algorithms could reduce unnecessary antibiotic use without compromising patient safety. The PROACT trial aimed to evaluate the effectiveness of procalcitonin-guided antibiotic prescribing for patients with suspected lower respiratory tract infection (LRTI) in the U.S. emergency department setting.

8.2 Study Design

Type: Multicenter, randomized, pragmatic, controlled trial
Population: 1656 adult patients presenting to U.S. emergency departments with suspected lower respiratory tract infections (including acute bronchitis, COPD exacerbation, and community-acquired pneumonia)
Intervention: Procalcitonin-guided antibiotic prescription using a predefined algorithm (encouraging withholding antibiotics at <0.25 ng/mL) vs. standard care based on clinician judgment
Primary Outcome: Total antibiotic exposure (in days) within 30 days of enrollment
Secondary Outcomes:

- Antibiotic initiation rates
- Antibiotic receipt by day 30
- Antibiotic-days during the hospital stay (among patients who were admitted)

8.3 Results

Primary Outcome: Procalcitonin-guided therapy was not superior to usual care in reducing total antibiotic exposure over 30 days (mean 4.2 days vs. 4.3 days; [95% CI: −0.6-0.5; p = 0.87]).
Secondary Outcomes:

- Antibiotic initiation rates in the emergency department were similar between groups (52% procalcitonin vs. 52% usual care; p = 0.96).
- There was no significant difference observed between groups in antibiotic receipt by day 30 and antibiotic-days during hospital stay.

8.4 Key Takeaways

- The trial tested whether procalcitonin-guided antibiotic prescribing reduced antibiotic use in U.S. emergency departments for patients with suspected lower respiratory tract infections.
- No significant reduction in antibiotic exposure was observed compared with usual care, with both groups averaging about 4 antibiotic-days within 30 days.
- Safety outcomes were similar between groups, and the trial demonstrated noninferiority of procalcitonin-guided care regarding adverse events.
- The findings suggest that in modern U.S. practice—where stewardship and shorter antibiotic courses are already emphasized—procalcitonin adds limited incremental benefit for reducing antibiotic exposure.

8.5 Clinical Application

- Use this trial to recognize that procalcitonin-guided algorithms may not substantially reduce antibiotic use in U.S. emergency departments where stewardship is already strong.
- Apply procalcitonin cautiously, understanding it should not override sound clinical judgment, especially in patients with COPD exacerbations or suspected bacterial infection.
- Consider procalcitonin testing most useful in cases of acute bronchitis or other low-likelihood bacterial infections, where it may help reduce unnecessary antibiotic prescribing.
- Avoid relying on procalcitonin as the sole determinant for starting or withholding antibiotics; instead, integrate it with clinical findings and guideline-based management.

8.6 When to Discuss on Rounds

Discuss this trial on rounds with the following scenarios:

- When evaluating biomarkers for guiding antibiotic decisions in pneumonia or COPD exacerbations.
- When addressing stewardship strategies in emergency or urgent care settings.

8.7 Relevant Guidelines

The **IDSA** and the **ATS** guidelines for community-acquired pneumonia do not recommend routine use of procalcitonin to determine initiation of antibiotics, emphasizing that treatment decisions should be guided by clinical judgment and standard diagnostic testing.

9 PREVENT TB Trial Summary [9]

Full Title: Three Months of Rifapentine and Isoniazid for Latent Tuberculosis Infection
Publication Year: 2011
Journal: New England Journal of Medicine

9.1 Background

Latent tuberculosis infection (LTBI) poses a significant risk for progression to active tuberculosis (TB). The traditional treatment was 9 months of daily isoniazid, but adherence was challenging. The PREVENT TB trial evaluated the efficacy and safety of a shorter directly observed, once-weekly regimen of rifapentine plus isoniazid compared to the standard 9-month daily isoniazid regimen.

9.2 Study Design

Type: Multicenter, randomized, open-label, non-inferiority trial
Population: 7731 individuals at high risk of progression from LTBI to active TB
Intervention: Once weekly rifapentine (900 mg) + isoniazid (900 mg) for 3 months (3HP regimen), directly observed, vs. daily isoniazid (300 mg) for 9 months
Primary Outcome: Development of culture confirmed tuberculosis
Secondary Outcomes:

- Completion rates

9.3 *Results*

Primary Outcome: The shorter rifapentine-isoniazid regimen was non-inferior to standard isoniazid therapy (0.19% vs. 0.43% progression to active TB; difference – 0.24% met non-inferiority criteria).

Secondary Outcomes:

- Completion rates: Significantly higher in the shorter regimen group (82.1% vs. 69%, $p < 0.001$).
- Adverse events: Generally similar, but the 3HP group reported slightly more hypersensitivity reactions.

9.4 *Key Takeaways*

- The PREVENT TB trial demonstrated that a 3-month regimen of once-weekly rifapentine plus isoniazid under directly observed therapy was noninferior to 9 months of daily self-administered isoniazid for the prevention of active tuberculosis in high-risk individuals.
- The combination regimen showed a trend toward superior protection, with fewer cases of tuberculosis developing compared with the isoniazid-only group.
- Treatment completion rates were significantly higher with the shorter rifapentine–isoniazid regimen than with 9 months of isoniazid, addressing one of the major challenges of latent tuberculosis therapy.
- Hepatotoxicity was less common in the rifapentine–isoniazid group, though hypersensitivity reactions were more frequently reported; overall rates of serious adverse events and deaths were similar between groups.
- Risk factors for developing tuberculosis despite therapy included smoking, HIV infection, and low body mass index, emphasizing the need for careful monitoring in these populations.
- The study reinforced the importance of directly observed therapy in improving adherence, which is likely a major contributor to the higher completion rates in the rifapentine–isoniazid group.
- These findings established the rifapentine–isoniazid regimen as a safe, effective, and more practical alternative to prolonged isoniazid monotherapy for latent tuberculosis infection.

9.5 *Clinical Application*

- Use the 3-month, once-weekly rifapentine plus isoniazid regimen (3HP) as an alternative to 9 months of daily isoniazid for latent tuberculosis infection in eligible patients.

- Consider the 3HP regimen particularly in close contacts of active tuberculosis cases or in patients with recent tuberculin skin test conversion, as studied in this trial.
- Monitor for hypersensitivity reactions in patients receiving rifapentine plus isoniazid, even though rates of severe adverse events were low overall.
- Recognize that hepatotoxicity is less common with rifapentine plus isoniazid than with isoniazid alone, making the 3HP regimen safer for patients with liver risk factors.
- Be cautious with drug–drug interactions involving rifapentine (e.g., warfarin, methadone, hormonal contraceptives, HIV protease inhibitors) and manage accordingly.

9.6 When to Discuss on Rounds

Discuss this trial on rounds with the following scenarios:

- When selecting treatment regimens for patients with newly diagnosed latent tuberculosis infection.
- When discussing adherence challenges and safety of TB prevention strategies.

9.7 Relevant Guidelines

CDC and **WHO** guidelines strongly recommend the rifapentine-isoniazid (3HP) regimen for LTBI treatment, directly citing PREVENT TBH trial outcomes.

10 CAP-START Trial Summary [10]

Full Title: Antibiotic Treatment Strategies for Community-Acquired Pneumonia in Adults
Publication Year: 2015
Journal: New England Journal of Medicine

10.1 Background

Community-acquired pneumonia (CAP) is commonly treated empirically, typically using beta-lactams with macrolides or fluoroquinolone monotherapy. The optimal empirical strategy was unclear. CAP-START compared three empiric antibiotic strategies: beta-lactam monotherapy, beta-lactam plus macrolide combination, and fluoroquinolone monotherapy, to determine whether any approach resulted in superior patient outcomes.

10.2 Study Design

Type: Multicenter, cluster-randomized, crossover trial
Population: 2283 adult patients non-ICU hospitalized with CAP
Intervention: Beta-lactam monotherapy (amoxicillin, amoxicillin-clavulanate, cefuroxime) vs. beta-lactam + macrolide combination therapy vs. fluoroquinolone monotherapy (levofloxacin or moxifloxacin)
Primary Outcome: 90-day all-cause mortality
Secondary Outcomes:

- Time to start oral treatment
- Length of hospital stay
- Occurrence of minor or major complications during the hospital stay

10.3 Results

Primary Outcome: There was no significant difference in 90-day mortality between treatment strategies beta-lactam monotherapy 9%, beta-lactam + macrolide 11.1% fluoroquinolone 8.8%; ($p = 0.59$).
Secondary Outcomes:

- Time to starting oral treatment: There was no significant difference observed between groups in median time receiving IV antibiotic treatment and starting oral antibiotic therapy.
- Length of hospital stay: The median length of hospital stay was 6 days between all groups. There was no significant difference observed.
- Complications during hospital stay: There was no significant difference observed between groups in the incidence of major or minor complications.

10.4 Key Takeaways

- The trial showed that empiric beta-lactam monotherapy was noninferior to beta-lactam–macrolide combination therapy and fluoroquinolone monotherapy for patients hospitalized with community-acquired pneumonia (CAP) outside of the intensive care unit.

- Mortality at 90 days was similar across all three strategies, supporting the safety of beta-lactam monotherapy as initial treatment.
- Beta-lactam monotherapy substantially reduced unnecessary atypical coverage, cutting macrolide/fluoroquinolone exposure by about two-thirds.
- There were no significant differences in length of hospital stay, complications, or clinical recovery between strategies.
- The study suggests that routine atypical coverage may not be needed in most non-ICU hospitalized patients with CAP, provided rapid diagnostic testing (e.g., for Legionella) is available for those at higher risk.
- These findings help balance antibiotic stewardship and safety, supporting narrower-spectrum therapy without compromising outcomes.

10.5 Clinical Application

- Consider beta-lactam monotherapy as a preferred initial empiric antibiotic strategy in non-ICU hospitalized CAP patients without atypical pathogen suspicion.
- Reserve macrolide or fluoroquinolone therapy for specific clinical scenarios (e.g., atypical pathogens, severe CAP).
- Empiric atypical coverage should still be considered in patients with risk factors for Legionella or in regions with higher prevalence of atypical pathogens.

10.6 When to Discuss on Rounds

Discuss this trial on rounds with the following scenarios:

- When initiating empiric antibiotics in hospitalized patients with community-acquired pneumonia.
- When emphasizing antibiotic stewardship and rational antibiotic selection with trainees.
- When reviewing antibiotic-related adverse events profiles in CAP treatment.

10.7 Relevant Guidelines

The **ATS** and **IDSA** guidelines recommend either a beta-lactam plus macrolide, a beta-lactam plus doxycycline, or a respiratory fluoroquinolone for hospitalized, non-ICU patients with CAP. However, they note that beta-lactam monotherapy is reasonable in low-severity cases when atypical coverage is not required.

References

1. Beigel JH, Tomashek KM, Dodd LE, et al. Remdesivir for the treatment of Covid-19—final report. N Engl J Med. 2020;383(19):1813–26. https://doi.org/10.1056/NEJMoa2007764.
2. Harris PNA, Tambyah PA, Lye DC, et al. Effect of piperacillin-tazobactam vs meropenem on 30-day mortality for patients with E coli or Klebsiella pneumoniae bloodstream infection and ceftriaxone resistance: a randomized clinical trial [published correction appears in JAMA. 2019 Jun 18;321(23):2370. Doi: 10.1001/jama.2019.6706]. JAMA. 2018;320(10):984–94. https://doi.org/10.1001/jama.2018.12163.
3. Iversen K, Ihlemann N, Gill SU, et al. Partial oral versus intravenous antibiotic treatment of endocarditis. N Engl J Med. 2019;380(5):415–24. https://doi.org/10.1056/NEJMoa1808312.
4. Li HK, Rombach I, Zambellas R, et al. Oral versus intravenous antibiotics for bone and joint infection. N Engl J Med. 2019;380(5):425–36. https://doi.org/10.1056/NEJMoa1710926.
5. de Gans J, van de Beek D, European Dexamethasone in Adulthood Bacterial Meningitis Study Investigators. Dexamethasone in adults with bacterial meningitis. N Engl J Med. 2002;347(20):1549–56. https://doi.org/10.1056/NEJMoa021334.
6. Conradie F, Diacon AH, Ngubane N, et al. Treatment of highly drug-resistant pulmonary tuberculosis. N Engl J Med. 2020;382(10):893–902. https://doi.org/10.1056/NEJMoa1901814.
7. Louie TJ, Miller MA, Mullane KM, et al. Fidaxomicin versus vancomycin for Clostridium difficile infection. N Engl J Med. 2011;364(5):422–31. https://doi.org/10.1056/NEJMoa0910812.
8. Huang DT, Yealy DM, Filbin MR, et al. Procalcitonin-guided use of antibiotics for lower respiratory tract infection. N Engl J Med. 2018;379(3):236–49. https://doi.org/10.1056/NEJMoa1802670.
9. Sterling TR, Villarino ME, Borisov AS, et al. Three months of rifapentine and isoniazid for latent tuberculosis infection. N Engl J Med. 2011;365(23):2155–66. https://doi.org/10.1056/NEJMoa1104875.
10. Postma DF, van Werkhoven CH, van Elden LJ, et al. Antibiotic treatment strategies for community-acquired pneumonia in adults. N Engl J Med. 2015;372(14):1312–23. https://doi.org/10.1056/NEJMoa1406330.

Conclusion

The practice of medicine stands on the shoulders of great trials. The studies summarized in this book are more than just statistics, they are the foundation of the care we provide every day. From the first blood pressure-lowering trials to modern immunotherapy breakthroughs, these pivotal investigations have shaped the protocols we follow, the questions we ask, and the lives we save.

Throughout your journey as a clinician, whether you're a medical student preparing for rounds, a resident writing orders at 3 AM, or an attending teaching on the fly, the relevance of these trials cannot be overstated. This book was designed not to overwhelm, but to empower. To give you the tools to speak confidently, think critically, and practice intentionally.

What This Book Should Remind You

- **Evidence matters — but so does judgment.**
  No trial applies perfectly to every patient. Use these studies to guide your decisions, not dictate them.
- **The "right answer" often changes.**
  Many of the practices we now take for granted were once controversial. As new evidence emerges, stay curious. Medicine is a living science.
- **Speaking in evidence builds trust.**
  Citing landmark trials during rounds or consults doesn't just demonstrate knowledge — it shows that your decisions are grounded in data, not dogma.

A. Love, *The Essential Evidence*, https://doi.org/10.1007/978-3-032-12399-2

Looking Forward

While this book focuses on the landmark trials that have stood the test of time, new studies are being published daily. Stay engaged with the literature. Consider reading trial summaries, joining journal clubs, or even conducting your own research. Someday, you may help write the next chapter of evidence-based medicine.

Thank you for letting this book be a part of your growth. May it serve not just as a reference, but as a companion on your path to clinical excellence.

Index

A. Love, *The Essential Evidence*, https://doi.org/10.1007/978-3-032-12399-2